FAMINIES IN ANCIENT INDIA

FAMINIES IN ANCIENT INDIA

(A Sudy of Agro-economy from Prehistoric to Early Historic Period)

By

Atreyi Biswas

GYAN

Faminies in Ancient India

ISBN : 978-81-212-0660-0

First Published 2000, reprint 2013 in India by
Gyan Publishing House
23, Main Ansari Road, Daryaganj,
New Delhi - 110002
Phones : 23282060, 23261060
Fax : (011) 23285914
E-mail: books@gyanbooks.com
website: gyanbooks.com

Printed at : Sagar Color Scan, New Delhi.

Introduction

Famine can be defined as 'a state of extreme hunger suffered by the population of a region as a result of the failure of the accustomed food supply.' (*Encyclopaedia of Social Sciences*, Vol. VI: 85). It can further be elaborated that 'famine is a lack of food over a large geographical area sufficiently long and severe to cause widespread disease and death from starvation.' (*Chambers Encyclopaedia*)

Food supply primarily depends on agricultural output which sometimes get hampered due to drought, flood, seismic disturbances, locust, mice, vermin and the geographical settings of a region, rivers, water resources, soil, climate, etc.

Droughts are caused by insufficient rainfall, untimely precipitation and intensity and long duration of a dry spell, during sowing and sprouting seasons leading to an increasing possibility of famine (*Famine Commission Report*, 1880;1-7). In present day India, there are a few regions which can be called drought-prone blocks. As compared to other areas, the drought-prone tracts are more vulnerable to ecological degradation. The areas which suffer frequently from drought and famine are those where the annual rainfall averages between 15" and 60". The drought-prone areas can roughly be divided into three zones:

(a) Extreme drought-prone areas: This covers the arid and semi–arid areas of western Rajasthan and Kutch which comprises portions of desert. The climate there is such that it does not permit high agricultural efficiency. Agriculture remains limited to cultivation of inferior quality of rain–fed crops.

(b) Severe drought-prone area: These include the regions surrounding Udaipur, Gwalior and Malwa plateau in northern India. Black and red loamy soils are common here and crop cultivation is limited.

(c) Moderate drought-prone areas: These cover Gujarat, two narrow strips running from the north of Madhya Pradesh to southern Uttar Pradesh, Bihar, south-west Bengal and Rajasthan in the northern zone (Reddy and Singh 1979:40-41).

The total agricultural areas of north India can be broadly divided into four categories (based on the analysis made by Aurora and Mehra 1974):

(i) Arid regions: The districts with annual rainfall of 14" and below comprise the arid regions.

(ii) Semi-arid regions: The districts in this region receive rainfall ranging from 15" to 30".

(iii) Dry sub-humid region: This region gets an annual rainfall ranging between 30" to 45".

(iv) Humid regions: For these regions the annual rainfall is 45" and above.

Agriculture continues to be the predominant sector of the Indian economy and the input of water is vital for realising the full potential of this sector. Farmers in India primarily depend on rain. The south-west monsoon brings most of the rainfall in northern India. In the plains rains are concentrated in the summer half of the year, though the winters are not totally dry. For agriculture it is the south-westerly monsoon during the months of June and July that are crucial. The fate of the *kharif* crop depends on them. Occurrence of agricultural droughts depend upon the erratic rainfall and bad nature of showers. Drought occurs when the seedlings of a particular crop suffer from insufficient moisture during the crucial period of its sowing and sprouting.

The monsoon season is by no means one of continuous rain. It is this pulsation of monsoon which is of great significance for agriculture. If there is no rain in June and

July during the sowing and sprouting of seeds for the *kharif* crops, no amount of rainfall later can save the situation. Similarly, for the success of the *rabi* crop, rainfall in December and January is of utmost importance. If the drought in June-July is followed by scarcity in winter rains, an agricultural famine becomes imminent (Bhatia 1967:6).

The provinces which suffer from annual inundation and heavy floods also cause irreparable damage to the crops of the farmers. The mid-Ganga plain which comprises mostly of Bihar and the lower-Ganga zone suffer from floods every year. North Bihar is intersected by numerous rivers. Not only in eastern India but even western semi-arid zone floods have been recorded. Occasionally, floods occur even in the Sindh province. For example, flooding in the Indus basin was recorded in 1882, 1892 and in 1914 that brought untold destruction to property and crops.

Besides droughts and floods another problem which the Indian agriculturists face is that of waterlogging. This situation arises when the water seeps into the crop root zone and saturates the soil. This is usually caused by the rise of the subsoil water table. Waterlogging can also be caused by excess soil moisture due to frequent flooding, excessive irrigation, seepage and impeded sub-surface drainage. These conditions affect the growth of crops. In due course such lands turn saline and alkaline and ultimately become unfit for cultivation. Large tracts of the Indo-Gangetic plain also suffer from waterlogging. Here irrigation is perennial and consequently the water flows into the subsoil constantly. The corresponding outflow is poorer due to the flat nature of the terrain and bad drainage system. Therefore, waterlogging is quite extensive here. A large part of the land between the Ravi and Chenab rivers in the semi-arid zone consists flood plains which are greatly waterlogged and highly saline. Some other areas between the Chenab and Jhelum rivers too suffer from the same problem. The areas with black soil suitable for cultivating black cotton are prone to waterlogging because of low permeability. The surroundings of ancient sites Harrappa sites have become completely barren at present due to salinity caused by waterlogging.

Therefore, we can pinpoint three main physical causes of famines namely drought, flood and depletion of fertility in soil. These natural hazards arise primarily due to geographical and climatic reasons.

In the recent past, famines occurred quite frequently. Devastating effects of famines had been regularly felt since the beginning of the British rule. The colonial and imperialistic policy of the British was thought to be the reason for it. Without repudiating this theory, we must confess that famines are not just a malady of the modern age. India has suffered, since time immemorial, from the devastating effects of natural calamities. At times, damage wrought by these natural calamities was worsened and accelerated by man-made causes. Detailed records of these calamities are not available currently due to the general apathy of the Indian writers to record the conditions of the ordinary people at that time.

Natural calamities and the resulting bad harvests were recorded in 1291 at the time of Ala-ud-din Khilji. However, an economic policy which resulted in financial and commercial chaos, was directly responsible for the severity of the famines during his reign. A similar lack of administrative foresight is noticed in Mohammed bin Tughlaq's time. Application of excessive land cess and the transfer of the capital caused famines in Delhi in 1337 (Moreland. 1929:50). Wars, which had been a regular feature during the Sultanate and the Mughal period, had resulted in scarcity and frequent occurrences of famine. In 1527 and 1540 famines were recorded in Sindh which happened mainly due to the unsuccessful war policy of the rulers of Sindh, Jam Ninda and Mirza Shah Humayun. They forbade the sowing of crops within their own dominion on either banks of the river and prohibited imports. This artificial famine was aggravated during the latter occasion due to the natural disasters caused during two consecutive seasons. Loveday (1914. *App.* A:25) is of the opinion that prior to the British rule, major famines occurred only once in every 50 years. From the beginning of the 11th century to the end of the 17th century there were fourteen major famines, almost all of them being confined to a limited region. (see Digby 1901:123)

Plague is looked upon quite often as a companion of drought and starvation. The epidemic broke out during the famines of 1345, 1399, 1574 and 1594. On the last two occasions, the conditions of people affected by famine and plague became so desperate that they were driven to eat of their own kind. The streets were blocked with corpses and no help was available to remove them (Elliot & Dowson 1869:193). The famines of 1630 and 1660 are recorded by Kafi Khan who stated that the former not only prevailed throughout India, but also extended over the whole of Asia (Loveday 1914:19). The outbreak of plague and a famine during 1630 was so acute that all efforts made by Shahjahan to improve the situation were in vain. "Life was offered for a loaf but none would buy, rank was to be sold for cake, but none cared for it." (Elliot & Dowson 1869: 24-25).

Gradually, famines became a regular feature. Digby (1901:121) has commented that "famine has become no more a stranger or a guest rather a child at home." As a result of famines, the mortality rate rose much above normal due to the physical hazards. This was natural since the ability of the people to resist diseases weakened owing to a lack of sustenance and deprivation. Hence epidemics took a heavy toll on life subsequent to famines. Some records are available on this aspect.

During the famine of 1033, a pestilence is claimed to have swept across the country and in less than four weeks forty thousand people were victims it in the city of Isphan (Dow 1973: I. 85). During the famine of 1291, so intense was the suffering of the people that entire families would go together to seek a less cruel death by drowning themselves in the rivers (Elliot & Dowson 1871:146). Famines brought a heavy death toll on livestock as well. In 1345, it is said that the total stock of horses and cattle in the country around Delhi perished due to lack of fodder (Elliot & Dowson 1871: 244). However, the most vivid description recorded of any famine is the one which occurred in 1630. Thirty thousand persons are said to have perished in the single city of Surat. Later, when the monsoon ultimately came, it brought rains so heavily that the surrounding country was inundated and the malady was prolonged for another year (Foster. 1906: 180-81). The famine of 1770 in lower Bengal and Bihar was extremely severe and it was officially estimated that a third of the population (or about 10 million people) had died. This became evident during the ensuing rainy season, when it was realised that the remnants of the population would not suffice to till the land. Some idea can be had of the mortality rate through the census report of 1891-1901. The provinces which were worst affected during this decennial period were Bombay, United Provinces, Central Provinces, Central India, Rajputana, Ajmer and Berar. The total population of these provinces as recorded in the census report of 1891 was 113,350,000 (including the native States) in contrast with 107,420,000 recorded by the census of 1901. Assuming the normal rate of increase in a decennial period to be 6 per cent as the most cautious approach, the population in 1901 should have naturally grown to 120,150,000. In actuality, population had decreased by 11:73 million. This deficiency represents the mortality due to famines, plague and diseases incidental to famines, migration and other causes. (Digby. 1901:131) has given a detailed study of the mortality records in British India. For our own understanding we may quote his conclusions thus:

1st 25 years of British rule—5 famines perhaps—1,000,000 deaths
2nd 25 years of British rule—2 famines perhaps—500,000 deaths
3rd 25 years of British rule—6 famines recorded—5,000,000 deaths
4th 25 years of British rule—18 famines estimated—26,000,000 deaths

Thus we may say that mortality had been very high during famines in medieval and modern times. A chronological table of the famines can give us a vivid idea about the frequency of its occurrence. We may compare the table with the available date of famines prior to British rule. Though we admit that the records are incomplete still it cannot be denied that famines become more regular since the beginning of British rule. (Chart I) region ... of the present environment of the past. A de... prerequisite to understand its given here bu... region is not intended to be and ecological fac... of the main geographical they influence the deve... to mention because of its inhabitants. This will p...ary ... decline of the culture during the study of its ancient ... framework of reference ... and geography.

India is a vast country which covers an area of 3,268,090 sq. kms. It ranks as the world's seventh largest country in area. In population, it is the second largest country in the world, next only to China. This land has been utilised by men and animals alike for thousands of years and now it has degenerated considerably to bring years of scarcity and famines frequently.

Within the continent of Asia, India, Pakistan and Afghanistan form a separate sub-continent. The sub-continent is isolated from the rest of Asia by continuous ranges of mountains and hills. North India is separated from the plateau of the Deccan by the central highlands consisting of a wide belt of hills, bordered in the west by the Aravalli Ranges. This, in turn, is succeeded in the south by the Vindhya Ranges, the Satpura Ranges, Mahadeo Hills and the Maikal Ranges, which separate north India from the southern peninsula. Thus, north India is itself a composite geographical unit in which cultural homogeneity had prevailed in succeeding eras.

North Indian cultural zone in ancient times spread over a vast region, south of the Pamir Knot and east of the plateau of Persia. The present survey includes the modern-day Afghanistan, Pakistan and north India. The areas of north India which are included in the present study are the Indus Plain, Punjab Plain, Indo-Gangetic Divide, Gangetic Plains, Upper Gangetic Basin, Middle-Gangetic Plain, Lower Gangetic region or Bengal, Rajasthan and the westcoast of India comprising mainly Kutch, Kathiawar and Gujarat.

Most of Afghanistan comprises of high mountains and elevated plateaus. These are six distinguished geographical [illegible] is surrounded regions in this country. (a) [illegible] (b) The barren and in the north by the valley [illegible]adakshan constitutes uninhabited Hindukush [illegible]listan which lies to the north east Afghanistan. It is an agricultural region south of Hindukush [illegible] Central Afghanistan consists of watered by Kabul ri[illegible] as Hazara district. (f) Deserts of mountain regions –the valley of the Helmund forms a the sou[illegible] and [illegible] land. Agriculture depends on irrigation gre[illegible] of fe[illegible] b[illegible] means of w[illegible]s, small streams and kerezes. Two harvest [illegible] a year is a normal practice. Crops consist of wheat and millet and rice cultivation is very limited.

Baluchistan lies outside the mountain wall of India and consequently outside the influence of monsoon. It comprises of several districts. At present, Quetta Pishin districts are most densely populated. Fertile soil in the valley, a good network of *kerez*, and a fair quantity of rainfall are some of the causes which have combined to give this district its leading agricultural position. The ramparts of Kirthar and Suleman ranges separate it from the Indus plains of the east.

The Gomal river forms its north–east limit, beyond which Baluchistan is bounded by the north–west province of Pakistan. Quetta-Pishin, Zhob and Lorlai districts are well watered by Zhob, Pishin and Anambar river systems. Marri-Bugti country comes to the south–east of Sibi district. It is composed of barren hills. Kalat district to the west and south–west of Sibi country takes up more than half of the whole area of Baluchistan. Northern Kalat is known as Sarawan, the southern portion as Jhalawan and in between lies the Kacchi territory. To the south of Kalat comes Makran. The landscape in Makran is bizarre. It is a vast territory, mostly barren. Baluchistan is basically barren and rainfall is scanty. A certain amount of irrigation is carried on by *kerez* system of irrigation. Nowhere in Baluchistan is rain as scarce as in the Kacchi plains. But this is the most fertile area in the whole of the province. Cultivation mainly depends upon flood irrigation. Baluchistan is far from being a hospitable land as the inhabitants have nomadic tendencies.

The Indus plain is confined within the Sibi lowland of Sewistan i.e., Kacchi area of Kalat, and on the north, the ridge of the Kirthar ranges and the Hab river on the west, the Nara river on the east, and the Arabian Sea and Rann of Kutch on the south. The river Indus intersects it through the centre. From a point east of Sukkur, Nara river runs parallel to the Indus to a distance of 60-75 miles. The stream possibly represents the lower course of the now dry Hakra or Ghaggar river. The northern portion of the Indus valley, between Jacobabad and Sibi, is formed of clay desert. The Indus–West Nara Doab is one of the most fertile lands of the Indus valley. It expands in the south into the marshy lake called Mancchar. Along the east Nara river small alkaline lakes are especially numerous. The characteristic feature of the climate is heat and aridity. The rainfall is scanty and irregular here. Agriculture in Sindh depends completely on irrigation facilities. Away from irrigation zone the land is a completely barren desert.

Geologically speaking, much of the Punjab plain has been built up by the silting action of its numerous streams, during the recent chapters of geological history. In its strict etymological sense the land of Punjab means the country enclosed and watered by five rivers—the Jhelum, Chenab, Ravi, Beas and the Sutlej. The Indus river forms its western boundary. On the east the Punjab plains mix up with the Gangetic Divide. To the south of the Sutlej, the land gradually becomes drier, till it meets the barren land of Thar desert. Though the region is apparently rich in rivers its greater part suffers from a lack of perennial rivers. In the winters the streams are comparatively empty. But, as all the big rivers of Punjab rise in the Himalayas, when the mountain snow melts with the approach of the hot season, the waters rise in the rivers and overflow the surrounding countryside. Between the Sutlej and Jhelum the region has been divided physiographically into four divisions by K.S. Ahmed, (1963::3).

(1) The active flood plains or *bet* lands.

(2) The meander flood plains or recently abandoned active flood plains.

(3) The cover flood plains, i.e. former meander flood plains which have been subjected to widespread sheet flooding and obscured by a blanket of alluvium.

(4) Scalloped interfluves or bar uplands, rising higher than the adjacent flood plains.

The soil of Punjab is primarily alluvial in character and at places. It is quite often deficient in nitrogen, phosphorus and potassium. In some places limestone concretion and useless expanses of alkaline efflorescence are found. In other areas land has been ruined by accumulation of salts resulting from evaporation. Waterlogging has caused the abandonment of large tracts, as in the Beas bend in the north–west corner. The monsoon currents extend only up to south–eastern regions, but diminish rapidly as the distance from the hills increases. The western part of Punjab, which is now in Pakistan, is the driest part with a usual rainfall of only 10" to 12" per annum. It is impossible to grow any crop here without irrigation. In some parts of Punjab which are a part of India at present, the maximum rain falls in Pathankot district in the north and in Ludhiana and Patiala, in the south–east. South–west and central Punjab have very scanty rainfall. Apart from the amount of rainfall, the seasonal distribution and reliability of rainfall have important bearing on agriculture. The rainfall in Punjab depends on wind currents from the Indian Ocean.

A definite regional division of the Gangetic plain is extremely difficult. The region, in general, falls within the drainage system of the Ganga, the Yamuna and their tributaries. This is a vast plain built up primarily by the various Himalayan rivers. The northern boundary is well defined by the curves of the Siwalik ranges. But on the south the boundary is very irregular. The whole region is primarily a recent alluvial expanse. But there are three important variations in this zone—*bhabar, tarai and bhur*. The soils of the plain which are primarily alluvial, range from the *usar* clay towards the west, with alkaline *reh* efflorescence in the more arid zones through the general loam to the sandy *bhur*. The flood plains of the rivers are generally covered with reasonably heavy *matiyar* clay of the soil. This variation is most widespread. The land comes under the monsoon zone. But still the rainfall variation depends on the distance from the sea, from where the moist winds usually blow. Taking the region as a whole, most of the crops are grown on irrigation land. Many important canal systems serve the area at present. The cause of scarcity or famine in this zone arises from the deficiency in rainfall in the south–west monsoon, resulting in the failure of the harvest. The tracts liable to famine are the drylands of Bundelkhand and Agra.

The middle Ganga plain lies simply between the upper Ganga plain and Bengal. The Ganga divides the region in two distinct parts—north and south Ganga plains. North can further be divided into (1) Ganga-Ghagra, (2) Ghagra-Gandak, (3) Gandak-Kosi, (4) Kosi-Mahanadi interfluves. There are many oxbow lakes, dead and deserted channels of the rivers. In the north Bihar plain the land is dotted with elongated temporary lakes. Kosi-Mahanadi interfluve has more of this feature as the river is notorious for its shifting channels. This has been responsible for enormous devastation by floods. Floods are generally a recurring feature in the middle Ganga plain region as a whole. Almost all the rivers of the region develop a capacity to spill over in the monsoon season. Most of the region is covered with alluvial soil. The soil is still immature specially in *khadar* and *bhur* land. *Khadar* soil covers the flood plains and replenish it annually by new deposits after inundation. The soil remains moist, even during dry weather. The crops can be grown on them without irrigation. They mostly consist of fine silts but are sandy along the banks of the Ghagra, the Gandak and the Son. The *bhangar* is the oldest alluvium and covers the upland tracks beyond the annual flood limit. It is highly productive for sugarcane.

From the annual amount of rainfall it may seem that droughts are rare, but the monsoon is sufficiently variable to introduce insecurity. What the region suffers most from is not inadequacy of rainfall but its faulty distribution, both in space and time. A few intensive rains, limited during 45 to 60 rainy days drains off, without benefiting the soil as such. Thus the rest of the year gets insufficient precipitation. The breaks of the monsoon are sometimes of long duration, causing droughts, and sometimes it ends up abruptly, without bringing the crucial *hatia* rains, so necessary for maturing and flowering paddy crop, resulting in considerable damage and creating difficulties for sowing of *rabi* crop. Sometimes the rain continues till late October, which also causes disadvantage to *kharif* harvesting and *rabi* sowing, and sometimes it brings floods.

Lower Gangetic region is the vast alluvial track and deltas of the Ganga and the Brahmaputra rivers. In the north it includes a small strip of *tarai* country, which lies in the lower reaches of the Himalayan region. Rainfall variability can be observed between the west and east Bengal. Western side gets between 50 and 60 inches of rainfall while eastern side gets 60 and 95 inches.

In western India a large portion comprises of drylands. The main Thar desert lies in Bikaner, Jodhpur (Marwar), and Jaisalmer districts of Rajasthan. But it also includes half of Bahawalpur, most of Khairpur, and Thar Parkar districts of Sindh. The last three are now units of Pakistan. The Luni river passes through it, but remains dry most of the time. In the desert, adjoining Khairpur, saline lakes are numerous. Annual rainfall is generally under 10 inches. South of this desert area, rainfall conditions improve slightly and during good monsoon grass grows. Bikaner lies on the old Ghaggar bed, where canal irrigation has facilitated some cultivation.

On the west coast of India lies the Kutch-Kathiawar-Gujarat region. To the north of this area lies the desert of Thar or dry valley of the Sindh, and in the south west the wet coast surrounds it. This is a transitional valley between these two extreme climates. The whole of the region is a low-land, bordering the sea zone in the west and is barely 100 ft. above the sea level. The Rann of Kutch is a vast expanse of barren tidal mudfalts. South of the Gulf of Kutch lies the Kathiawar peninsula drained by the Bhadar river flowing west and the Shetrunji river flowing toward the east. Further south, along the plateau, the land is marshy and often saline. The rainfall here is low and unreliable. The Bhadar basin is the most productive area in the whole of Kathiawar. Gujarat is primarily composed of alluvium brought by the rivers like Sabarmati, Mahi and other minor streams and is mainly dry. Irrigation is independable, as most of the streams that drain this land remain dry most of the time. Cultivation can only be done with the help of tanks. Black cotton soil is found in south Gujarat which is the wettest part of the region. The narrow coastal strip has salty soil, which harms the cultivable fields. Beyond this the black soil provides good condition for rice and cotton cultivation.

1

THE GOLDEN AGE

The story of famines starts from the beginning of civilization in Indian history. In the evolutionary process of pre-history, historians have generally named three phases—'savagery', 'barbarism', and 'civilization'. Human history commenced with the palaeolithic period of the archaeologists. While people were leading a 'savage' state of life, they used to collect fruits, go fishing and hunt animals for food.

Different stages of cultural development can be postulated on the basis of archaeological data, which shows the different levels of subsistence settlement types. The earliest was the food gathering stage. This can be divided into three steps.

(1) When hordes of human beings were enjoying the free-wandering habits. They had started to 'fashion' their tools to some extent, but had not yet achieved any norms of standardization.

(2) They were still freely wandering and depended on food collection for their subsistence but their tools were mostly shaped in a standardized tradition (i.e., the earlier core-bifaces, flake, and chopping tools). They mostly lived in open air sites.

(3) Their wanderings became to some extent restricted as they were commonly occupying the caves, wherever they existed. The tools had taken a standardized form and there was somewhat of a 'tool industry'. The regional restrictions can also be traced in the distribution of any

particular industry. The second stage of cultural development was when food collection depended on seasonal basis which further restricted their free-wanderings. Regional variations now marked the tool types. Food collection became a season bound activity. They intensified hunting. Gradually they adopted semi-permanent to permanent sedentary types of groups. The third was the food producing stage. In this stage of development agriculture and animal breeding became important. Animal breeding became important specifically in those areas where natural food resources were less. People in game and food rich regions in Africa, America and Australia did not domesticate animals (Herre and Rohrs. 1976:512). Domestic animals only attained importance over a very long course of development. Some of the features with which they even helped to alter the social milieu of mankind were wool and fur production, early maturation, high meat yield, efficient use of food, high and rapid reproduction rate and production of milk.

A reasonably well established hypothesis is that the origin of a cultivated plant is a process not an event (Anderson 1960:71). The incipient agriculture, "involving potential manipulation of the potential domesticates within a subsistence milieu within an environment of natural habitat for the potential domesticates restricted wanderings to some permanent settlement groups" (Braidwood 1960: 143).

Whether people suffered famines during these earliest stages of human history or not cannot be ascertained. Famine conditions probably occurred with the beginning of settled 'civilization'.

'Civilization' commenced at the culmination of this process of continuous progressive changes. The drastic population rise provided incentives which the neolithic societies needed. New means were discovered to extract food resources to fulfil the enlarged demands. The change from the tribal to peasant societies are also due to the increase in population. Smith (1972: 409-42), suggests that changes in population pressure on the available resources, bring about in some cases developments in technology and exploitative efficiency of the groups concerned. Boserup (1965) thinks that 'level of development and production is determined by the availability of the labour in a pre-industrial society'. Population increase had an effect on the production methods. Primitive agriculturists usually followed long fallowing methods. But with the pressure of population density the demand more food forced the cultivator to adopt the short fallowing methods. The cultivator is only forced to produce surplus output of agriculture when a certain critical level of population density is reached and carrying capacity of the available land cannot produce sufficiently for all. At this stage the concerned social group either intensifies its cultivation by rejecting long fallowing methods and accepting short fallowing method or they migrate to more productive lands (Childe, 1979: 12-17). Shortening the recovery intervals between sowing of crops have both advantages and disadvantages. Of course the immediate benefit is the increase in agricultural output, but by doing so the farmer relinquishes his own leisure hours for the benefit of society. Smith (*ibid*) rightly thinks that 'the cultivators will be reluctant to sacrifice part or all of their traditional period of leisure unless they are compelled to do so by another tax imposing group'. Thus the concept of the state becomes a prerequisite for the beginning of 'civilization'.

Another criterion of 'civilization' is that it maintains considerable number of non-food producing population. When a particular social group reaches the stage of surplus agricultural yield it can support a number released from work of primary food production. Childe (1979: 12-17) points out that it is very difficult to categorize at what stage of development the 'civilization' begins. 'Civilized' state is definitely later than the 'savage' stage and 'barbarian' stages of society.

Population changes can also be noticed in these three stages of early society. In the 'savagery' stage the social group remained very small. They roved around in small bands in search of food. In neolithic times the situation changed. Farmers lived almost always near a place where plentiful water was available for their daily consumption and irrigation and moved from a chosen locality when water supply became insufficient, or the productivity of soil decreased due to various reasons or when the population increased so much that carrying capacity of soil could not bear with it. The population increased but density of population in units of settlements, was yet small, therefore, the settlements were not enlarged, instead but they multiplied. The subsistence economy of this neolithic stage was based on 'slash and burn' cultivation. Archaeologists think that extensive agriculture is associated with shifting settlements and intensive agriculture with stable ones (Childe, 1953: 198). In this neolithic level people reached "a self sufficiency in food producing economy" (Childe, 1956). Everyone supported directly or indirectly to food production. Their technical advancement was not of so high level that they could afford to sustain, with their surplus production, a large number of nonfood-producing members of the society. This became possible only at the more advanced stage, when use of metal and proper irrigation methods could provide substantial surplus. This stage is the 'civilized' stage. Only after reaching this stage the question of famines and scarcity arose. The social group settled down in a specific portion of land for varying reasons, e.g., the geographical suitability of land, irrigation facility, centres for raw materials which were essential for making other artifacts, or strategic position of the area for trade and military purposes. Therefore, when this sort of stable social group was afflicted with any natural calamity, they could not easily abandon their favoured places and as a result faced hardships. Natural calamities like floods, droughts, pest attacks, or any disease, if persisted for a few consecutive years, then it ultimately resulted in famines, mass migration or heavy death toll. In retrospect, we may say that famine is primarily related to 'civilization' and could not be traced back to the time when human groups were following a nomadic migratory life style.

Population increase can be observed in two ways, i.e. (1) multiplicity of the settlements, (2) density of the settlements. The first stage was reached earlier. With the increased population the social groups scattered around in numerous small settlements but remained confined in a more or less comprehensive geographical zone. Their technical expertise was not very highly developed that they could exploit the resources more intensively or could produce enough surplus food to maintain a big non-producing community. So they made small settlements, which were more or less self sufficient. They had minimum equipment and technology. Their technicians were probably not full time. They procured their own food by rudimentary agriculture and substituted it with fishing and hunting. In some societies the technicians kept themselves engaged wholetime in their work. But then they had to be mobile, selling their products from village to village. Because no village produced enough surplus to maintain non-food producing groups of technicians throughout the year, they later developed into artisan tribes.

The second stage could only be reached with three essential prerequisites. (1) They learnt to exploit their resources more profitably by improving quality of the tools. (2) They learnt the use of metal, which could improve their technical knowledge considerably. (3) They could control the river water for irrigation and transport. Water transport supplemented by wheeled vehicles and pack animals made it easy to collect foodstuffs at a few centres. At the same time dependency on river water for the irrigation of the crops influenced the selection of the sites. Floods in rivers remained a constant threat for the surrounding villages. To protect the inhabitants from the annual disasters concentration of population became a necessity, as only a joint social endeavour could construct safety devices. The canals and dykes were constructed to utilize the river water at its maximum capacity. Gorden Childe (1979: 15) has rightly commented that "about 5000 years ago irrigation cultivation (combined with stock breeding) in the valleys of Nile, the Tigris-Euphrates and the Indus had begun to yield a social surplus, large enough to support a number of resident specialists, who were themselves released from food production". In the beginning cultivation depended on 'natural irrigation', i.e., it depended on natural rise and fall of the river. The earliest cultivation of Egypt, Mesopotamia and Indus valley was done in this method. The rivers flowed through their slightly conclave and sloping plains and carried water and silts over the fields. Heavy part of the silts would settle down near the river banks. This built up their banks higher than the surrounding plains. Floods water thus was unable to wash a large portion of land and slowly it became essential to build dykes and canals to conduct the river water to the distant fields. This was the basis of basin irrigation, which became popular in Egypt and Mesopotamia. (Forbes, 1955: Vol. II: 59). When farmers were in need of building these utility constructions, it became essential for them to have big density of population in the required places. Thus it is quite evident that the controlled irrigation provided the basis for the density of population.

Famine prone zone in this earliest phase of our history were naturally limited to the riverine belts where human concentration had been immense. They were affected with droughts and floods, both depending on the vagaries of nature. These droughts and floods were the basic physical causes for the famines in ancient India.

A concise account of the present environment of the region under study is a prerequisite to understand its past. A detailed record of the region is not intended to be given here but a short account of the main geographical and ecological factors is necessary to mention because they influence the development and decline of the culture of its inhabitants. This will provide a framework for reference during the study of its ancient ecology and geography.

India is a vast country which covers an area of 3,268,090 sq. kms. It ranks as the world's seventh largest country in area. In population, it is the second largest country in the world, next only to China. This land has been utilised by men and animals alike for thousands of years and now it has degenerated considerably to bring years of scarcity and famines frequently.

Within the continent of Asia, India, Pakistan and Afghanistan form a separate sub-continent. The sub-continent is isolated from the rest of Asia by continuous ranges of mountains and hills. North India is separated from the plateau of the Deccan by the central highlands consisting of a wide belt of hills, bordered in the west by the Aravalli Ranges. This, in turn, is succeeded in the south by the Vindhya Ranges, the Satpura Ranges, Mahadeo Hills and the Maikal Ranges, which separate north India from the southern peninsula. Thus, north India is itself a composite geographical unit in which cultural homogeneity had prevailed in succeeding eras.

North Indian cultural zone in ancient times spread over a vast region, south of the Pamir Knot and east of the plateau of Persia. The present survey includes the modern–day Afghanistan, Pakistan and north India. The areas of north India which are included in the present study are the Indus Plain, Punjab Plain, Indo-Gangetic Divide, Gangetic Plains, Upper Gangetic Basin, Middle-Gangetic Plain, Lower Gangetic region or Bengal, Rajasthan and the westcoast of India comprising mainly Kutch, Kathiawar and Gujarat.

Most of Afghanistan comprises of high mountains and elevated plateaus. These are six distinguished geographical regions in this country. (a) Bactria – which is surrounded in the north by the valley of river Oxus. (b) The barren and uninhabited Hindukush region. (c) Badakshan constitutes north east Afghanistan. (d) Kabulistan which lies to the south of Hindukush ranges. It is an agricultural region watered by Kabul river. (e) Central Afghanistan consists of mountain regions known as Hazara district. (f) Deserts of the south and west—the valley of the Helmund forms a green belt of fertile land. Agriculture depends on irrigation by means of wells, small streams and *kerezes*. Two harvest in a year is a normal practice. Crops consist of wheat and millet and rice cultivation is very limited.

Baluchistan lies outside the mountain wall of India and consequently outside the influence of monsoon. It comprises of several districts. At present, Quetta Pishin districts are most densely populated. Fertile soil in the valley, a good network of *kerez*, and a fair quantity of rainfall are some of the causes which have combined to give this district its leading agricultural position. The ramparts of Kirthar and Suleman ranges separate it from the Indus plains of the east.

The Gomal river forms its north–east limit, beyond which Baluchistan is bounded by the north–west province of Pakistan. Quetta-Pishin, Zhob and Lorlai districts are well watered by Zhob, Pishin and Anambar river systems. Marri-Bugti country comes to the south–east of Sibi district. It is composed of barren hills. Kalat district to the west and south–west of Sibi country takes up more than half of the whole area of Baluchistan. Northern Kalat is known as Sarawan, the southern portion as Jhalawan and in between lies the Kacchi territory. To the south of Kalat comes Makran. The landscape in Makran is bizarre. It is a vast territory, mostly barren. Baluchistan is basically barren and rainfall is scanty. A certain amount of irrigation is carried on by *kerez* system of irrigation. Nowhere in Baluchistan is rain as scarce as in the Kacchi plains. But this is the most fertile area in the whole of the province. Cultivation mainly depends upon flood irrigation. Baluchistan is far from being a hospitable land as the inhabitants have nomadic tendencies.

The Indus plain is confined within the Sibi lowland of Sewistan i.e., Kacchi area of Kalat, and on the north, the ridge of the Kirthar ranges and the Hab river on the west, the Nara river on the east, and the Arabian Sea and Rann of Kutch on the south. The river Indus intersects it through the centre. From a point east of Sukkur, Nara river runs parallel to the Indus to a distance of 60-75 miles. The stream possibly represents the lower course of the now dry Hakra or Ghaggar river. The northern portion of the Indus valley, between Jacobabad and Sibi, is formed of clay desert. The Indus–West Nara Doab is one of the most fertile lands of the Indus valley. It expands in the south into the marshy lake called Mancchar. Along the east Nara river small alkaline lakes are especially numerous. The characteristic feature of the climate is heat and aridity. The rainfall is scanty and irregular here. Agriculture in Sindh depends completely on irrigation facilities. Away from irrigation zone the land is a completely barren desert.

Geologically speaking, much of the Punjab plain has been built up by the silting action of its numerous streams, during the recent chapters of geological history. In its strict etymological sense the land of Punjab means the country enclosed and watered by five rivers—the Jhelum, Chenab, Ravi, Beas and the Sutlej. The Indus river forms its western boundary. On the east the Punjab plains mix up with the Gangetic Divide. To the south of the Sutlej, the land gradually becomes drier, till it meets the barren land of Thar desert. Though the region is apparently rich in rivers its greater part suffers from a lack of perennial rivers. In the winters the streams are comparatively empty. But, as all the big rivers of Punjab rise in the Himalayas, when the mountain snow melts with the approach of the hot season, the waters rise in the rivers and overflow the surrounding countryside. Between the Sutlej and Jhelum the region has been divided physiographically into four divisions by K.S. Ahmed, (1963::3).

(1) The active flood plains or *bet* lands.

(2) The meander flood plains or recently abandoned active flood plains.

(3) The cover flood plains, i.e. former meander flood plains which have been subjected to widespread sheet flooding and obscured by a blanket of alluvium.

(4) Scalloped interfluves or bar uplands, rising higher than the adjacent flood plains.

The soil of Punjab is primarily alluvial in character and at places. It is quite often deficient in nitrogen, phosphorus and potassium. In some places limestone concretion and useless expanses of alkaline efflorescence are found. In other areas land has been ruined by accumulation of salts resulting from evaporation. Waterlogging has caused the abandonment of large tracts, as in the Beas bend in the north–west corner. The monsoon currents extend only up to south–eastern regions, but diminish rapidly as the distance from the hills increases. The western part of Punjab, which is now in Pakistan, is the driest part with a usual rainfall of only 10" to 12" per annum. It is impossible to grow any crop here without irrigation. In some parts of Punjab which are a part of India at present, the maximum rain falls in Pathankot district in the north and in Ludhiana and Patiala, in the south–east. South-west and central Punjab have very scanty rainfall. Apart from the amount of rainfall, the seasonal distribution and reliability of rainfall have important bearing on agriculture. The rainfall in Punjab depends on wind currents from the Indian Ocean.

A definite regional division of the Gangetic plain is extremely difficult. The region, in general, falls within the drainage system of the Ganga, the Yamuna and their tributaries. This is a vast plain built up primarily by the various Himalayan rivers. The northern boundary is well defined by the curves of the Siwalik ranges. But on the south the boundary is very irregular. The whole region is primarily a recent alluvial expanse. But there are three important variations in this zone—*bhabar, tarai and bhur*. The soils of the plain which are primarily alluvial, range from the *usar* clay towards the west, with alkaline *reh* efflorescence in the more arid zones through the general loam to the sandy *bhur*. The flood plains of the rivers are generally covered with reasonably heavy *matiyar* clay of the soil. This variation is most widespread. The land comes under the monsoon zone. But still the rainfall variation depends on the distance from the sea, from where the moist winds usually blow. Taking the region as a whole, most of the crops are grown on irrigation land. Many important canal systems serve the area at present. The cause of scarcity or famine in this zone arises from the deficiency in rainfall in the south–west monsoon, resulting in the failure of the harvest. The tracts liable to famine are the drylands of Bundelkhand and Agra.

The middle Ganga plain lies simply between the upper Ganga plain and Bengal. The Ganga divides the region in two distinct parts—north and south Ganga plains. North can further be divided into (1) Ganga-Ghagra, (2) Ghagra-Gandak, (3) Gandak-Kosi, (4) Kosi-Mahanadi interfluves. There are many oxbow lakes, dead and deserted channels of the rivers. In the north Bihar plain the land is dotted with elongated temporary lakes. Kosi-Mahanadi interfluve has more of this feature as the river is notorious for its shifting channels. This has been responsible for enormous devastation by floods. Floods are generally a recurring feature in the middle Ganga plain region as a whole. Almost all the rivers of the region develop a capacity to spill over in the monsoon season. Most of the region is covered with alluvial soil. The soil is still immature specially in *khadar* and *bhur* land. *Khadar* soil covers the flood plains and replenish it annually by new deposits after inundation. The soil remains moist, even during dry weather. The crops can be grown on them without irrigation. They mostly consist of fine silts but are sandy along the banks of the Ghagra, the Gandak and the Son. The *bhangar* is the oldest alluvium and covers the upland tracks beyond the annual flood limit. It is highly productive for sugarcane.

From the annual amount of rainfall it may seem that droughts are rare, but the monsoon is sufficiently variable to introduce insecurity. What the region suffers most from is not inadequacy of rainfall but its faulty distribution, both in space and time. A few intensive rains, limited during 45 to 60 rainy days drains off, without benefiting the soil as such. Thus the rest of the year gets insufficient precipitation. The breaks of the monsoon are sometimes of long duration, causing droughts, and sometimes it ends up abruptly, without bringing the crucial *hatia* rains, so necessary for maturing and flowering paddy crop, resulting in considerable damage and creating difficulties for sowing of *rabi* crop. Sometimes the rain continues till late October, which also causes disadvantage to *kharif* harvesting and *rabi* sowing, and sometimes it brings floods.

Lower Gangetic region is the vast alluvial track and deltas of the Ganga and the Brahmaputra rivers. In the north it includes a small strip of *tarai* country, which lies in the lower reaches of the Himalayan region. Rainfall variability can be observed between the west and east Bengal. Western side gets between 50 and 60 inches of rainfall while eastern side gets 60 and 95 inches.

In western India a large portion comprises of drylands. The main Thar desert lies in Bikaner, Jodhpur (Marwar), and Jaisalmer districts of Rajasthan. But it also includes half of Bahawalpur, most of Khairpur, and Thar Parkar districts of Sindh. The last three are now units of Pakistan. The Luni river passes through it, but remains dry most of the time. In the desert, adjoining Khairpur, saline lakes are numerous. Annual rainfall is generally under 10 inches. South of this desert area, rainfall conditions improve slightly and during good monsoon grass grows. Bikaner lies on the old Ghaggar bed, where canal irrigation has facilitated some cultivation.

On the west coast of India lies the Kutch-Kathiawar-Gujarat region. To the north of this area lies the desert of Thar or dry valley of the Sindh, and in the south west the wet coast surrounds it. This is a transitional valley between these two extreme climates. The whole of the region is a low-land, bordering the sea zone in the west and is barely 100 ft. above the sea level. The Rann of Kutch is a vast expanse of barren tidal mudfalts. South of the Gulf of Kutch lies the Kathiawar peninsula drained by the Bhadar river flowing west and the Shetrunji river flowing toward the east. Further south, along the plateau, the land is marshy and often saline. The rainfall here is low and unreliable. The Bhadar basin is the most productive area in the whole of Kathiawar. Gujarat is primarily composed of alluvium brought by the rivers like Sabarmati, Mahi and other minor streams and is mainly dry. Irrigation is independable, as most of the streams that drain this land remain dry most of the time. Cultivation can only be done with the help of tanks. Black cotton soil is found in south Gujarat which is the wettest part of the region. The narrow coastal strip has salty soil, which harms the cultivable fields. Beyond this the black soil provides good condition for rice and cotton cultivation.

1

THE GOLDEN AGE

The story of famines starts from the beginning of civilization in Indian history. In the evolutionary process of pre-history, historians have generally named three phases—'savagery', 'barbarism', and 'civilization'. Human history commenced with the palaeolithic period of the archaeologists. While people were leading a 'savage' state of life, they used to collect fruits, go fishing and hunt animals for food.

Different stages of cultural development can be postulated on the basis of archaeological data, which shows the different levels of subsistence settlement types. The earliest was the food gathering stage. This can be divided into three steps.

(1) When hordes of human beings were enjoying the free-wandering habits. They had started to 'fashion' their tools to some extent, but had not yet achieved any norms of standardization.

(2) They were still freely wandering and depended on food collection for their subsistence but their tools were mostly shaped in a standardized tradition (i.e., the earlier core-bifaces, flake, and chopping tools). They mostly lived in open air sites.

(3) Their wanderings became to some extent restricted as they were commonly occupying the caves, wherever they existed. The tools had taken a standardized form and there was somewhat of a 'tool industry'. The regional restrictions can also be traced in the distribution of any

particular industry. The second stage of cultural development was when food collection depended on seasonal basis which further restricted their free-wanderings. Regional variations now marked the tool types. Food collection became a season bound activity. They intensified hunting. Gradually they adopted semi-permanent to permanent sedentary types of groups. The third was the food producing stage. In this stage of development agriculture and animal breeding became important. Animal breeding became important specifically in those areas where natural food resources were less. People in game and food rich regions in Africa, America and Australia did not domesticate animals (Herre and Rohrs. 1976:512). Domestic animals only attained importance over a very long course of development. Some of the features with which they even helped to alter the social milieu of mankind were wool and fur production, early maturation, high meat yield, efficient use of food, high and rapid reproduction rate and production of milk.

A reasonably well established hypothesis is that the origin of a cultivated plant is a process not an event (Anderson 1960:71). The incipient agriculture, "involving potential manipulation of the potential domesticates within a subsistence milieu within an environment of natural habitat for the potential domesticates restricted wanderings to some permanent settlement groups" (Braidwood 1960: 143).

Whether people suffered famines during these earliest stages of human history or not cannot be ascertained. Famine conditions probably occurred with the beginning of settled 'civilization'.

'Civilization' commenced at the culmination of this process of continuous progressive changes. The drastic population rise provided incentives which the neolithic societies needed. New means were discovered to extract food resources to fulfil the enlarged demands. The change from the tribal to peasant societies are also due to the increase in population. Smith (1972: 409-42), suggests that changes in population pressure on the available resources, bring about in some cases developments in technology and exploitative efficiency of the groups concerned. Boserup (1965) thinks that 'level of development and production is determined by the availability of the labour in a pre-industrial society'. Population increase had an effect on the production methods. Primitive agriculturists usually followed long fallowing methods. But with the pressure of population density the demand more food forced the cultivator to adopt the short fallowing methods. The cultivator is only forced to produce surplus output of agriculture when a certain critical level of population density is reached and carrying capacity of the available land cannot produce sufficiently for all. At this stage the concerned social group either intensifies its cultivation by rejecting long fallowing methods and accepting short fallowing method or they migrate to more productive lands (Childe, 1979: 12-17). Shortening the recovery intervals between sowing of crops have both advantages and disadvantages. Of course the immediate benefit is the increase in agricultural output, but by doing so the farmer relinquishes his own leisure hours for the benefit of society. Smith (*ibid*) rightly thinks that 'the cultivators will be reluctant to sacrifice part or all of their traditional period of leisure unless they are compelled to do so by another tax imposing group'. Thus the concept of the state becomes a prerequisite for the beginning of 'civilization'.

Another criterion of 'civilization' is that it maintains considerable number of non-food producing population. When a particular social group reaches the stage of surplus agricultural yield it can support a number released from work of primary food production. Childe (1979: 12-17) points out that it is very difficult to categorize at what stage of development the 'civilization' begins. 'Civilized' state is definitely later than the 'savage' stage and 'barbarian' stages of society.

Population changes can also be noticed in these three stages of early society. In the 'savagery' stage the social group remained very small. They roved around in small bands in search of food. In neolithic times the situation changed. Farmers lived almost always near a place where plentiful water was available for their daily consumption and irrigation and moved from a chosen locality when water supply became insufficient, or the productivity of soil decreased due to various reasons or when the population increased so much that carrying capacity of soil could not bear with it. The population increased but density of population in units of settlements, was yet small, therefore, the settlements were not enlarged, instead but they multiplied. The subsistence economy of this neolithic stage was based on 'slash and burn' cultivation. Archaeologists think that extensive agriculture is associated with shifting settlements and intensive agriculture with stable ones (Childe, 1953: 198). In this neolithic level people reached "a self sufficiency in food producing economy" (Childe, 1956). Everyone supported directly or indirectly to food production. Their technical advancement was not of so high level that they could afford to sustain, with their surplus production, a large number of nonfood-producing members of the society. This became possible only at the more advanced stage, when use of metal and proper irrigation methods could provide substantial surplus. This stage is the 'civilized' stage. Only after reaching this stage the question of famines and scarcity arose. The social group settled down in a specific portion of land for varying reasons, e.g., the geographical suitability of land, irrigation facility, centres for raw materials which were essential for making other artifacts, or strategic position of the area for trade and military purposes. Therefore, when this sort of stable social group was afflicted with any natural calamity, they could not easily abandon their favoured places and as a result faced hardships. Natural calamities like floods, droughts, pest attacks, or any disease, if persisted for a few consecutive years, then it ultimately resulted in famines, mass migration or heavy death toll. In retrospect, we may say that famine is primarily related to 'civilization' and could not be traced back to the time when human groups were following a nomadic migratory life style.

Population increase can be observed in two ways, i.e. (1) multiplicity of the settlements, (2) density of the settlements. The first stage was reached earlier. With the increased population the social groups scattered around in numerous small settlements but remained confined in a more or less comprehensive geographical zone. Their technical expertise was not very highly developed that they could exploit the resources more intensively or could produce enough surplus food to maintain a big non-producing community. So they made small settlements, which were more or less self sufficient. They had minimum equipment and technology. Their technicians were probably not full time. They procured their own food by rudimentary agriculture and substituted it with fishing and hunting. In some societies the technicians kept themselves engaged wholetime in their work. But then they had to be mobile, selling their products from village to village. Because no village produced enough surplus to maintain non-food producing groups of technicians throughout the year, they later developed into artisan tribes.

The second stage could only be reached with three essential prerequisites. (1) They learnt to exploit their resources more profitably by improving quality of the tools. (2) They learnt the use of metal, which could improve their technical knowledge considerably. (3) They could control the river water for irrigation and transport. Water transport supplemented by wheeled vehicles and pack animals made it easy to collect foodstuffs at a few centres. At the same time dependency on river water for the irrigation of the crops influenced the selection of the sites. Floods in rivers remained a constant threat for the surrounding villages. To protect the inhabitants from the annual disasters concentration of population became a necessity, as only a joint social endeavour could construct safety devices. The canals and dykes were constructed to utilize the river water at its maximum capacity. Gorden Childe (1979: 15) has rightly commented that "about 5000 years ago irrigation cultivation (combined with stock breeding) in the valleys of Nile, the Tigris-Euphrates and the Indus had begun to yield a social surplus, large enough to support a number of resident specialists, who were themselves released from food production". In the beginning cultivation depended on 'natural irrigation', i.e., it depended on natural rise and fall of the river. The earliest cultivation of Egypt, Mesopotamia and Indus valley was done in this method. The rivers flowed through their slightly conclave and sloping plains and carried water and silts over the fields. Heavy part of the silts would settle down near the river banks. This built up their banks higher than the surrounding plains. Floods water thus was unable to wash a large portion of land and slowly it became essential to build dykes and canals to conduct the river water to the distant fields. This was the basis of basin irrigation, which became popular in Egypt and Mesopotamia. (Forbes, 1955: Vol. II: 59). When farmers were in need of building these utility constructions, it became essential for them to have big density of population in the required places. Thus it is quite evident that the controlled irrigation provided the basis for the density of population.

Famine prone zone in this earliest phase of our history were naturally limited to the riverine belts where human concentration had been immense. They were affected with droughts and floods, both depending on the vagaries of nature. These droughts and floods were the basic physical causes for the famines in ancient India.

SECTION I

NATURAL CALAMITIES

2

DROUGHTS

The people of the earliest civilization selected the areas of arid and semi-arid zones for settlement. They were primarily dependant on water from rivers and their perennial tributaries. Sometimes even small hilly brooks or big lakes provided them sufficient water and irrigation facilities. Their subsistence economy depended primarily on animal breeding and incipient agriculture. This stage was usually reached by the neolithic period. The region of present-day Afghanistan was populated by small village societies as early as 5th millennium B.C. Afghanistan in general has very scanty and unreliable rainfall. Drought possibilities are ample in this region. Therefore, the early agriculturists selected areas near perennial water sources. Northern Afghanistan is essentially part of the Oxus valley system. Whatever small sites are found here they are located near sources of perennial waters. Early prehistoric villages were confined mainly to inner fertile valley, among the foothills, where perennial springs supplied them with water throughout the year. In southern Afghanistan the river Helmund makes the region of Seistan an oasis amidst desert. Many prehistoric sites have been discovered here by Stein (1928). In the south of Afghanistan in Kandahar area early neolithic and chalcolithic artifacts were discovered. Sites are located at the foot of the Koh-i-baba range, where the Argandab river and tributaries like the Tarnak, debouch from the mountains. East of Kandahar, lies the Suleman range and penetrating through them one reaches the valley of Baluchistan. Afghanistan provides us with proof that early village communities of the mountainous regions of Hindukush were confined only to small village settlements. They remained mostly confined to sites around perennial mountain streams. They could never develop into big urban centres, even though they supplied the trade commodities to the centres of the later period, which developed in more productive zones. The small village settlements of Afghanistan were more or less self sufficient. If ever there had been any natural disaster, the population could shift to nearby areas, as there plenty of vacant places in the neighbourhood. In this way major catastrophes could easily be averted and no large scale famine could afflict them.

Next to Afghanistan, Baluchistan was the other important zone where early or pre-Harappan culture flourished. At present Baluchistan falls in category of drought prone area. Rain is scarce and unreliable. Average annual rainfall in Quetta-Pishin is 12.4 inches, Zhob district is basically barren and rainfall is very scanty. A certain amount of irrigation is carried on by *kerez* and streams, chiefly from the Zhob river. Early agriculturists realized this physical constraint and selected the zones where perennial river waters were available. Recent explorations show that the Bolan basin provided an excellent location for this kind of incipient agriculture, since the river flooded large tracts of lands during the summer months. Simply by planting cereals in the fertile alluvial soil at the end of summer, people could have raised a considerable quantity of winter crop, without requiring extra labour to clear forests or to build irrigational projects. Excavations at Mehrgarh (Jarrige 1979: 93-114) in Baluchistan is particularly interesting as it takes back the history of organized agriculture to 6th millenium B.C., or even earlier. The concentration of population is visible mainly in the areas where the water and soil situations were favourable, for example in the Kolwa area, which is situated at the head of the Kej valley and in the valleys south of Surab. In central Jhalawan districts Nal type culture flourished. Thus the settlement pattern of Baluchistan indicates that the people were selecting the sites which were nearer to perennial river sources so that they did not have to depend on rain water for their irrigation necessities.

The other areas where the chalcolithic Harappan cultures flourished were north-west Punjab and Sindh. Archaeological remains and settlement patterns of various stages of Harappan culture suggest that the people selected the regions where the perennial water sources were easily available.

The entire area of Afghanistan, Baluchistan, North-west Frontier, west Punjab and Sindh, where neolithic and chalcolithic civilizations developed, formed a composite geographical entity—for they can all be counted as arid and semi-arid zones. The major factor which gives geographical homogeneity to this whole area is the nature of rainfall. This area falls outside the limits of the monsoon zone and therefore, scanty summer rains occur in this region. It forms the eastern most limits of the west Asian rain zone. In west Asia, rainfall is restricted to the winter months (November to April). Due to their effects some precipitation occurs in the north west regions of Indian sub-continent during these times. The major problem for this whole zone is scarcity of rain.

These areas where the Harappan culture flourished are presently either having desert or steppe type climate. In most of this region, comprising of Sindh, west Punjab, north-west Rajasthan, and Gujarat, the rainfall level varies between 'extreme low' and 'very low'. It can be seen that 30 inches *isohyet* forms the eastern boundary of Harappan zone, and the civilization never really penetrated into regions of more rainfall. The climate of northern Sindh is semi-arid (annual rainfall less than 10 inches). Since the temperature goes up to 90° F., the evaporation of surface water is very rapid.

Some scholars are of opinion that in pre- and proto-historic times the whole north-western region of the Indian subcontinent which was the cradle land of the earliest civilization had a more conducive climate. The rainfall was sufficient for primitive agriculture activities to flourish. On the basis of a recent meteorological study, it is indicated that in circa 2000 B.C., deep troughs in the upper westerlies must have extended into west Pakistan, far more frequently than they do now, Ramaswamy (1968: 628) has suggested that there was the possibility of frequent active monsoon conditions over the entire Indus valley.

Earlier, in 1931, Stein had made the observation that there had been a definite decrease of rainfall in north western regions comprised of Baluchistan, west Punjab, Sindh, etc. since the prehistoric times due to a change of climate. The same theory was propounded by Marshall (1931: 2), Vats (1940: 4), Piggot (1950: 134-35), Wheeler (1953: 5-6), and Spate (1954: 145). On the basis of the *gabarbunds* (dams) found in many sites in Makshai-Jhalawan areas of Baluchistan, Stein holds the view that during Harappan times much precipitation occurred in those areas against which protective dams were constructed to save the sites from recurrant floods. Alternatively, these were possibly the 'store dams' which preserved the excess rain water. But this interpretation of the archaeological remains of *gabarbunds* has not been generally accepted by historians. The objection on this issue is sustained by the observation that the capacity of the *gabarbunds* as storage dams is negligible. Besides this they are mostly situated on the porous gravel fans, where storage is not possible for a long duration. They seem to have been check dams in fact, which were created to make a cultivable patch of land. Water probably passed through those dams, but the silt was preserved on the upstream side of the *gabarbunds;* which could provide cultivable patch of fertile land. Thus the existence of *gabarbunds* does not indicate a wet climate but a dry one, where the agriculturists were in a desperate position to save whatever silty, moist land they could save for their utilization. Besides this, the dates of the construction of these *gabarbunds* have not yet been confirmed. They may not even belong to prehistoric times. Thus, on the basis of these hypotheses alone, the theory of different types of climatic conditions cannot be postulated. Piggot (1950) had argued that more abundant rainfall and a denser forest in Sindh and Punjab can be inferred from the fauna which gave the wood needed to burn many millions of bricks and the implication of a flourishing agricultural background. Wheeler (1953) also concurs with this view. He thinks that the exquisite representation of elephant, tiger, buffalo, rhinoceros and crocodile on the Indus seals postulates the existence of "broad jungles and intermittent marshes in this region".

Attention should be given to the latest available palaeobotanical and palaeozoological data of the region. The mention of wheat, rice, *jawar, bajra* generally indicates four kinds of soil, differing in a very marked manner as to their character and facilities for irrigation and in most cases these would be sufficient guide to its water privileges.

The palaeobotanical evidence definitely precludes the possibility of a moist tropical forest or a wetter climate in the north-western parts of the Indian subcontinent. Cereal remains, as discovered from the excavated sites of the region, show the prominence of wheat and barley cultivation, which are the main crops grown even at present time. Absence of rice as staple part of diet, indicates that this crop could not be extensively grown due to limited rainfall. Though at sites like Pirak, Loebanr and Aligrama rice remains are found but that was introduced in the later period, which became possible probably due to the closer cultural contacts with the rice growing areas of the east. This crop remained strictly limited to a few marshy surroundings. Its availability thus, does not indicate the existence of a wetter climate in that region on the whole. On the other hand Pirak has produced samples of *sorghum* too, which basically is a dry crop and is usually raised in arid conditions. (see chart II)

As far as arboreal evidences from north-western regions are concerned not much reliance can be placed on them. In general, it seems that the forest land comprised of *babul, tamarisk, kandli, sissoo,* and *bahan* trees. But owing to economic demands much timber was imported from far away regions too, as and when they were required by the people of mature Harappan culture. In such cases the types of trees found in the archaeological sites do not always indicate the types of locally grown forest trees, which may have helped to determine the climate of the region.

More than the arboreal data, we can depend on the faunal evidence, as a standard to determine the climate of the past. The chart (Chart III) on animal remains of the north-western regions shows that the wild animals, whose existence is proven by their skeletal remains, survived on grassland and open forest zone. Had there been greater rainy climate, where a thick riparian forest developed then the animals would have been different. A thick forest is usually infested with smaller mammals such as moles, mice, reptiles, etc., the evidence of which types are completely lacking in north-western zones. The evidence of rat, mole and lizard are found in eastern regions of Punjab (Ropar) or in the southern regions of Gujarat, i.e. Jokha, Dhatva and Kanewal, which indicates that the north-western region of the Indian subcontinent had far more arid conditions than eastern Punjab and Gujarat.

The presence of the water buffalo and *nilgai* in several sites of north-west regions are of course of special significance. Water buffaloes can be traced in Mehrgarh, Balakot and Loebanr, whereas the skeletal remains of *nilgai* are discovered in the first two sites. The natural habitat of the water buffalo is swampy area, whereas that of *nilgai* is grassy plains, accompanied with bushes and scattered low trees. *Nilgais* are rarely found in the thick forests. Thus their existence in the north-western region shows that no riparian forests existed in those parts, though a few swampy patches near the river valleys may have existed, where the water buffaloes dwelt.

In the same manner the availability of the skeletal remains of molluscs in the Bannu basin is of immense interest. The specific species of mollusc discovered in the Bannu basin usually shows them native to the arid and semi-arid regions (Thomas, 1979: 227).

The problem arises with the availability of the bones of elephants. They seem to have been residing in the neighbourhood of Mehrgarh. In the same manner camel bones are found in Loebanr. These solitary evidences of elephant and camel are rather puzzling. Elephants usually survive in thick forests and camel prefer to live in desert lands. Though typically desert like environment may not have existed in Baluchistan, but we must note that even in present times camels are found around these regions. On the whole a general survey of the faunal remains of the north-western region does indicate that a grassland open forest existed in the area, which indicates in its turn, a dry arid climate.

The animal remains of Baluchistan, Sindh and Punjab testify the existence of a large number of domesticated animals, most of whom depended on the pasture land. The percentage of bones of wild animals decreases after the aceramic neolithic age. With the increase in settled habits hunting did not figure prominently in in the settlers' economy. Their subsistence economy depended on animal breeding and agriculture. Grass grazing animals were instrumental in denuding the surrounding tracts through incessant grazing. Probably in the years of drought the scanty grassland used to dry up which forced the herdsmen to move towards the river valleys of Sindh and Punjab, in pursuit of pasture land.

Geomorphic studies done in the last decade in the dry zone of Rajasthan, prove the existence of a buried red soil, with fully developed soil profile, in much greater depth than any soil formation today. Underneath the buried red soil there is a sand sheet formation and above the red soil there is another layer of aeolian sand, which includes considerable mixture of lime concretion. The existence of buried red soil proves that its formation could have materialized under greater humid conditions or in other words, this indicates that Rajasthan had heavier rainfall in earlier days than it has now. The aeolian sand dunes in lower and upper levels of the buried red soil confirm the theory that there had been alternate dry and wet spells in prehistoric times (Allchin and Allchin 1983: 13-20).

On the basis of geological and geomorphological studies in Luni valley, R.N. Ghosh (1977: 157-166), has formulated the theory of climatic changes in that region. He thinks that the semi arid climate set in about 1000 B.C., when the pronounced landscape became an aeolian one. He thinks this was not a local but worldwide phenomenon, affecting even Europe where dry climate postulated to exist around 1200-600 B.C.

Major climatic changes had been suggested in the province of Rajasthan, especially in the northern parts. Agarwal and Sood (1982:225) have suggested that in 5000 B.P. the climate of Rajasthan was much wetter and onset of aridity should be placed in C. 3500 B.P.

The theory of climatic fluctuations was discussed by Gurdip Singh in 1971. He thinks that climatic changes in 8th mill. B.C., brought about the beginning of agriculture based life. The polynological evidences of Singh's theory were provided from Lunkaransar, Sambhar, Didwana and Pushkar lakes of Rajasthan. According to Singh the pollen records from these lakes show the climatic sequence thus:

Phase I : Prior to 8000 B.C. severe arid conditions existed as proven by wind-borne sand deposits at the base of lake sediments.

Phase II : Pollen zone A: C. 8000 B.C. to c. 7500 B.C. In this period the rainfall increased, as proven by the first sedimentation in the lakes.

Phase III : Pollen zone B: C. 7500 B.C. to 3000 B.C.: In this period slight decline in rainfall occured but more or less a constant ecological pattern continued. Cerealia type pollen and carbonized vegetable remains indicate that agriculture had been introduced.

Phase IV : pollen zone C: C. 3000 B.C. to C. 1000 B.C.: This phase is subdivided into two phases.

IV(a) : C. 3000 B.C. to 1800 B.C. Sudden increase in rainfall is noted because cerealia type pollen is available in plenty. This was more or less the period which was contemporary to chalcolithic pre-Harappan cultures of Rajasthan.

> IV (b) : 1800 B.C. to 1500 B.C. Lunkaransar lake in the arid region dried up and Sambhar lake, which is in the semi-arid region, turned saline. He thinks that this was the time when the Harappan cultures in the arid and semi-arid areas weakened, (Singh G. *et.al.* 1974: 489-99).

The dating of the alternate climate fluctuations have been questioned by many scholars. We must point out that we are not concerned here particularly with the geological history. We will only concentrate on the periods when civilized human settlements can be distinctly located. Singh's suggestion that the decrease in rainfall occurred around 1800 B.C. is questionable. He suggests that due to this arid spell the Lunkaransar lake dried up around 2000 B.C., as also the Sambhar lake around 1000 B.C. It is interesting to observe that these two lakes are separated by no more than a distance of 200 km. and Singh does not have any concrete theory as to how this discrepancy arose between the drying up periods of the two lakes. Similarly, Singh thinks that due to this dry spell after 1800 B.C., there was hiatus between the Harappan and painted gray ware (PGW) cultures. The recent archaeological findings at Bhagwanpura (in Kurukshetra district of Haryana), Dadheri (Ludhiana), Nagar and Katapalon (both in Jullunder district), Manda (Jammu) have shown that PGW cultures in fact coexisted with the late Harappan cultures and thus there had been no substantial time gap between the two. Besides PGW can be traced along with black and red ware (BRW) in Rajasthan itself. This goes to prove that there was no real hiatus between the BRW of late Harappans and PGW in Rajasthan too. In fact it was only in north Rajasthan that a drastic gap can be noticed between the Harappan levels and the succeeding cultures. But for the desiccation of north Rajasthan the climatic changes could not have been responsible, as climate is not a local phenomenon. Whether a drastic climatic change occurred and affeced vast areas is not indicated. The climate of Rajasthan remained more or less constant, where aridity and dry weather were a prominent feature. If desiccation of north Rajasthan is noticeable in post-Harappan period, it may be due to changes in the drainage pattern, rather than due to changes in climate.

After arriving at this conclusion that there had been no major climatic change in Baluchistan, Sindh, Punjab and Rajasthan, we may now survey the province of Gujarat, which also witnessed the chalcolithic Harappan civilizations. A glimpse of the floral and faunal remains of ancient Gujarat can elucidate their climatic conditions. (See Chart IV and V)

Available records of the cereal remains as found in the pre- and proto-historic Gujarat gives rice the status of most preferred crop. *Bajra* was introduced later and no direct proof is available about wheat cultivation. But at present wheat is the most widely cultivated crop. *Bajra* and thereafter rice come in order of preference. This data does not corroborate with our polaeobotanical knowledge of pre- and proto-historic period. Can we presume, therefore, that a wetter climate prevailed in earlier times, as the cultivation of rice needed a moist weather condition?

Rice was known to the people of Gujarat from the pre-Harappan times. In the later period millet (*bajra*) was also introduced of Gujarat. Rice requires plenty of water for its growth. But it should be kept in mind that much of the rice husk found of pre-historic Gujarat, was discovered as binding material. Whether rice was duly cultivated, its grain used as cereal for food consumption and its husk utilized as binding material for plaster, or it grew wild in the nearby marshy patches, is not yet clear. The coastal areas of the province and valleys of principal rivers, probably provided the necessary water for its natural growth. At present rice is grown in those part of Gujarat where adequate water is available either through perennial rivers or through artificial irrigation. Therefore, the existence of rice in pre-historic times does not necessarily mean that the climate was wetter. It could even grow in marshy patches, which definitely existed then even if the climate in general remained as dry as at present. On the other hand cultivated variety of *bajra*, though a late introduction, proves the aridity of the climate then prevailing in the region.

There is no positive evidence of wheat cultivation in Harappan times in Gujarat. But is not unlikely that they had known about this cereal as they had inherited its knowledge from mature Harappan people of Sindh and Punjab, for whom wheat was the staple. At present the primary area where wheat and barley is cultivated is limited to the vicinity of Ahmedabad, through Dhandhuka *taluk*. Three important Harappan centres situated in this strip of land are Lothal, Koth and Rangpur. This indicates that the currently wheat growing zone was at least duly utilized in the Harappan period too.

To understand the climate of pre- and proto-historic Gujarat the study of wood remains is helpful. The plant remains excavated from Rangpur are fairly rich in information. *Acacia* was the most common though the other trees are *Albizzia*, *Tamarix*, etc. (see chart IV). These trees grow in Gujarat even at present. Thus a comparison between present and past flora of Gujarat does not indicate any climatic difference and we may presume that the climate has not gone through any drastic change since pre- and proto-historic times.

The study of faunal remains reflects some aspects of their climate and economy. Most of the skeletal remains are of common domestic animals. They were instrumental in denuding the land of its scanty grass coverage, as in the drylands of Gujarat no vast pasture grounds can be conceived. But Gujarat was not as dry a country as Sindh or west Punjab were. Some swampy areas existed, as *chital* or spotted deer survived in swampy surroundings. Kanewal from where *chital* bones are found, has natural water reservoirs. *Chital* bones are also available from Jokha and Dhatva in Surat district. This district received better rainfall in the monsoons than other parts of north Gujarat. The land near Jokha shows the existence of *nalas* and low lands, which probably used to get filled up with water in the rainy seasons. Similarly, rhinoceros too survives in swampy areas. The existance of this animal can be proven from the skaletal remains found in Lothal and Kanewal. Other wild animals which roamed around in the ancient forests of Gujarat, were those which usually live in dry forests, like *barasingha, nilgai*, etc. (see chart V).

On the basis of paleo-botanical and palaeo-zoological evidence it may safely be concluded that no significant climatic difference can be postulated in ancient Gujarat. The people had to survive under similar climate restraint as at present times. Aridity and drought-prone environment were the basic features of Gujarat. Nevertheless, Gujarat was probably slightly better than northern Rajasthan and north-western parts of the Indian subcontinent. Even at present Gujarat falls under the category of moderate drought-prone area, whereas northern Rajasthan falls under the category of severe drought-prone area.

Climate as known through ancient literary sources

As has been seen through archaeological, palaeo-botanical and palaeo-zoological evidences that no significant climatic difference can be postulated in pre- and proto-historic times, the various literary sources of the times also corroborate this conclusion further.

The *Rig Veda*, the earliest literary composition of India, reflects similar sentiments. Though basically Rig Vedic people were leading a pastoral nomadic lifestyle, there is no doubt that primary agriculture had been introduced too. The people were cultivating primarily rain-fed crops. Rig Vedic people were inhabiting the Punjab, Sindh and Saraswati valley zones. These regions fell under arid and semi-arid zones. The scarcity of rain was a dominant feature even in Rig Vedic times. This is amply clarified when we come across innumerable prayers composed for the rain god Indra. (e.g. *RV.* VII. 101. 3.; X. 105. 1.; X. 50. 3.; IV. 57. 1. etc.) Indra was the chief god of the Aryans, who brought rains by battling and destroying the demons *Vrtra* and *Ahi*, who were regarded as the serpents of clouds and 'demons of drought'. Ragozin (1984: 190-194) has called it a great aerial drama, which the Vedic Aryans perceived and conceived in their poetic imagination as a battle between Indra and his friends *Marutas*, fighting with *Vrtra* and *Ahi*, the demons of clouds, who kept the clouds enfolded inside their mountain caves. As nothing can be more disheartening than to see the clouds floating around in the atmosphere and not pouring down the precious water which was the life of their crops and animals. *Vrtra* is referred 27 times in the *Rig Veda* Bk. I, 5 times in Bk. II, 15 times in Bk. III, 12 times in Bk. IV, 7 times in Bk. V, 17 times in Bk. VI, 2 times in Bk. VII, 20 times in Bk. VIII, 2 times in Bk. IX, and 17 times in Bk. X. It goes to that especially in the time of Bk. I, Bk. VIII and Bk. X, which were composed comparatively later, when agriculture had become a major activity, fear of *Vrtra*, who caused scarcity of rain or drought, was deeply felt. Winds which brought rain were anxiously awaited by the Rig Vedic people. *Marut* was the wind god who brought the clouds for the Aryan cultivators (*RV.* I. 19. 7). They were the makers of waves in the sea and hence were invoked to bring down rain for the good production of crops. *Vata* was another regular word for the wind in the *Rig Veda* (I. 28. 6.; II. 38. 3.; III. 14. 3. etc.). In one passage (*RV.* V. 53. 8), Zimmer (1951) points to a reference to the north-eastern monsoon. He compares this verse with *RV.* X. 17. 2 which refers to two winds. *Rig Veda* V. 83, sings of the blessings heaped on Earth by *Parjanya*, another rain god, who was described as the protector.

In later Vedic times too the clamour for rain is vivid in the literature. Importance of rain was so great for them that the 'year' was named '*varsa*' (*Sat. Br.* II. 2. 3. 7.). All the prosperity of land and people depended on climate and weather. *Atharva Veda* mentions a foreteller of weather (V. 12. 1-4) and gives spells by which the evil effects of *anavrsti* (i.e., drought) could be countered (VII. 18).

Arid conditions, sandstorms and aeolian activities can be supported by Vedic literacy evidences. Vedic seers have referred to *pamsu-varsa* (i.e., duststorm or sand rain *A.V.* VII 109. 2.; XII. 1. 26.; *Tait. Br.* II. 6. 10. 2.; *Nirukta* XII. 19. etc.). The area where sandstorms could be expected was probably northern Rajasthan, where once the mythical Saraswati river flowed in full capacity, and which disappeared in later times.

The hymns of the *Rig Veda* refer to three deserts (I. 35. 8) the exact location of which are yet a matter of conjecture. We can only presume their locations on the basis of the rivers referred to in their contexts. One of the deserts was situated near the sea. Through this desert the rivers Sindhu, Arjikiya and the Marudvrdha cut their way. The other two deserts were also in north India. Through one of them the rivers Sindhu, Vipasa, and the Satudri flowed. And the third desert was the one through which the Sarayu, Saraswati, Apaya, and the Drsadwati cut their way (Bhargava 1964: 28-29). It seems that all these three deserts refer to different sides of present Thar and Rajasthan deserts. The existence of deserts in the Rig Vedic times also prove that arid climate prevailed. If it would have been wet climate the deserts would have become green.

These desert lands sometimes got heavy rainfall too. In some of the Rig Vedic hymns (IV. 17. 2.; IV. 19. 77.; V. 53.6.) rainfall or even floods in desert rivers are mentioned. Similarly, in modern times a few heavy showers or floods in desert rivers are not an unusual thing. All these comparisons show that there had been not much climatic difference in north-west India in past and present.

In the post Vedic periods too no significant different can be noticed. Scarcity of rain was not uncommon in the days of Pāṇinī. *Varṣā pratibandha* (drought or failure of rain) was referred to as an *avagraha* (III. 3.51.). Panini (III. 4.32.) mentions to *varsa pramana* (or measurement of rainfall). Land could be classified into three types, namely, *jāngala, anūpa, sādhāraṇa,* according to the nature of soil and climatic conditions. *Jāngala* was dry deserted land. *Anupa* was wet swampy and marshy land. *Sādhāraṇa* land was where all types of vegetables grew (G.P. Majumdar, 1935). Kautalya wrote about the quantity of rain (*varsa pramana*) in *jāngala* and other parts of the country. He mentioned that 16 *droṇas* of rain falls in the country of *jangala,* half as much more in *anūpa* country, 13½ *dronas* in the country of *asmakas* (Maharashtra), 23 in *Avanti,* an immense quantity in *Aparantam* (western country) and foot-hill of the Himalayas. (Bk. II. Ch. XXIV. 116-117). Kautalya

(Bk. II. Ch. 24) further says "when one third of requisite quantity of rain falls both during the commencement and closing months of the rainy season, two third in the middle, then the rainfall is (considered) very even (*sushmarupam*)". A forecast of such rainfall can be made by observing the position, motion, etc. of Jupiter, Venus and the Sun. In the southern parts of the Jhelum-Chenab *doab*, the tract was known as *jangala* country by the Puranic writers. *Jangala* as a kingdom of Madhyadesa is referred to many times in the *Purāṇa* (*Br.* II. 16. 40.; *Vāyu.* 45. 109.; *Matsya.* 114. 34.). Therefore, many regions of north India it seems, had dry and deserted or *jāngala* type climatic conditions.

Classical writers also refer to desert-like conditions in Punjab and Sindh. When Alexander marched against Mallas of Punjab, not far away from the river Akesines, he had to march through a desert country (Arrian's VI. 7.; Majumdar. 1960: 64). Cunningham (1963; 175) identifies this waterless desert tract with Kot Kamalia, situated in the bar land of the river Chandra, and only 16 miles away from the ancient site of Harappa. It seems that in the times of Alexander the bar land of west Punjab suffered due to lack of rain and other water resources. Similarly, the lowland belt which run parallel to the Indus along its western bank has always been an extremely dry and sandy tract. Ptolemy mentions only about a dozen towns of some importance here (Majumdar, 1960: 370-371).

But when the colonization efforts of more eastern regions materialised and these eastern provinces became centres of power, the prominence of wet climatic zones was evident. We know that even at present the lands of eastern U.P. and Bihar are more moist than western U.P. and Punjab.

In the *Jātaka* stories, which were composed in the geographical backound of eastern U.P. and Bihar, many references occur about 'dark clouds' (*Jāt. 163*), continuous rain (*Kurudhamma Jāt* No. 276), 'heavy downpur' (*Gijjha Jāt.* No. 52), rainy season for 4-5 months (*Mahāsutasoma Jāt*, No. 537), Pavarana festival at the end of the rainy season (*Kanha Jat* No. 29), etc. This climatic condition prevailed in eastern India, instead of the west, where dry arid conditions prevailed in the times of the *Jātakas* too. In *Apannaka* (No. 1) *Jātaka* the story teller refers about desert like lands towards the western region. But even in eastern India, references of droughts and failure of rain are numerous. We know that even in present times droughts do occur in the wet climatic zones.

To conclude the discussion on the climatic conditions of ancient times, it can now be said that the climate remained more or less of similar type as that of today. Western side of the Indian subcontinent comprising Baluchistan, Sindh, west Punjab, Gujarat, north-western Rajasthan, and western U.P. had dry arid type of climate, where scarcity of rain was a common feature. While obversely, the eastern side of the country, i.e. east U.P. and Bihar had wet climate. Here more than *anāvṛṣṭi ativṛṣṭi* was a common feature. On the basis of this study it can be concluded that drought prone and flood prone zones of ancient India, were more or less similar to that of present times.

But even so the earliest civilization flourished in the western region. Why did early men prefer these arid and semi-arid areas more than the valleys of the Ganges and the Yamuna, where the rainfall was definitely much more and where the land was surely more productive? The answer is very simple. The technological advancement until copper or bronze age was not sufficient enough to clear the deep forests of monsoon zone, and thus make them habitable. Instead they preferred dry zones, but where the drought possibilities remained constant.

Chalcolithic Harappan culture (in all its phases, namely pre, mature and late) was basically a riverine culture. It flourished in arid lands and, therefore, depended for its survival on river water. Even in Baluchistan, the pastoral agriculturists preferred the zones which had the benefit of riverine tracts. But Baluchi hills did not have vast cultivable lands. Therefore, with the increase in population, the people shifted from the rugged countryside to the vast alluvial lands of Sindh and Punjab.

Flood waters in the Indus had always provided the best cultivable land. But shifting of flood regimes was not an unusual phenomenon. In present times the most lucrative cultivable lands are to the east of the Indus—in the *doab* region between the Indus and eastern Nara river. During Mughal period summer floods affected most the western areas above Sukkur (Raverty, 1880). These types of changes in flood regimes may have happened earlier too. In the east of Indus, which is affected with present flood regime, only a few Harappan sites are known, like Kot-diji, Chanhudaro and Garhi Bhiro. The distribution of Harappan sites in the northern and western side of the Indus, imply that the flood water reached most of these areas. It can be expected to flow to the west, passing between Jacobabad and Ratodero and Larkana in the south, and may have even provided the cultivable lands for Judeirjodar. But it is quite possible that any change in this flood regime may have brought their end. Rivers had played a very significant role in the agricultural prosperity of India, especially in the days when artificial irrigation was very sparse. Wells were, of course, known to the Harappan people. The wells in the *bet* land were shallow and simply scooped out the earth, as the water level in the river valley remained quite high. Wells in the *kadir* land were seldom lined with bricks as they were of permanent nature. But how far they were used for agriculture is still a matter of conjecture. Most settlements were in the riverine valleys and benefited from its direct supply of water. Therefore, when a river did change its course, it brought desiccation to its neighbouring land. If the river passed through an arid region, where rainfall was unreliable, change of river beds meant complete destruction of the nearby settlements. This becomes vivid when we see the settlement patterns in pre- and proto-historic times. In pre-Harappan and mature Harappan periods rivers of Punjab, Sindh, and Rajasthan supported innumerable colonies. But in the later Harappan periods these settlements met a natural death. It seems that with changes in river routes, the collapse of earlier settlements became inevitable. Geographical area of this pre- and proto-historic cultural horizon belonged to the drought areas.

Therefore, the changes in river routes and their flood regimes became more hazardous.

On the basis of aerial photos and ground surveys, Louis Flam (1986; 65-89) has shown that during the prehistoric period two independent river courses flowed through the lower Indus basin, one in the western portion of the region which was the Sindhu river and the other in the eastern portion of the region which was the river Nara. Throughout the ages Sindhu (Indus) had remained a perennial river. It supported many chalcolithic sites of Harappan affinity. In later periods it was known through literary sources. *Rig Veda* and later Vedas mention it innumerable times (*RV.* I. 97. 8.; 125. 5.; II. 11. 9.; III. 53. 9.; IV. 54. 6.; V. 53. 9.; X. 64. 9.; *AV,* XII. 1. 3.; XIV. 1. 3.; Vaj. *Sam.* VIII. 59, etc.). The might of Sindhu is said to have surpassed all the streams that flowed (*RV.* X. 75. 1.). It is praised for its fair fields (*RV.* I. 122. 6.). It is remembered for its "far resounding billows of the flood" (*RV.* I. 44. 12.). This river had enough flow of water throughout the ages, but some changes in its river beds can be noticed. Flam (*Ibid.* p. 16) has pointed out its old river bed, which is different from its present course. In prehistoric times, according to Flam, 'the river Sindhu had taken a south-westward route. A short distance from modern town of Khandhkot, it took a turn west of Shikarpur and Ratodero—through Warah and west of Mehar. South of Mehar the river took a southernly direction down to the western flank of the lower Indus basin, passing through just north of the Mancchar lake. It then followed an easterly route near the town of Sahwan. To the east of Sahwan land forms of the river Sindhu are diluted by the more recently active courses of the present Indus'. Present course of Indus, which passes through the limestone/hills near Sukkur was adopted, according to Arab geographers, some time between 10th and 13th century A.D. (*Ibid.* p. 66). How many times the river Indus had changed its bed cannot be precisely stated. But the decline of later Harappan settlements along its banks indicates that it changed its course at least once around that time.

The second important river in the lower Indus basin, was the eastern Nara river. This was once a perennial river and was known by various names along its course. In its northernly reaches inside Pakistan borders, from Fort Abbas to Fort Derawar, it was known as the Hakra river, and at present is marked by a depression, which is clearly visible from the aerial photographs of the region. 'South-west of Fort Derawar the course of the Hakra becomes increasingly unclear, and intermittently becomes lost beneath sand dunes. Remnants of the river course emerge where dunes are less numerous. It gets aligned with the Raini and Wahind channels. South of these two channels the eastern Nara river can be clearly traced as a depression southwards along the eastern edge of the lower Indus basin, where it was eventually joined by Sindhu river' (L. Flam: 1986; 68).

The eastern Nara/Hakra river is known as river Ghaggar in its upwards region, which is in India. Nara/Hakra/ Ghaggar river has been identified with the ancient Saraswati river. Ghosh (1953: 31-34) has explored the valleys of Saraswati.

In Harappan times the Hakra/Ghaggar was a perennial river. It is quite possible that it met the river Nara and flowed directly to Rann of Kutch, without meeting the Indus. The presence of archaeological sites in the vicinity of these palaeo-channels gives a possible data for the time of 'wet' period, when the Hakra/Ghaggar was flowing in its full capacity.

The Saraswatī was referred many times in the *Rig Veda* (VII. 95. 1-2.; 64-9; VI. 52. 6.; VII. 36. 6.).. It was one of the most favoured rivers of the age. Most of Rig Vedic hymns were composed on the banks of the Saraswati. The Saraswati flowed as an independent river, and not as tributary to the Indus. *Mahābhārata (Vana Parva* LXXXII) states that the Saraswatī joined the sea near Prabhas, which was situated on the western sea coast.

But in the later Vedic period, probably some geomorphic changes occurred in the Saraswatī valley, which affected its full flow. Medaieval Sanskrit lexicons (*Śabda Kalpadruma* Vol. IV: 400) refers to *Vinasana* as the place where the Rig Vedic river Saraswatī disappeared in the sands. The reference of Saraswatī's disappearance in the desert, however, goes back to the time of the *Brāhmaṇas (Ait. Br.* II. 19; *Pan Br.* XXV. 10. 1.; *Śat. Br.* XIV. 1. 1. 8.). Exact location of *Vinasana* cannot be conjectured, as it looks that the length of its flow varied according to the intensity of rainfall in the lower Himalayan slopes, from where it received its maximum source of water. At present, Ghaggar almost ceases its flow at Hanumangarh, occasionally extending of course, a few more miles, if there is heavy rain in the catchment areas. Most likely, therefore, '*Vinaśana*', or the place where the Saraswatī vanished underground, varied from period to period. But whether the Saraswati was completely lost in post Rig Vedic period cannot be finally ascertained, because as late as 8th century A.D., Arab conquerors of Sindh have mentioned that in the east of Indus, another great river named Mihran, which has been identified by many scholars as eastern Nara/ Wahind/Hakra river, i.e. the ancient Saraswati.

The flow of Saraswati depended on the supply of water through its tributaries. Many palaeo-channels have been located in the upstream regions of the Saraswati, which had contributed in its uninterrupted flow. But whenever the tributaries had either changed their course, or had dried up due to various geographic and geomorphic reasons, the quantity of water in the Saraswati was reduced. And as this river passed through climatically arid parts of India and Pakistan, there had always been a chance of its drying up, at least partially.

Camasodbheda is said to be the place where Saraswati was joined by other rivers. From this place Sindhu is described as close by to it. Bhargava (1964: 82) identified this place in north of Alore, near Rohri in Sindh, Pakistan. Sutlej or ancient Śutudri, was one of the tributaries of the Saraswatī. This ran westwards below Ropar and joined the Saraswatī further down in the district of Hanumangarh. In the Vedic literary sources Śutudri is often mentioned together with the Vipāśā (modern Beas) (*RV* III. 33. 1. 2. 3. 5. 11.; II. 53. 9.). Sutlej played an important role in the rise and fall of civilizations settled along its riverine tracks. The Sutlej had a tendency to change its course even in comparatively recent times. Around A.D. 1000 the Sutlej was stated as a tributary to Ghaggar (*Imp. Gaz. of Ind.* XXIII. 179). In A.D. 1245 Sutlej had taken a more northernly course and was not contributing to Ghaggar. The diversion of the Sutlej can again be noticed in A.D. 1593 and A.D. 1796. Repeatedly it left Ghaggar and repeatedly it contributed to its flow. Similar shifting of river Sutlej and resultant dryness of the Ghaggar can be visualised even in pre- and proto-historic times. To prove this, a thorough ground-based fieldwork was conducted by Singh and Ghosh (1977; 135-45) and by Agarwal and Sood (1982: 223-233). They have argued that the Sutlej was captured time and again either by the Beas or by the Yamuna. Beas, (*Vipasa*) as we have seen, was mentioned along with the Sutlej (*Sutudri*) in Vedic literature. But the palaeochannel of river Beas, which is quite conspicuous in Landsat imagery, joined the Indus independent of the Sutlej.

Similarly, there is a distinct palaeochannel which shows that the Sutlej flowed through the Nara directly into Rann of Kutch, without meeting the Beas, on its way. The role of Beas in capturing the Sutlej is, therefore, doubtful. It is more likely that the Sutlej was captured by the Yamuna river.

The ancient bed of river Yamuna has been recognised and named by Agarwal and Sood (*op. cit.*) as *Y1, Y2, Y3*. Y1 channel was once connected to Ghaggar, which implies that the Yamuna supplied water to the Ghaggar, which ultimately as river Saraswatī, passed on water to river Nara. In later period the river changed its course and *Y2* channel was formed. *Y2* channel merged with Chautang (ancient *Driṣadwatī*), which on its part met the Ghaggar near Suratgarh. Thus, through *Y2* channel course as well Yamuna supplied water indirectly to Ghaggar or Saraswatī. The third course was *Y3*. It flowed further east and south-east and finally joined the Ganga. Thus the Yamuna was ultimately captured by the river Ganga and became disconnected with the Ghaggar/Saraswati/Nara river system. Most likely it was *Y3* which ultimately took the course of present-day Yamuna. Ghaggar/Hakra/Nara

(Sarawati) river thus gradually dried up because its main tributary Sutlej stopped supplying water to it.

Raikes (1968: a: 286-91) believes that Yamuna was captured alternatively by the Indus and the Ganga river systems. In his table he gives a date-wise sketch of this alternative capture of Yamuna:

1. Westward diversion to Indus (2500-1700 B.C.) coinciding with Harappan occupation of the Indus basin.
2. Eastward diversion to Ganga (1750-1100 B.C.) coinciding with the abandonment of the Indus region in late Harappan period.
3. Westward diversion to Indus (1100-500 B.C.) coinciding with the PGW sites.
4. Eastward diversion to Ganga (500-100 B.C.) coinciding with abandonment.
5. Westward diversion to Indus (100 B.C. to 500 A.D.) coinciding with the early historic period.
6. Eastward diversion to Ganga in about A.D. 500 coinciding with abandonment.

The first two periodic diversions propounded by Raikes, seems to be accurate, but as far as the hypothetical diversion of the later periods are concerned, one is not too sure. The idea that the Ghaggar basin could again become popular zones in PGW or in Early Historic period does not seem feasible. Dikshit (1977: 61-66), Gupta, Asthana, Amarendra Nath (1977: 79-92), and Pande (1977: 55-60) have worked on the archaeological remains of the now dried up river beds sites. Suraj Bhan (1972: 125-128) has also tried to locate the channel of the Yamuna, with the help of archaeological sites. He finds out an old channel of the Yamuna which starts near Indri, 20 km. north of Karnal, and is traceable for 180 km. up to Tigrana. The channel is lost in sand. Suraj Bhan has identified 18 Harappan and 2 PGW sites along this channel. The scarcity of PGW sites indicates that the Yamnua had already shifted eastwards by the time of PGW, and thus we cannot accept

Raikes view that Yamuna had reoccupied its western diversion towards Indus in PGW times.

Chautang (Drisadwatī) was another river which had contributed its water to river Saraswatī. *Rig Veda* (III. 23. 4) mentions the two rivers together. This river had also received water of Yamuna, as we have already seen, through *Y2* channel. But later this supply was stopped and the river gradually dried up. *Pañcha Vimśa Brāhmaṇa* (XXV. 13. 4.) and other later Vedic literature (*Sānkhāyana Śr. Sū* XIII. 29. 33; *Lātyāyana Śr. Sū*. X. 19. 9.; *Katyayana Śr. Sū*. XIV. 6.39) refer to *Tripalaksa* as the place, where Drişadwatī disappeared. Drying up of Saraswatī and Drişadwatī rivers are not only referred to in the literary sources but can be corroborated by modern proto-geological studies as well. R. N. Ghosh (1977: 157-166) has shown that soon after the wet phase of Harappan period (300-1800 B.C.) some major ecological changes had occurred in the river valleys of Rajasthan. This had an effect on the valleys of Luni, Saraswatī and Drişadwatī rivers. Goudie et.al (1973: 243-257) have argued that climatic changes were the root cause for this dissection of river valleys. They think that the present arid climate of north Rajasthan, was set in about 1000 B.C. During this arid phase the pronounced landscape in Rajasthan became an aeolean one. The active sanddunes blocked the river courses. And possibly due to this dry climatic phase perennial flow of the Saraswatī and Drişadwatī got dried up.

This theory of climatic changes is not fully acceptable. The climate in pre- and proto-historic times were not basically different from what it is at present. We think that drying up of the river courses were not due to increased aridity in climate, but due to changes in the river courses. Ghaggar or Saraswatī had a full flow through desert regions of north Rajasthan, Bahawalpur and Sindh and as long as Sutlej and Drişadwatī contributed their waters to it. Sutlej on its part was getting water from the Yamuna. But when the Yamuna was captured upstream by the Ganga river system, it stopped supplying water to Sutlej. Thus Sutlej did not have much to contribute to Ghaggar/Saraswatī either. In similar way, Yamuna had once contributed to Drişadwatī (Chautang). But when Yamuna was captured by the Ganga it stopped supplying to Chautang. In this way the main two tributaries of Ghaggar, Sutlej and Chautang themselves became nominal rivers and could not contribute much to Ghaggar. This was the main reason which interrupted the full flow of the Saraswatī. Due to scarcity of water in the Saraswati arid valleys of the rivers became more dry and aeolean activities increased, which hampered its flow further.

Our study of the changes in ancient river systems, thus, indicates that this was one of the main reasons to transform arid lands into unproductive, dry, drought-prone zones. This phenomenon effected drylands of west Punjab, Sindh, north Rajasthan, Gujarat where settlements thrived till the mature Harappan period. But then with the increasing biotic pressure, forests and grassland gradually got depleted. This affected the ecology. Land became more arid. Climate had always been dry. With minimum availability of rain water, when the rivers changed their courses too, the old beds got dried up. It definitely brought drought conditions. Drought was a major cause of famines in these north-western and western parts of India. Drought and famines forced people to migrate en masse from large tracts of affected areas. This can be seen through a study of their settlement patterns. The areas which were thickly populated till Harappan times, were abandoned in late Harappan and post-Harappan times, mainly because droughts in the areas caused famine conditions.

Some archaeological sites give us indications of calamities that stemmed from drought. To elucidate this we can take Gujarat as example. Aridity and drought might have brought sufferings to many settlements in Gujarat in chalcolithic period. For example, Jokha was a chalcolithic site of Gujarat situated in Surat district. Surat district is marked by comparatively heavier rainfall. As a result this district has fewer years of crop failure. Instead of this advantage the site shows that there was a very long gap period between its earliest chalcolithic period and its later occupation by iron using people. There was a distinct mark of weathering of the potteries of period I. The excavators think that "the site was deserted after period I, possibly due to drought of potable water" (Mehta, Choudhury, Hegde, Shah: 1971: 15). Rundhi Mora was another small settlement in the environs of Dhatva, in the Surat district. The chalcolithic settlement of this place was abandoned for a long period till it was reoccupied by the iron using people. The excavators suggest that drought seemed to be the reason for the abandonment (Mehta, Choudhury: 1975, Mehta: 1982: 167-175). Similar situation can be perceived in the site of Kanewal. Probably drought was the reason for its abandonment. This area quite often had failure of rain (Mehta, Momin, Shah: 1980: 70-72). Temporary abandonment of sites can be traced in later periods as well. Hastinapur excavation shows that the site was abandoned in between C. 600-800 B.C.; Mathura was abandoned after the NBPW phase and was occupied only at the Kusana 'red ware' times. Several occupational breaks can be traced in Tamralipti as well (Thakur: 1981: 326). Those towns most likely lost their importance due to some natural disasters, like drought or famine, which forced its occupants to leave the areas for some time.

Literary References to Droughts

India is a vast country. It has diverse types of climate, rainfall pattern and soil. This phenomenon was well realised by our ancient thinkers. Kautalya says that the 'quantity of rainfall was never even all over the country. Sixteen *dronas* were the normal rainfall in desert country (*Jangala*), half as much greater than in moist country. Thirteen and a half *dronas* in the country of *Asmakas* (i.e. Maharastra), twenty-three *dronas* in Avanti. The rainfall was considered very even when one third of the required quantity of rain falls both during the commencement and closing months of the rainy season and two-thirds in the middle' (II. 24). Of course, there are many rivers which provide water to its cultivable fields, but still there are large tracts of lands in between the riverine belts. Therefore, dependency on rain water was inevitable and clamour for adequate rain can be perceived in every step of our recorded history.

Till the Rig vedic times, the Aryans were leading a tribal mobile pastoral type of life. Therefore, it was quite likely that if any region got afflicted with drought the settlers moved out of that place and thus could avert famine situations. But still it looks like that on few occasions too the people suffer agricultural scarcities, which was probably generated due to drought situation.

The *Rig Veda* and the *Nirukta* provide the earliest references of such possibilities. Griffith in his translation of the *Rig Veda* has referred famine at least six times in the text (I. 112. 11.; III. 8. 2.; III. 53. 15.; VIII. 18. 10-11.; VIII. 55. 14.; X. 41. 10.). We have tried to check the hymns in detail. We cannot find any exact word in these verses which can be literally translated as 'famines'. The word '*amatim*' which appears in these verses may signify the 'poor condition' or 'poverty', but not exactly 'famine'. Thus we cannot admit that famine was a common phenomenon in the early Vedic period. The people had not yet coined any particular word for 'famine'. But that does not necessarily mean that droughts did not occur in those days.

A reference to drought occurs in the *Rig Veda* I. 112. 11. Dirghasavas, according to the story, was forced to leave the occupation of his forefathers, who were *risis*, and was compelled to live by trade, as the 'drought' had enveloped the whole region where he lived. This tragedy had forced him, along with his community, to migrate northwards, crossing the river Parusni. These are a few stray references to droughts in early Vedic literature, but of course droughts were not threatening the society on a large scale.

Yaska's *Nirukta* (II. 10) provides us with a story of king Santanu and Devapi, who belonged to the family of the Kurus. It is said that a prolonged drought in the realm of the Kurus, brought innumerable miseries for king Santanu, who in fact had usurped the throne of his elder brother Devapi. When the improper deed brought in his realm he was compelled to ask his brother Devapi to assume kingship. Devapi, of course, refused this offer but performed a sacrifice which produced rain in the Kuru region. Traces of this story can be found in the *Rig Vedic* hymn X. 98. 1. But all that is stated in this context is that 'Devapi Aristasena obtained rain for Santanu'. There is no hint of any relationship at all between the two personalities. Kurus came into prominence in later Vedic period, therefore, it can be argued that this reference of 'drought, during the time of Santanu', should be dated to later Vedic times and not in the early Vedic times.

In later Vedic times, references to droughts and famines became more common. By now the Aryans had developed stationary habits and had settled down as village cultivators. Therefore, whenever any part of their land was affected by drought, they usually did not evacuate the area, till they were starved due to aggravated situations like famines. In later Vedic literature numerous times it is said that the people depended for the success or failure of their crops on rainwater. *Chhāndogya Upaniṣad* specifically mentions that plentiful growth of crops depended on the timely availability of the rains (IV. 15. 7. 18.; IV. 15. 2.; IV. 15. 2-11. 16; XX. 17. 7.). Rain was so much important for the Vedic Aryans that the 'year' was named '*varsha*' (*Śat. Br.* II. 2. 3. 7.). Hymns were composed in the *Atharva Veda* for abundant rainfalls (IV. 15. 1-10.; VII. 18. 1-2.). It recites charms for the hastening of rains (IV. 15). In *Chhāndogya Upaniṣad* (1. 10. 6.) king of Kurus is mentioned, performing a sacrifice in order to provide relief for the drought affecting his populace. Besides this we get a reference of a 'great disaster' which befell on the Srinjayas. But the nature of this disaster is not very explicit. It is only said, that Srinjaya king Vitihavya had offended priest Bhrigu, and therefore, 'great distress' came on them (*AV.* V. 19. 1.; V. 18. 10.). There was of course a general belief that if any Brahman was offended by a certain king, then due to his curse no rain fell on that realm (*AV.* 19. 15.). Therefore, it is not unlikely that the Vitihavyas, whose destruction came through the curse of Bhrigu, perished due to scarcity of rain, resulting in drought. In another place, the king of Mahavrisas, Jñānaśruti Pautrayana, is referred (*Chhāndogya Upaniṣad* IV. 1.1.) as anxious for the welfare of his people. Jñānaśruti was a pious giver. He built *avasthas* everywhere in his kingdom, so that people throughout his realm could be provided with staple food. Rice and barley seems to have been the main items of food supplied by the king. Lentil (*masha*) was quite widely available. But it is said that in the days of severe droughts, when famine situations prevailed, even the rich people survived on minimum subsistence. In *Chhāndogya Upaniṣad* (I. 10. 2.) another tale is told about Usasti Cakrayana, who was begging from a rich person while there was 'a drought in the Kuru land'. As the rich man himself was eating bad *māsha*, so Usasti was unable to get any help from him and was forced to lead a miserable life along with his wife.

In the later Vedic period the settlements have thrived mostly in the eastern India. The later literary sources, therefore, refer to drought which mostly afflicted the eastern regions. Eastern parts of India have a wetter climate. Here green fields and thick forests cover the land. But even so in drought years vegetation was badly effected. River water became minimal during drought seasons and caused tension amongst the tribes who utilised the river water for irrigating their fields. One such incidence is referred in the *Dhammapada* (XV. 1). The water of river Rohini became very insufficient that it originated a feud between the Sakyas and the Koliyas, who use to utilize water of this river for irrigating their fields. *Jataka* stories describe the drought situation in eastern India, when water of ponds and reservoirs evaporated. *Kacchapa Jātaka* (No. 178 para 80) refers about a drought in the land of Benaras when the ponds got dried up. *Maccha Jātaka* (No. 75 para 331) refers to a similar drought in the kingdom of Kosala, when 'crops withered and everywhere the ponds, tanks and lakes dried up'.

The regions where droughts occurred quite regularly can be scanned for evidence in literary sources. We hear of droughts in Banaras (*Kacchapa Jāt.* No. 178 para 80; *Nalinika Jat.* No. 526 para 194; *Mahāvagga* VI. 23, 11-14), in Kosala (*Kacchapa Jāt* No. 75 para 331), in Kalinga (*Dhammapada* 25, 2 a; III. 276; 547), in Veranja (*Dhammapada* VI. 8; *Pārājka Samantapasādikā nāma*

Vinaya Atthakathā I. 164), in Vajji country (*Vinaya text* I. 211, 15), in Nalanda (IV. 323-24), in Rajgrha (*Mahavagga* V. 17, 7-8; *Cullavagga* VI. 21), in Anga (*RĀM. Bālkāṇḍa.* IX. 7-9), in Magadha (*Sthavirvadi Charita* IX. 55-59), in Ujjain (*see* J.C. Jain 1947), and in Kosala (*Vyavahāra* 10, 557-60).

All these regions mentioned are located in eastern India. This shows that droughts were not only prevalent in northern and western India, where dry climate predominated, but scarcity and failure of rain was quite common even in those regions where normally the climate was wet.

Sometimes droughts lingered for very long durations. A three year drought in Kasi is referred to in *Nalinika Jataka* (No. 526 para 193). A twelve year drought is referred to in *Divyavadana* (XX. 291-93) and in Jain traditions (*Sth. Ca.* IX. 55-59). A long duration drought of twelve years is referred to in the *Yuga Purāṇa* (Manka's ed. lines 177-180).

The *Ramayana* (II. 62-10; IV. 23. 8.) admits that the success of crops depended on timely rainfall. It was believed that the king could ensure timely rainfall by his righteous conduct (I. 8. 12.). Several times in the *Ramayana* (V. 38. 2.) and the *Mahābhārata*, waiting with extreme eagerness is illustrated with the simile of a peasant waiting for rain (XII. 349. 6.; XIII. 59. 14.; XIII. 62. 20.; XIII. 24. 49.; XIII. 70.10). According to Varahamihira's *Brihat Saṃhitā* cultivation of soil mainly depended on rains (*B.S.* XXI. 1; XIX. 2). He makes elaborate meteorological observations for the occurrence of rain (Shastri : 1969: 407-18). Rain gauge (*varsa pramana*) was known to Varahamihira (II. 24). *Arthaśāstra* (II. 8) also speaks of rain gauge. According to Kautalya a forecast of rainfall could be made by observing the position, motion and pregnancy of Jupiter, the rise and setting and motion of Venus and the natural or unnatural aspect of the Sun (*AS.* II. 24. 7-8.). Kautalya (VIII. 2) says that the scarcity of rain is worse than excess of rain. The same idea occurs in the *Nārada Smriti* (XI. 18). *Mahāvastu* (II. 153), *Manu* (II. 76), *Rāmāyaṇa* (II. 32. 13.; II. 112. 12.) and *Milindapanho* (VII. 6. 13.) all indicate that the success of crops and all other kinds of vegetation depended on the rain.

Scarcity of rains even affected the river courses. Due to paucity of rain the rivers got dried up, which affected the settlements, that survived on the supply of water from the rivers. *Brihat Saṃhitā* (XVVI. 47) says that if rivers in course of time recede from towns or if deep lakes in the neighbourhood should become dry, such towns would be deserted by the inhabitants. When scarcity of rain reached acute stage it dried up ponds, tanks and lakes (*Maccha Jāt Bk.* I, No. 75, para 331; *Kacchapa Jāt Bk.* II No. 178 para 80).

Droughts, when not so severe, caused bearable inconveniences. Buddhist sources suggest that whenever there were scarcity of food in any region due to drought, the Buddhist monks did not receive enough alms (*Mahavagga* VI. 19. 2.; VI. 32. 2.; *Cullavagga* VI. 21). In most cases droughts continued for fairly long duration and those caused famine conditions. During severe famines people fought for their bare survival. They consumed anything available. *Mahavagga* (VI. 23, 10-13) refers about a famine when the people even ate the flesh of dogs and elephants. During famines the hunters or those who basically lived in forest areas had nothing to eat as no food supply from the cultivators could be expected and due to drought even the natural forest products dried up.

Droughts were the natural cause for a number of famines. It is quite often said that during the famines people had to survive on the flesh of wild animals like those of tigers and hyenas (*Mahavagga* VI. 23. 14.). *Vyavahāra Bhāṣya* (10. 557-60) refers to a famine in Kosala when *sadhus* were forced to commit suicide. In the *Rupavatī Avadāna* of *Divyāvadāna* a tragic story is related, when a mother is depicted as devouring her own son when afflicted with extreme hunger during a severe famine.

To sum it up can be said that drought had caused famines many times in the past. The reference of famines which had resulted due to drought are not lacking, but dating them is not practically possible. Only Jain sources refer to about to a 12 year drought and resultant famine which occurred 200 years after the death of Mahavir, when Chandra Gupta was reigning and when Jain monk Bhadrabahu led the Jain community to the south. But all the other literary references of famines are very vague about the exact dating of episodes and it seems a futile attempt to suggest any possible date for them.

3

FLOODS

The basic changes in settlement history arose due to man-water-land relationship. Selection of land depended on easy availability of the perennial water sources. The earliest major civilization of India, the Harappan civilization flourished in the alluvial riverine valleys. The distribution of Harappan sites in northern and western Sindh shows that they were largely situated on active and meandering flood plains. Cover flood plains probably consisted of the forest areas. These forests were essentially xerophytic forests including trees such as *acacia*, *capparis*, *zizyphus* and *tamarix*. There were hardly any Harappan sites in these forest hinterlands. Without the knowledge of iron technology it was not easy to use the bronze implements by the Harappan people to develop this region and make it cultivable. Therefore, they had no option but to remain in the limited areas of the river flood plains.

The annual inundation of river banks during the rainy season, when the rivers were in spate due to rains in upper catchment areas, was a normal thing. After the flood water receded, it would leave behind the silt, which was extremely fertile. Cultivation on these river banks would bring good crops, without any need for manuring or furrowing the fields. This is called *sailabi* method and was utilized even in the recent past in Sindh.

The Punjab region is also covered with alluvial plains. Punjab has a multi-river system. The Jhelum, Chenab,

Ravi, Beas and Sutlej irrigate its vast tracts. On the basis of land–use the whole zone can be subdivided into four categories: (1) the active flood plains or *bet* lands, (2) meander flood plains or *kadir* lands, (3) the cover flood plains, (4) the bar uplands. The lands belonging to zone I are mostly benefited with the seasonal floods, which brings alluvial soil to these riverine tracts. Leshnik (1973 : 67-84) believes that most probably the Harappans avoided the immediate riverine tracks, as they must have had faced enormous difficulties to cope with the devastating floods. We think that they probably constructed some flood protection devices but they utilized the flood irrigation methods. The *kadir* land was also used, but it could not have given them enough agricultural support alone, if we presume that *bet* lands were altogether abandoned due to possible menaces.

The Punjab can be very productive, but only through a great human effort and community organisation. Sindh-Sagar *doab* region suffers with aridity and hard soil conditions. But in south Punjab, *doabs* of the five rivers created a mass of alluvial soil. A proper canal system is an essential prerequisite for the cultivation of crops in Punjab, as the rains are unreliable, aridity is maximum and the temperature rises very high. At present most productive cultivable fields in Punjab are situated in the cover flood plains and in the bars. But they can only be useful through vast canal systems. As there was no proof of canal system in Harappan times, the inhabitants probably could not utilize these productive fields. They used active flood plains and meander flood plains. Mohenjodaro itself was situated on meander flood plains.

The Punjab rivers bring heavy floods quite often and unless proper drainage is arranged the cultivable areas become waterlogged, which bring salinity to the soil and turns the lands unproductive. This malady has infected the regions surrounding ancient Harappa; the whole area at present has become absolutely unproductive due to waterlogging and salinity.

A great demand existed for the flood plains. Most of the pre– and proto–historic settlements in Sindh, Punjab, Bahawalpur north Rajasthan, Kutch and Gujarat can be traced on the flood zones of their respective rivers. The region from where the Hakra river flowed in modern Pakistan is known as Bahawalpur state (or Cholistan), which lies to the east of river Sindh. The oldest known assemblage in this region is named Hakra ware. The Hakra river which was a full fledged river system during pre– and mature Harappan period served the people living on its flood regime.

Though the settlements enjoyed the benefits of fertile riverine tracts, there were also occasions when they were completely devastated and washed out due to heavy floods in some of their rivers. The archaeological evidence of Mohenjodaro, situated on the river Indus, showed that the city was buried by 30 ft. of silt above ground level, which does not indicate a normal inundation of the river banks by the annual floods of the river (Sahni 1956 : 101-107). Moreover, 1964 test borings have revealed that the silt deposits also exist below the ground level. When the layers of silt deposits above ground level are added to those of below ground level, the total thickness of the silt comes to above 70 ft., which is divided into layers. The accumulation of such a huge silt deposit could have been possible only if we presume that the city had been destroyed by floods many times in the past (Raikes. 1965 : 196). The citizens tried to rebuild their city a number of times after flood waters receded. But their patience and repeated endeavour to rebuild this settlement could not withstand the devastating nature of the Indus river floods. The prosperity declined in the later phases of the site occupation. Many factors were responsible for the decline of the Harappan culture. This is not an appropriate place to indulge in that academic discussion but it cannot be denied that flood havoc also played a major role in the process of their gradual downfall.

The floods in Sindh basin were often aggravated by the tectonic movements. The huge silt deposits around

Mohenjodaro had induced Sahani to imagine the possibility of an unprecedented flood in Harappan times, which had devastated this big metropolitan centre. He compares it with 1819 flood in the Indus river, which occurred near Hyderabad in Sindh. 'A sudden local uplift of the part of flood plain of the Indus, had caused flooding of about 2000 sq. miles and which endured for about two years. This uplift of a strip of land—50 miles long and 15 miles wide—to an average height of 15 ft. above the ground level occurred due to some earthquake. This sort of incidence could have very well happen during Harappan times in Mohenjodaro.' R.L. Raikes (1984 : 455-60) has also given enthusiastic support to Sahnis theory. Raikes is basically a hydrologist. He thinks that "the huge deposits of silt in different levels of Mohenjodaro could not have got accumulated by occasional normal floods. It could have resulted only in a situation when the city was submerged under a stagnant water or was under a slow moving water for long duration." He argues that "'there is abundant geological evidence of rock faulting on a large scale near Sehwan. Faulting could easily be accompanied by massive extrusion of mud, aided by the pressure of accumulated underground gases. Such mud extrusions are not uncommon in Sindh. If this mud extrusion created barriers near Sahwan, it would stop the flow of the Indus to the sea and accumulated water upstream would engulf the surrounding villages and towns." This sort of fear always probably existed for the citizens of Mohenjodaro. That might have been the reason that they constructed huge surrounding walls to prevent the flood water. But the thrust of the flooding river was so enormous that the walls were unable to save the city. Raikes also points out that "the excavation of the uppermost levels in HR mound of Mohenjodaro reveal a squatter type occupational level. The buildings of this level were rudely constructed of second hand bricks. But before building this latest level, the abandoned rooms and alleyways of the previous occupation were completely filled in with rubble and gray dirt. Also crudely made packing walls were made to face portions of these fillings. When such fillings were removed it was found that the structure so filled were quite adequate for habitation." Why the people of Mohenjodaro took pains to fill these lower constructions to make a sort of platform on which they rebuilt their houses ? It looks like that this was the last effort of the inhabitants to save themselves from recurring floods, by artificially raising the whole city. Thus this platform and mud brick fortification wall indicate the danger of floods which constantly hung over the city. Flood episodes might have had occurred many times and ultimately a sudden local uplift in a part of the flood plain of the Indus might have demolished the city for a longer period, due to which the people were forced to abandon the city.

Sahni and Raikes' theory had not gained universal support. Lambrick (1967 : 313-322) has suggested that 'the sand borne winds, which is naturally composed of lighter grains can be accumulated inside the hollows of the ruins, and when these get consolidated by rains, the texture becomes silty clay, resembling very closely to the substance resulting from deposition in a lake or by very slow moving river flood.' Therefore, what Raikes considered as silt accumulated in Mohenjodaro ruins due to stagnant water overlapping the site may not be necessarily so. Lambrick presents a modern equivalent episode, which occurred in Sheikh Bhirkio village, 20 miles south east of Hyderabad. This village was completely obliterated by air-borne river silts.

The flood marks were not only found in the big metropolitan city of Mohenjodaro, but also some other neighbouring towns as well. Even Chanhudaro (Mackay; 1943; 63) and Amri (N.G. Majumdar; 1934) seem to have been effected to floods. The floods in the Indus river devastated the sites located primarily in the lower regions of this river valley. The lower regions accumulated a great amount of silt deposits along its banks and therefore, the ground level was raised up. Whenever there was a heavy winter in the mountainous regions, where the river is fed by the melting snow, the flow of water in the ensuing summer was much more and if accompanied by a heavy rainfall then floods were unavoidable in the lower regions of the river path. The people of Chanhudaro suffered repeatedly due to recurring floods (Wheeler 1968 : 56), as the site was located in the lower region of the river Indus. They were forced to make their way to lands of higher elevation and this original site was ultimately abandoned. Harappa was another important site, remains of which can now be traced on the old river bed of Ravi. Today the dry river bed extends to 6 miles from the north of the site, but once it must have been much closer as the traces of flood havoc can be ascertained in this settlement as well (Wheeler *Ibid* : 30).

The Ghaggar (Hakra, the ancient Saraswati river) had supported many settlements along its banks. According to hydrologist Raikes (1968 : 286-291) the Ghaggar was captured alternatively by the rivers of Indus system and of the Ganges system in pre– and proto–historic times which affected its westward and eastward diversions. During the period of its westward diversion it had brought seasonal floods to the north Rajasthan region. Kalibangan was one of the important sites which reached the status of urbanization in pre– and mature Harappan periods. Kalibangan, which was situated on the Ghaggar river provide us with proof of thick clay among the ruins of the city. Raikes (*op. cit*) considers that it resulted due to 'unprecedented floods which might have engulfed the city and brought about its ruin.' The controversy persists due to the conflicting archaeological reports, B. B. Lal (1979 : 85-97) thinks that there is no evidence of the destruction of the site through floods.

Gujarat including Kutch was another area which was colonized by Harappan people. This region became popular due to trade. Gujarat supplied the raw materials to the Harappan cities of Punjab and Sindh. It had a long sea coast. Some centres evolved around trading ports. Lothal, in Ahmedabad district was one of the major trading centres. Excavator S.R. Rao (1973 : 54-60) considers that this town, which witnessed days of prosperity, declined due to great floods, 'which occurred quite a number of times and ultimately reduced the city to a heap of ruins'. The dockyard, which was the source of its maritime activity was also 'rendered unserviceable because of accumulation of silt.' The later phase of its occupation consist of jerry built houses with mud floors, reed walls and thatched roofs, which clearly depict its decaying economy.

Floods affected the nearby areas as well. Koth, which was situated 12 miles north east of Lothal, in Dholka taluk of Ahmedabad, was also damaged by floods. A 4 ft. thick deposit of flood loam and fine sand caps an 8 ft. thick occupational debris. It is clear, therefore, that a heavy flood of long duration, brought the end of Koth settlement (S.R. Rao 1963:181). Kanasutaria was another small Harappan site in the Ahmedabad district which lies north of Lothal. This site is covered by a thick fluvial deposit of sand and gravel, thus providing us with the proof, that the settlement was destroyed by a heavy flood (*Ibid* : 188-89). Another site of much importance was Rangpur, in Surendranagar district of Gujarat, situated on the river Bhadar. Most of the structures of this site are reported to have been either washed away by floods or disintegrated in a mass of clay (*Ibid* : 188; Ibid : 24; *IAR* : 1954-55). Desalpur a small site in Kutch, situated in the bank of river Bamuchela (Morai), an affluent of the river Dhrud, was destroyed in the same way (*Ibid* : 1963 : 188). Bhagatrav, in Bharoach district of Gujarat, was situated on the river Kim. The backwaters of the sea which entered the creek, together with the flood in the Kim, had brought devastation to the site (*IAR* : 1957-58 : 15).

This short sketch of the flood disturbances in Harappan and late Harappan times, in Punjab, Sindh, North Rajasthan and Gujarat, shows that in spite of the sufferings the in habitants underwent through year after year, they were forced to live in the flood zone areas. The reason behind this, as we have already seen, is that the technological base of the Harappans was still very premature.

It was a bronze age culture, and as we know bronze or copper are not very strong metals and inadequate for making agricultural tools. Besides, bronze is used very sparingly, because it was not available locally in abundance.

The inhabitants had no other choice than to reside near the flood zones and alluvial areas of the riverine tracks, where flood water solved their irrigation demands and receding water left a soft silt on the embankments, which could be easily cultivated even with the use of a hoe. But they had to pay a heavy price for it. Floods had often devastated their settlements and recurring floods may have brought famine situations, which forced them to evacuate their favoured areas as well.

In late Harappan periods noticeable shifts in population concentration can be seen. From west Punjab, Sindh and Rajasthan, people were now moving towards east Punjab, Haryana and western parts of Uttar Pradesh. These areas had better prospects of rain. But as their technical knowledge was not progressing, rather declining, they could not enter the thickly forested areas and still remained clinging to the riverine tracts. As a result there was no rescue from flood menaces. Many sites provide us this proof. The people with Harappan background were settling down in Haryana. Banawali was one of their important centres. Flood damage could not be avoided here (*IAR* 1983-84). Hulas was another late Harappan colony in Saharanpur district of U.P. Precautions were taken against flood havocs, which proves that this danger persisted in western U.P. too. (Dikshit : 1979 : 213;1861 : 70-75). Manda was a small late Harappan site, situated in the north–west of Jammu, on the banks of Chenab river which gives evidence of flood destruction (Joshi and Madhubala 1982 : 185-197). The site of Bhagvanpura, in the district of Kurukshetra, Haryana, was situated on the river bank of Saraswati. The excavation of this site reveals an inter–locking stage of the Harappan and ensuing PGW cultural levels. The late Harappan period shows traces of mud platform which was damaged by a devastating flood, though this did not lead to people evacuating the site for ever, as they continued to live in the area after flood waters receded. Here we find the traces of later cultural levels, including those of Ochre Colour Ware (OCW) and Painted Gray Ware (PGW) people. OCW are mostly available from flood effected trenches. G.R. Sharma (1969) reporting on the excavation of Kausambi has brought to light in late Harappan cultural context a fortification wall. This site lies on the river Yamuna, which endangered its safety. Therefore, the Harappan people built this defensive wall.

With the extinction of different phases of Harappan culture, an unsettling situation prevailed in north India. The following cultural level is named Ochre Colour Ware and Black and Red Ware. Their stratigraphical sequences differed according to regions. The region of OCW culture was quite extensive from Bahadarabad, Hardwar district, U.P. in the north to Noh in Bharatpur district, Rajasthan in the south and from Katapalon in Jullundhar district, Punjab in the west to Saipai in Etawah district of U.P. in the east.

The OCW deposits are of shallow nature. Excavation at Ambakheri (*IAR* 1963-64 : 53-55), Baheria (*IAR* : 1966-67 : 43-44), Bahadarabad (IAR : 1971-72 : 54), all in Saharanpur district, Jhinjhana (*IAR* : 1962-63 : 70) in Muzaffarnagar district; Lal Qila (*IAR* : 1969-70 : 38) in Bulandashahr district; Atranjikhera (Gaur : 1983) in Etah district; and Saipai (*IAR* : 1971-72 : 46-47) in Etawah district show that the depth of OCW deposits vary between 0.5 m. and 1.5 m. The material culture of the OCW sites are found sporadically. No habitational deposits are found in OCW levels. Some scholars connect the OCW cultures with the 'copper hoards', as some specimens of 'copper hoard' have been discovered along with the OCW in some sites. OCW potteries are brittle in nature. This could have been due to lack of proper firing of potteries. But Krishna Deva (1969 : 75-82) has rightly pointed out that we cannot imagine that the people of OCW culture who knew the technique of smelting copper at a high temperature did not know how to fire pottery well. Therefore, the condition of OCW indicate that they reached this stage of brittleness due to waterlogging. One of the important OCW site was Hastinapur (Lal 1954-55 : 138-146; 1955 : 31-32) in Meerut district U.P., which was situated one the river Burhi Ganga. Lal (1969 : 83-94) has undertaken a detailed study of soil samples from OCW sites of Hastinapur, Jhinjhana

(*IAR.* 1962-63 : 70), Achichatra (*IAR.* 1963-64; 1964-65) and Nasirpur (Dikshit : 1968 : 47). The chemical analysis of the OCW deposits suggest that they were water-laid. The presently dried–up river Burhi Ganga, which was once a great affluent, flowed along the site of Hastinapur. The site started its history from OCW level and continued till the NBPW period. The definite gap between each period indicates that the site was abandoned due to flood havoc and reoccupied repeatedly. The absence of any habitational traits in the OCW level indicates that these people had a very short stay and they had a poor socio-economic infrastructure. Probably they were of migratory nature, as no burnt brick houses, or any structural evidence is found from any of the OCW sites. Gaur (1983) while excavating OCW levels in Atranjikhera had noticed fluvial sediments in the OCW horizon (*IAR* : 1965-66; 1967-68; etc.) Prof. Fakruddin Ali Ahmad has also independently examined the soil sample of Atranjikhera, which has yielded OCW in a substantial amount (Gaur : 1983 : 23). He has reached the conclusion that the area had been flooded by the river and remained waterlogged for a considerable period (*IAR* 1962-63; 1968-69), Lal (1968 : 857-63), suggested that a major tectonic activity during OCW period brought about a great flood in the upper valleys of the Ganga, the Yamuna and their tributaries which took the form of a deluge and affected OCW sites extensively. We have seen that in Bhagvanpura also OCW remains are found in flood effected trenches (Joshi and Madhubala : 1982, 185-97). Atranjikhera, Etah district, U.P. provides us with four cultural levels. The site is situated on the right (western) bank of Kali-nadi, tributary of the Ganga. On the north-eastern side, the river flows closest to the mound, the distance being hardly 50 m. The area had been quite prone to floods from the very beginning of its occupation. It had been flooded many times. This natural calamity exists even in present days. During rainy seasons the whole area is deluged with water. Therefore, in the days of its earliest occupation, i.e., OCW period, there are clear indications that the area had been flooded by the river and remained waterlogged for a considerable period. There seems to have been a gap between OCW period and the succeeding BRW period. The latter had a very thin distinctive layer. Probably the BRW people occupied the area after horrifying memories of flood destruction of OCW site were forgotten (Gaur : 1983 : 4-5). BRW cultural level again met with destruction due to flood. A mud filling which seems to have been deposited by floods in the river Kali separates the BRW and PGW phases (*IAR* : 1963-64; 1968-69). Their knowledge of copper was possibly their only significant achievement. But as pastoral nomads, they did not need to settle down permanently anywhere and therefore did not need to support their settlements with diverse economic activities. Due to weakness of their infrastructure, no evidence of constructional activity is available at their sites. They could not therefore have taken any precautionary measures against floods. Their sites were so badly damaged due to flood havoc that hardly any traces of their civilization are available to us. B. B. Lal (1954-55 : 21-23) has suggested the pre-1200 BC period as the chronology of OCW people. Though Wheeler (1959) has suggested the pre-800 B.C. period as the age of this culture.

OCW deposits are found in a large area. Now if a major flood has washed away the OCW sites and because of this natural calamity the ware has received its present character, then the floods must have been of the major scale. B. B. Lal (1968 : 857-63) has suggested a major tectonic activity during the OCW period, which may account for the drying up of river Ghaggar, which could have resulted for the diversion of some of its tributaries to the neighbouring river systems, in this case the Yamuna, and the flooding of the OCW sites.

The floods may have effected the OCW settlements of Rajasthan too. The rivers Kantli, Kasaunti, Dohan, Gambhiri, Pandoli, etc. which have given support to late Harappan and the OCW sites may have had devastating floods, which submerged the OCW sites for a long period and brought its wares to this brittle and off-slip condition.

After OCW period comes the cultural level of Painted Gray Ware (PGW) people. PGW deposits, which probably belonged to later Vedic civilization, have been found in a wider horizon. They were getting better equipped with new technology as iron was definitely introduced by this time. But no improvement can be perceived in their flood-prevention measures. They were still constructing mud-embankments, similar to those of the earlier days. In some of the PGW sites this cultural level was found overlain by flood deposits, causing desertion of the settlement. For example Surdargarh, a small site in Bikaner district, Rajasthan which represents PGW period, was evacuated till long after PGW level, after which it was reoccupied by Rangmahal culture. A flood deposit separates the two cultural periods (V. Tripathi 1976 : 28). Noh in Bharatpur district, Rajasthan, is situated near a small rivulet known as Ruparel. But in rainy season this rivulet quite often gets flooded. The PGW strata of this site, which is termed as period III by the excavator, is found in a highly disturbed condition. River gravel is mixed with rolled sherds of PGW. It is interesting to see that the inhabitants of this site had tried to save their colony from these floods. Period II has 3 m. thick filling beneath it which was made to raise the ground level against flood damages (*IAR* 1962-63 : 28; 1968-69; 1970-71). We have seen repeated flood menaces in the Bhagvanpura in the district of Kurukshetra. The river Saraswati had once again brought disaster to PGW cultural levels (Joshi and Madhubala 1982 : 185-97). In the same way, Atrarjikhera, which was ruined twice earlier came under flood destruction for a third time in the PGW period. In the PGW period, floods occurred a number of times. The worst of these floods occurred in the river Kali towards the end of the middle phase of this period. The flood washed away considerable portions of the settlement. The excavator Gaur finds the deposits of eroded materials, sometimes redeposited in the trenches and sometimes near the river bed. He feels that some time after the flood the site was probably shaken by an earthquake, effects of which can be traced in trench D.1 (N.W.) (Gaur 1983 : 122). A mud embankment with a basal width of about 7 m. can be noticed in Atrarnjikhera—which belonged to PGW period. Jakhera was a site in the district Etah (*IAR*

1974-75 : 43) which is situated on the left bank of the river Kali. It is 16 km. from Atranjikhera. Period II b. of Jakhera which has wielded PGW remains can be correlated with period III of Atranjikhera. PGW people in Jakhera were facing the same flood menace. They built a mud-embankment with an extant basal width of 4.80 m. and a moat channel to protect their site from harassment (Sahi 1978 : 102). Similarly PGW people of Kampil, Farrukhabad district, built a mud-embankment to save their settlement from the flood-fury, the traces of which can be seen in the excavation of that site (*IAR* 1975-6). In the same way floods had brought destruction to PGW people in Dadheri, in district Ludhiana (J.P. Joshi 1978 : 98-101) and in Hastinapur (B. B. Lal 1955 : 5-151).

Cultural extent of PGW civilization can be fixed on the basis of available C-14 dating and from the excavation report of its various sites. Twenty-five C-14 dates for PGW culture from ten sites are noted by Lal (M. Lal 1986 : 94). These dates come from the middle and late phases of PGW deposits—providing a time limit between 1155-660 B.C. They mainly belong to Rajasthan and west U.P. Thus it seems that PGW deposits belonged to the late Vedic age.

Iron was found in all the phases of PGW levels, but their use was confined to weapons, craft-tools, household objects and ornaments. The use of iron in agricultural activity had not yet become common. Concentration of population and surplus of food production did not reach their climax and hence big utility projects could not be mounted on a large scale. PGW settlement pattern had not made any drastic changes. Most of the sites are located on the river banks, not away from it, which shows that the infiltration into the forested hinterlands was not yet a practical possibility. PGW people colonized, primarily upper Saraswati valley, Yamuna and Ganga valleys. Maximum number of PGW settlements in Haryana existed in the alluvial plains (*Bhangar* land). Nearly 186 PGW and Gray Ware settlements have been located in the *Bhangar* land by Breham Datta (1980 : Table 3-4), 47 PGW and GW sites have been found on direct flood plains. In addition a number of PGW sites have been located on the flood plains of the Saraswati and Markanda rivers. This settlement pattern indicates that PGW people were mainly settling down along the natural drainage system, which provided them with potable water along with irrigation facilities. A study of the PGW settlements in Ganga-Yamuna *Doab* also indicates the same pattern. (M. Lal : 1984 : b: 171-72). Barring few, most of the settlements in Ganga,Rind and Yamuna Rind *Doab* are situated on the river banks and not away from it. Though they may have initiated the process of expanding their cultivable land by burning the forests, as the *Satapatha Brahmana* refers to it, but they had not yet infiltrated much into the thick hinterland forest areas and thus primarily depended upon the river-side tracks. Flood irrigation was a basic source of cultivation. Of course, now they were occupying wetter areas where rain was much more dependable, but had always been erratic. In the Rig Vedic period they prayed to the rain god Indra, for more water. They were scared of drought, not excessive rain or flood. Their settlements survived on the flood-water irrigation. References to floods occur many times in Vedic literature (e.g. in *RV.I.61.11; II.13.12;* IV.19.6; VIII. 31.10). But in many Rig Vedic hymns they are invoked and praised for their beneficial deeds. For example in *Rig Veda* (X.17.10) the flood is called 'mother who gives brightness and shining'. In *Rig Veda* (X. 36.1) while invoking all the gods, the poet even invoked floods. In *Rig Veda* (X.109.1) it is called 'heavenly flood'. It has been suggested (N. N. Bhattacharya, 1975 : 10-11, 57) that the importance given to sacrifices and rituals in ancient society was an economic necessity. Vedic sires had introduced sacrifices and rituals with a notion that the sacrifices exercised power over gods and could even influence things and events. All the Vedic *yajnas* were primarily connected to economic motives. They were directly connected with food production. Either they were to appease the rain god Indra, who could help them to irrigate their fields or to desist the menace of droughts so that their food production was not hampered. In fact the sacrificial details of the *Vajapeya* was a simple magical performance employed as a productive technique to obtain food and drink (Kane 1930 : 58 : 1206). But it is interesting to notice that there were no rituals connecting with stopping the flooding of the rivers. This definitely indicates that the Vedic society welcomed the floods, even if it may have brought destructions to its river-side settlements.

The favourable attitude towards floods which inundated the cultivable fields of the Aryans were sometimes lost, when flood destructions led to complete devastation of the sites. This suggests that floods probably became the causative factor for famines, at least during excessive situations. A great flood has been referred to in a story of the *Mahabharata*. According to this episode, during the reign of Nicakshu who was sixth in succession after Pariksita, a great flood occurred in the Ganga, which destroyed the capital Hastinapur completely and forced its inhabitants to flee. Thereafter, Nicakshu had to establish a new capital called Kausambi (Pargitar 1913 : 5-6). The episode may be related with the later Vedic times.

The next stage of our history can be seen with the arrival of the people using Northern Black Polish Ware (NBPW). The chronological sequence of NBPW can be determined through available C-14 dates. Most of the dates fall within the time range of 700-100 B.C. This is quite a long period when seen through the eyes of literary sources. It includes Buddhist, Mauryan and post Mauryan periods. Our literary sources of this vast period are of diverse types-which include early Buddhist canons and goes up to the period of the *Jatakas*. In archaeological terms this period has been generally studied under three phases—Early, Middle and Late. The early NBPW period corresponds to C. 600 B.C. The Middle phase can be restrained between 500-350 B.C. and the Late phase between 350-100 B.C. dealing with the post Mauryan remains.

Flood menaces continued in NBPW period as well. Great destructions by flood led the people to evacuate their land. Like present times, heavy floods created unbearable situations as the residential centres of the people collapsed, and their crops failed, which led to extreme hunger. Quite often stagnant water after floods brought epidemics and created famine situations, which forced the people to evacuate the land. The archaeological excavations have revealed many sites, which were affected by furies of flood. The–river side settlements, which have grown much bigger in size, were quite often shattered due to flood havocs. This can be seen from the evidence in Kausambi, where river Yamuna threatened its safety (Sharma 1969 :6; *IAR* 1962-63 : 33). The site had been affected by floods many times, the earliest vestiges of this flood menace can be perceived in sub-period I-2, where the traces of a sandy layer can be seen, which probably got accumulated due to flood (*Ibid* : 27). Again in sub-period III. 8, in spite of the precaution taken by the inhabitants of the site, by building huge rampart walls, the site witnessed the furies of the flooded Yamuna. Sandy earth full of *kankar* nodules cover the rampart wall. Similarly in Rajghat (Roy, Narain 1976:22), which was ancient Benaras, in spite of protective devices constructed there, in the early levels of the site, damage by the flood of the Ganga can be proved, as the traces of flood can be found in the form of salt, *kankar*, and shells strewn amidst the habitational deposits. In Ujjain also, which was situated on the eastern bank of the river Sipra, a formidable danger from flood always existed, especially because the town was situated on a bend in such a way, that flood water would have invariably entered in it (*IAR: 1956-57*).

Excavation reports in the eastern region of Bihar confirm the above observation. Flood destruction in Bihar was more common, as the area is drained by numerous rivers. Even in modern times this state is afflicted with annual inundation during rainy seasons. In early historic period, Bihar had to suffer due to heavy floods many times. Chirand, an ancient site, situated on the banks of the river Ghaghra, was several times eroded by floods. Excavation at Charittarvan (Buxar) also presents the same evidence of flood destruction. The Ganga probably washed away a major portion of the habitational area after its period II. This may have forced its inhabitants to abandon this town as well (*IAR* 1965-66:11). Silt deposits can also be traced in other smaller sites of Bihar, like Balirajgarh (*IAR* 1962-63:5),

Rajbadidanga (*IAR* 1964-65:50). An effort to save their settlements were constantly made by the inhabitants. Brick-concrete ramps or massive fortifications were constructed on the riversides for the safety of the sites (Mate: 1969-70: 58-69). But these precautionary measures could not save the settlements, as the vagaries of the floods were too massive.

Even during early centuries of the Christian era, when settlement pattern had much changed, and people were expanding in all directions of available land, the flood havocs affected the riverine zones. The climatic phenomenon always had such an imperative constraint that in spite of all the inconveniencies created by floods people adhered to the sites nearer to the rivers. Vaisali, an important urban centre, provides distinct flood deposits in the period II, representing the Kusana-Gupta phase (IAR 1960-61: 6). Probably the site was ultimately abandoned after a few devastating experiences of flood havocs. Pataliputra was a prominent urban centre in Bihar. The town was crucially surrounded by four rivers—Ganga, Son, Punpun and Gandak. The city seems to have been destroyed by a devastating flood of the Son in C. 6th century A.D. Kumrahar excavation done in 1912-13, shows about 8 to 10 ft. deep silt and thick layer of ashes, near the famous pillared hall of Pataliputra. Waddell (1975:8) suggests that the place may have been destroyed by floods. Besides the sand and mud of the river Son, that of the river Punpun too was found at Kumrahar during 1951-55 excavations (Pandey 1963:75). The city was probably ultimately abandoned around A.D. 750., as Cunningham suggests on the basis of a Chinese account (*ASIR* XI:155-156).

The archaeological data can be supplemented by the literary evidences. Floods often occurred due to heavy rains in the catchment areas and sometimes even in upper reaches of the river, which affected villages in the downstream regions. Heavy rains and floods are quite often recalled in *Jātaka* stories. *Gahapati Jātaka* (No. 199, para 135) refers a heavy rains in the region of Kasi, which carried away all the grain and brought famine. In

Padakusala Manava Jātaka (No. 432, para 508) a heavy rain which brought flood in Kasi is also referred to. Sravasti also suffered due to flood havocs (*Champeya Jātaka* No 506; *Dhammapada* IV.3.338). A heavy rain in the upper reaches of the rivers Achiravati, which brought a devastating flood in Saraswati, seems to have had an everlasting memory as it was recalled in many Buddhist stories (*Tevijja Suttanta*-I.24; *Kāma Jātaka*-No. 467; *Khadirangara Jāt* No. 40). Sometimes small streams also flowed in spate and brought havoc in the nearby villages (*Chulla Dhanuggaha Jātaka* No. 374). The *Champeya Jātaka* tells the story of a big flood in the river Champa, which lay between the realms of Anga and Magadha (No. 506, para 454). Buddhist legends speak of Gautam Buddha giving warning to the monks of his monastery about the calamities of excessive rain which brought floods to the villages. In *Gahapati Jātaka* (No. 199) famine conditions are mentioned as having arisen due to heavy floods. The period reflected in the Buddhists *Jātaka* probably belonged to the beginning of the Christian era, which shows that even with the advancement of technology, state mechanism, man mobilization and social consciousness, the menace of floods could not be avoided. Other Buddhist works like *Milindapañho* (II.1.10) and *Mahāvaṃśa* (XXXI.25) also refer to the floods.

The menace was noticed by the classical writers too. Strabo notices that quite often rivers overflowded the banks, causing settled areas to be evacuated and deserted (R.C. Majumdar 1960 : 254). The later Buddhist literature, which were composed in early Christian eras, refer to the river torrents which brought sorrow and devastation by assailing the dams (*Buddhacarita* : IX : 15 : 94 ; XIII:6:138).

To conclude it can be said that the floods had created unprecedented difficulties on numerous occasions in ancient India. Sometimes they were manageable. People probably vacated the towns temporarily and came back as the flood water receded; as they do even at present times. But no doubt, on some occasions floods brought ultimate destructions. It all depended on the waterlogging situation.

If the site remained under the layers of water continuously for a considerable length of time, then the whole eco-system collapsed. Floods have brought famine conditions even in modern times. We know that many times Bengal and Bihar floods had brought famines in 19th and 20th centuries. Even in west of India where the floods are not so frequent, the famines had followed after the flood situations persisted for a long period. (*See* Introduction.) Similar situations can be imagined in the ancient times. We have seen that many settlements in the valleys of the Sindh, the rivers of Punjab, the Saraswatī and Ganga Yamuna valleys, were utterly destroyed due to floods and even mass migration and evacuation of the the settlements became inevitable. These situations indicate that the floods had brought famines in the affected areas.

A large number of casualties, resulting in a drastic decline of the population is another criteria, to know whether the flood conditions had created famine situations or not. In most of the sites reported above the levels which have the marks of flood destruction was followed by a comparatively dilapidated cultural levels. These ensuing levels show that the size of site had become smaller the habitational area has shrunken, the construction of the houses were of inferior types, mostly using used bricks and there is a general decline in every sphere of their civilization. This is a simple indication that a large number of deaths had occurred due to the flood menace and those who survived even after this calamity could only fulfil their minimum needs.

SECTION II

MAN-MADE CALAMITIES

Famine conditions arose due to ecological degradation of a particular region. When a settled social community due to its ignorance or negligence towards ecological factors, interfered extensively in the surrounding land profile, it depleted its natural resources. Concentration of population on a limited zone was followed by unplanned clearing of grassland and forests. Ecological degradation could have been resisted only with improvements in technology and environmental consciousness. But if both these balancing elements were lacking then famine conditions could not be averted. Natural calamities had always been common features in ancient times. Denudation of grass cover, deforestation and over–exploitation of land fertility due to concentration of population in a limited area, were some of the human factors responsible to aggravate the ecological imbalance and cause famine situations.

4

ECOLOGICAL DEGRADATION DUE TO CONCENTRATION OF POPULATION

When population is concentrated on a limited zone for a considerable length of time, it brings undue pressure on the bearing capacity of land. This adverse effect is more vivid in dry climatic areas. Baluchistan, western Punjab, Sindh, north-western Rajasthan, Cholistan (Bahawalpur state), Gujarat and Kutch were the main areas where numerous settlements flourished in neolithic and chalcolithic phases of Indian history. Most of these areas, at present fall under arid and drought-prone regions. The depletion of land profile in arid zones was a gradual process and human factors had been largely responsible for it.

As long as the population remained sparce, ecological degradation remained under control. For example in Mehrgarh we find seven continuous, and successive cultural periods which proves that the site survived for more than 3 million years (Pd. I roughly—6th-5th mill. B.C. and Pd. VII till the middle of the 3rd mill. B.C.). Similarly, Kili Gul Muhammad reveals four distinct periods, without any break. Charcoal samples collcted from the upper surface of Kili Gul Muhammad I takes its antiquity back to C. 5000 B.C. (C.14-5300 + -200 B.P) (Fairservis 1956 : 1971). Gradually the population multiplied. India is a vast country. If the people would have settled down all throughout its length and breadth, there would have been no concentration of population in selected zones.

But in prehistoric times people were settling down in the river valleys only, near the sides of lakes and streams, because they depended completely on the perennial water resources for their requirements. Therefore, they had a limited scope for the selection of sites. The forests were impregnable as the people suffered from technological limitations of clearing and providing water facilities. It is the water, and not the land that prescribed the man-land relationship to a large degree. We may explain our ideas with the help of a chart. (See chart VI) The earlier settlements when the population pressure was less, survived longer than the later period when the population multiplied. Due to excessive population concentration on a limited zone the effected regions were soon depleted of its fertility which affected the longevity of the settlements. In the north-western boundaries Gomal and Quetta valleys provided an excellent situation for the rise of neolithic and chalcolithic cultures which flourished on the Zhob, Lorlai Quetta and Pishin river valleys. Moving southwards in Baluchistan one encounters the sites belonging to Nal and Kulli cultures. Nal culture settlements are spread over the valleys of the Hingol, the Porali and the Hab rivers. A number of Nal settlements have been reported by N. G. Majumdar (1934) around the Gaj river pass. Majumdar's survey reveals that most of the Amri sites were located on the flood plains of the river Nara and Lake Mancchar.

Louis Flam (1984 : 77-82) has surveyed the settlement pattern in the province of Sindh. He observes that there are a total of 61 pre-historic sites in Sindh. In Sindh Kohistan region there are 30 sites, 10 sites in Kirthar mountain-Kirthar piedmont region and 20 sites in the river plains of lower Indus basin. Of the 30 sites in Sindh Kohistan 20 sites are located near perennial streams, and the remaining 10 sites are located near ephemeral streams. In the Kirthar mountain piedmont region all 10 sites are located near ephemeral streams. In the lower Indus basin all 21 sites are located near perennial rivers with seasonal floodings.

Mughal's (1982 : 85-95) survey in Cholistan (Bahawalpur State) region confirms the above settlement pattern. In the earliest period i.e. the Hakra ware period, the settlements are generally located in the *dahars* (mud flats). A great concentration of sites are along the Hakra flood plain. In early Harappan period the sites are along the river bank but not on that specific stretch of land where the Hakra ware sites are found. They shifted away from the previously occupied centres. In the mature Harappan period again the shifting of the settlements are noticeable, but they remained confined to the riverine belts. In the ensuing post-Harappan-PGW period the sites are located in the middle of the former Hakra bed. This study show that due to the extreme arid climate of Cholistan region, even the perennial river source had limited water. In this sort of climatic conditions ecological degradation was quite quick (see Chart VII).

In South Rajasthan the existence of the chalcolithic culture is revealed by the excavations at Ahar and Gilund. Nearly 50 sites of this culture discovered so far show that the culture was centered in the valleys of the Berach and Banas rivers in Udaipur and Chittorgarh districts. This culture even extended eastwards along the course of the Banas and its tributaries. The site of the Bagor is situated on the left bank of a tributary of the river Banas. Its habitational deposits can be divided into three cultural phases. The earliest settlers were hunters and food gatherers. The radiocarbon dating of Bagor can take back the dates of its cultural phase I to about 3800 B.C., while the chalcolithic culture here began about 2800 B.C. There is no break in between. Such a long survival of settlements is not found in north Rajasthan. The upper portion of the Hakra valley, which passes through north Rajasthan, is known by the name of Ghaggar and is identified as the ancient Saraswatī river. Stein (1943) and Ghosh (1953 : 31-34) have explored the valleys of the river Saraswatī. In the Harappan times the Hakra/Ghaggar (Saraswatī) was a perennial river. It is quite possible that it met the river Nara and could have flowed directly into the Rann of Kutch, without meeting the Indus. The presence of archaeological sites in the vicinity of these channels give us a possible data for the time of the 'wet' period, when the Hakra Ghaggar was flowing to its full capacity.

More than 25 mounds of Harappan cultural affinity are traced by A. Ghosh (1989 : 98-106) on Saraswati Drisadwati valleys. Beginning right from the Pakistan border up to midway between Hanumangarh and Suratgarh in the Saraswatī valley and about 15 miles east of Bhadra in the Driṣadwatī valley near the border between Bikaner and Punjab. Stein's (1943, S. P. Gupta. e.d. 1989) archaeological tour along the Ghaggar/Hakra river is of much value for the study of the region. His observations can be summarised thus: From Suratgarh up the bed of Ghaggar as it stretches towards Hanumangarh, Rangmahal sites 23. In Anupgarh *tehsil*, which extends up to Bahawalpur border, late prehistoric mounds 10. In Bahawalpur region from Kudwala Ther to Marot, Harappan sites 30. From Lurewala Ther to Derawar, Harappan ware sites 16.

Suraj Bhan's (1976, 1977, 1978) explorations in Haryana has located 133 sites in the river valleys of the state. In mature Harappan period there were 3 settlements in the Saraswatī valley, 22 in the Driṣadwatī valley, 3 in the Sabi valley and 8 in the Yamuna valley. In late Harappan period there are 43 sites located in the Saraswatī valley, 51 in the Driṣadwatī valley, 7 in the Sabi and 32 in the Yamuna valley. In PGW period the Saraswatī supported 100 settlements, the Driṣadwatī 171 settlements and the Yamuna 87 settlements (see Chart VII).

In western Uttar Pradesh, Dikshit, (1984 : 260) observes that Harappan sites have a heavy concentration in Saharanpur district. These settlements here are generally located on the tributaries of the Yamuna. In the Yamuna Gangetic *doab*, Dikshit has located nearly 75 sites of Harappan culture. Most of these are located on the tributaries of the Yamuna and not on Yamuna proper, probably ensuring against the recurring floods.

Similar survey has been conducted by Makhan Lal (1978, 1981, 1984) in Kanpur district. The earliest culture identified in this area is that of BRW (Black and Red

Ware). The total number of BRW sites in Kanpur is 9, of which 6 are in the Ganga Rind *doab* and 3 in the Yamuna Rind *doab*. All the sites are located on the river banks. The total number of PGW sites is 46, out of which 31 are located on the Ganga Rind *doab* and 15 on the Yamuna Rind *doab*. All except 6 are located on the river banks. Six sites located away from the river banks are near large low-lying swampy areas, where water accumulates during the rainy seasons. Here most of the sites located on the rivers are on elevated lands, away from the reach of floods. Belonging to NBPW (Northern Black Polish Ware) period 99 sites are found. Of these 65 sites are located along the river banks and 39 away from the rivers. The number of sites in Kanpur district during the EH (Early Historic) period is 141. Of these 89 are on river banks and 52 away from them. T. N. Roy (1986 App.) has provided a list of 413 NBPW sites, out of which 71 sites are located on river banks which demonstrates that people were gradually breaking new lands and moving away from the limited riverine zones (see Chart VII).

In the southern districts of Harappan settlement pattern, a survey has been conducted by Possehl. An important geographical factor which can be noted is that Harappan sites of Saurastra, Gujarat are all located directly adjacent to source of flowing water. Possehl (1980 : 50) specifically mentions that within his survey zone he had rigorously searched to find out if any Harappan site can be traced away from the riverine tracks, but he could not find any site which existed away from the river valleys. These 'interior places', of course, contain archaeological sites dating from early historical times, late in the first millennium B.C: (see Chart VII).

The interior of Gujarat, which definitely was more wooded than what it is today, needed to be cleared up for human habitation. Instead the riverine belts were automatically cleared up due to frequent heavy floods, as they occur in the Gujarati rivers. A special feature of the rivers of Gujarat (like the Ghelo and the Kalubhar rivers) is that due to short but heavy precipitation sudden floods overflow the embankments and wash away the big trees from the area. These floods are short lived, therefore, the grassy outcrops of shrubs are not much effected. Only big trees cannot exist on the riverine belts. This must have provided them with enough cultivable land on the riverine tracks. Chitalwala (1979 : 113-20) has surveyed the Rajkot district of Gujarat. He has shown that in the Harappan and post Harappan periods, the number of sites which were located along a perennial water course are 17, whereas the number of sites on non-perennial water courses are eight. The number of sites on rocky prominence are 10.

Thus a survey on various regions of pre- and proto-historic north India, makes it clear the most of the population concentrated on the limited tracks of river valleys. We think that when a limited geographical unit had excessive population concentration then the ecological degradation became inevitable. In such conditions the population was forced to migrate to new productive areas. Thus a popular zone become 'an area of isolation'.

Density of population which effects the ecology of a region can be judged on two basis 1) multiplicity of sites, 2) emergence of bigger sites. Surveying it area wise a study of settlement pattern in Baluchistan can be done on the basis of Fairservis' work (see Chart VIII). It can be noticed that whenever multiplicity of the sites occurred, in a limited geographical zone, which indicated density of population, it effected ecology. Probably over exploitation of land resources depleted the soil fertility. As a result in the ensuing period the population migrated and the number of sites decreased. For example in Quetta Pishin, Jhalawan, and Makran areas the number of sites increased noticeably in between 2500-1400 B.C. As a result in the following period between 1400-600 B.C. the number of sites decreased remarkably. It looks like that over exploitation of land resources of a limited area depleted the land so greatly that whenever a natural hazard happened, a famine-like situation occurred, and therefore, people migrated from the effected regions. Which is represented by the decrease of number of sites.

Population escalation can be estimated on the basis of the size of the settlements in Baluchistan (see Chart IX). Baluchistan was thickly populated in the pre/early/mature Harappan periods. To sustain this increased population Baluchistan lacked large cultivable fields. The region suffered with scarcity of rain water. Most of the rivers which mark the map of Baluchistan are not perennial. It seems that gradual degradation of Baluchi lands due to over exploitation of its land resources by excessive population concentration brought disasters. Lean years might have been quite regular, as the climate was basically arid. People could not develop new techniques of irrigation, so that they could move out of the much used riverine tracks. Neither they had much knowledge of preserving the fertility of soil and therefore, when due to excessive population pressure the bearing capacity of the land diminished, they had no other alternative but to migrate in large numbers towards fertile lands of Sindh and Punjab. When bearing capacity of a region is reduced then the famines become quite possible, specially in the years of natural disasters. The evacuation of Baluchi hills in later period prove by itself that such conditions were becoming quite common.

Sindh areas were geographically in advantageous situations, in comparison to Baluchistan. They have large riverine tracks, perennial water resources and through 'flood irrigation' methods they could procure better harvests. Therefore, Punjab and Sindh could sustain population pressure for a longer period. But climate was more or less the same type. Aridity was common feature. Rains were unreliable. Therefore over exploitation of the natural resources depleted its ecology easily. Population concentration in a limited zone showed its adverse effects very soon. Density of population can be checked through settlements pattern of the region (see Charts X, XI).

Majumdar's (1934) and Casal's (1964) works had traced pre/early Harappan trends in Amri. Amrian wares are distributed over a vast area. In the Kirthar Kohistan region,

Amri-Kotdijian wares can be found in 30 sites. This type of wares are found only in 3 sites in Lower Indus valley.

Find spots of the Amrian wares show that the people were settling down on the flood zones of the rivers. Population concentration in Sindh reached its maximum utilization period in mature Harappan times. In Kirthar Kohistan region mature Harappan culture can be traced in 19 sites, and 20 sites are found in Lower Indus valley. Soon after this period decrease in the number of sites and the reduced size of the sites are noticeable. This shows that the area was losing its fertility and therefore, migrations became inevitable (see Chart XI).

Similar observations can be made in Punjab. Early Harappan sites are frequently encountered to the north and the west of Harappa, especially in the Indus-Jhelum interfluve and along the west bank of the river Indus. Dani (1970. 1 : 177) has located a number of sites of this early phase on the Gomal plains in the vicinity of the Dera Ghazi Khan. Sarai Khola near Taxila. Tikrial, Jhumg are other important early Harappan sites of this region. Early Harappans, were mainly settling down in the west of the Indus. There is only one site of Musakhel which produces early Harappan cultural penetration in the east of the Indus river. The "favoured zone" of early Harappan period in north western Punjab, lost their privileged position in the mature Harappan period, probably due to over exploitation of the natural resources. Whereas 25 early Harappan sites can be located in western Punjab, there is hardly any mature Harappan site in that region. Emergence of bigger sites in Punjab starts with early Harappan period. Jalilpur, situated in the former flood plains of river Ravi covers and area of 15 hectares (Dales : 1973:121). But larger population concentrations happened during mature Harappan period. Harappa developed into big urban centre, spread over 45 hectare area. Over-utilization of the lands of Punjab happened during mature Harapan period. This can be estimated on the basis of increase in the size of the settlements (see Chart XII).

In the upper Sindh, on the east of river Indus, in a distance of 30 miles from Mohenjodaro, is the pre/early Harappan site named Kotdiji. The place was excavated by F.A. Khan (1959) of Pakistan Department of Archaeology. Kotdijian type wares, though it has its own local variations, is still considered as related with Nal and Kulli type wares. Kotdijjian pottery covered a large area, almost 140,00 sq. miles. Mughal (1970, Ch. III) thinks that Kotdijian wares were near contemporary to Amrian wares. Both the types are of course pre-Harappan. Cholistan (Bahawalpur) region marks the centre of Kotdijian culture. River Hakra flows through Cholistan. The passage of the Hakra river was first explored by Stein in 1943 (S.P. Gupta Ed. 1989). Further through Mughal's explorations altogether 414 sites have been mapped along 300 miles of Hakra river bed. Fourth millennium B.C. artifacts of this region are closely associated with Jalilpur I wares; they are termed Hakra wares by explorers (see Chart XIII).

Mughal estimates that about 60 per cent of the early Harappan (Kotdijian) sites are smaller than 5 hectares; 25% are between 5 and 10 hectares. Whereas 47.7 per cent of the total mature Harappan sites are comparatively bigger settlements. 45.4% of the total mature Harappan sites are industrial sites, out of which 19% sites combined both residential and industrial functions.

In the late Harappan period industrial sites account for only 18 per cent of the total late Harappan sites. 26 per cent of the late Harappan sites are merely camp sites. In the post Harappan (PGW) period except Satwali, the rest are less than 5 hectares in size. It is interesting to note that quite often evacuated sites were rehabilitated after a short or long gap of period. In the early Harappan period the maximum concentration of population occurred around Derawar fort. The over exploitation of this area seems to have depleted its bearing capacity. In the next phase we find a shifting of population concentration. They were moving towards the north east of the Hakra valley. Now the most populous area was between Yazman and Fort Abbas. But once again in the mature Harappan period they came back to the south west around and beyond Derawar fort, where a profusion of industrial sites can be located. This shifting is very meaningful. It proves that due to over utilization of land resources in pre-Harappan period the north eastern parts of the Hakra valley, around Derawar fort became depleted of its natural resources. Therefore, the land was evacuated for a few hundred years. During this epoch of absence the region regained its basic components and thus mature Harappan people could utilize the area once again. 174 sites of the mature Harappan phase has been noted down. This was the period of excessive population concentration. As a result soon this area lost its ecological balance. In the ensuing period, i.e. in late Harappan phase the number of sites are 50. The size of the sites in the late Harappan phase was also reduced (see Chart XIV). In PGW phase they became smaller. Out of the 14 OCP sites of this Hakra valley 13 sites were below 5 hectares, and only one site Satwali was of 13.7 hectare. The study of settlement pattern in Hakra valley, supports our view that over exploitation of arid region increased the possibility of famines, specially whenever natural calamities occurred there.

Similarly in north Rajasthan Harappan sites are reported from the valleys of the Saraswati and the Drisadwatī. They sometimes yield a pre-Harappan cultural phase. (e.g. in Kalibangan). Maximum exploitation of land occurred during the mature Harappan phase. That might have depleted its natural fertility and no late Harappan assemblages are found here. K. N. Dikshit (1979 : 123-133) has revisited the earlier explored sites from Sherapura near Bhadra up to Pakistan border in 1978, but no late Harappan assemblages were found in them.

The climate of Rajasthan varies considerably between its northern and southern parts. North and north western Rajasthan were afflicted with basic phenomenon of aridity. At present Sikar district of North Rajasthan receives 631'9 mm rain water in its wettest month and 269'2 mm in its driest month. Ganganagar and Bikaner districts of north-western Rajasthan receive 640'6 mm rain waters in their wettest months and 123'4 mm and 29'0 in their driest months respectively. These northern and north-western parts of Rajasthan, due to their problems of aridity could not sustain the population pressure for a long period. They were basically depending on the river waters of the Saraswatí and Drisadwati. When these perennial sources of water were gradually drying up then it affected its ecology. Bearing capacity of these arid lands got depleted and population shifted away at least for a considerable duration. In the years of its abandonment the region regained its fertility and then it could be repopulated. A survey of their settlement pattern can explain this statement better (see Chart XV).

Ganganagar district of Rajasthan was thoroughly dotted with Harappan cultural sites. Kalibangan was thriving with cultural activities since the pre/early Harappan stage. Comparable with Kalibangan, another site is recently discovered, named Ganwariwala, which was even larger than Harappa and was almost the size of Mohenjodaro. The city was located in the midway between Mohenjodaro and Harappa. Probably through it two major metropolis drew the Rajasthan resources.

Soon after mature Harappan period the Saraswati river valley sites of Hanumangarh district suffered a setback. During mature Harappan period the most thickly populated area was between Bijnor and Kalibangan. But there is hardly any site which can be spotted in this particular region, and can be dated in the late Harappan period. In the following cultural level, i.e., in the PGW cultural horizon total 20 sites had been located by Ghosh (1952 : 41) in the whole of the Saraswati basin of north Rajasthan. But at this time the concentration of population had shifted between Ramsimhapura and Suratgarh. Therefore it seems quite a possibility that even the Ghaggar (Saraswati) could not sustain the population pressure for a very long time.

The whole of north western Rajasthan was basically arid and in such climatic zone depletion of soil was quite prompt. But it is interesting to note that after a lapse of period the regions could regain its ecological balance. Stein's observation has shown that Ghaggar/Hakra valley could be rejuvinated once again in the period of Rangmahal pottery (i.e. 1st 2nd century A.D.). This region remained more or less vacated after the Harappan period, thus giving a period of more than a thousand years to regain its ecological balance. Ahar culture has been identified as one of the copper using cultures, which flourished in and around Udaipur, Chittorgarh and Dungarpur. It spread along the Berach Banas group of rivers. (R. C. Agarwal 1984 : 157-162). Explorations of archaeological survey of India between 1956-59 (*IAR* 1956-59) have revealed nearly 40 sites belonging to painted Black and Red Ware. V. N. Misra counts 49 sites of this culture (1967 : 148). This culture flourished in the valleys of Banas and its tributaries in the district of Udaipur, Bhilwara, Ajmer, Jaipur and Tonk in Rajasthan. The affinites of this culture can be traced with Harappan culture of Gujarat and with the chalcolithic culture of Nagda and Navdatoli. According to our latest count 78 sites can be traced which belong to Ahar (or Banas) cultural zone. Udaipur does not lack in rain water. During the wettest months it acquires enough rain water. Therefore the aridity did not affect its ecology and south Rajasthan was able to provide shelter to quite a few succeeding cultures (see Chart XVI).

In south Rajsthan we do get OCP and PGW culture vestiges in those areas which were occupied since the Pleistocene period. Almost all these sites kept their cultural continuity till 2nd century A.D. This indicates that for nearly 4000 years south Rajasthan could sustain its ecological balance, whereas the north-western Rajasthan of Ghaggar valley was badly mutilated soon after the mature Harappan period. In fact, between 1700 and 800 B.C. this part of north-western Rajasthan seems to have been completely deserted. In the period between 800 and 400 B.C. a few PGW sites can of course be traced here. But the previous flourishing situation which existed in pre-Harappan and Harappan times was not to be observed. Therefore we can conclude that ecological degradation was more pronounced in north and north-western Rajasthan than the southern and eastern Rajasthan, where climatic situations were more favourable and thus ecological loss was limited. Over exploitation of the land resources by population concentration in a particular area were more definite in arid zones.

Somewhat similar situation can be noticed in Gujarat. Kutch and Saurastra were primarily populated in the mature Harappan period. Kutch is at present quite a drought-prone area. Precipitation, except for the extreme eastern parts of the area, is less than 400 mm per annum. In Saurastra rainfall ranges between 400 and 700 mm per year. In north Gujarat plains it varies between 400 and 800 mm per year. South Gujarat is the wettest area. Here it varies between 800 and 1000 mm. per annum.

Pre/early Harappan phase is practically absent in this region. Probably due to some natural calamities, an influx of refugees from Punjab and Sindh occupied the lands of Gujarat in mature Harappan times. They used the corridor of Kutch to enter Saurastra and Gujarat. This was the reason that a number of sites can be traced in Kutch, belonging to mature Harappan period. They gradually settled down in various river valleys of the province. The rivers of Gujarat due to sudden floods in them are not very adequate for irrigation purposes. It may not have attracted agricultural activities on a big scale. They substituted it with pastoralism and trading activities. When agriculture was not their main subsistence activity, depletion of soil fertility did not affect them much. In mature Harappan times urban centres grew because of their trade with Sindh and Punjab. In late Harappan period when trade declined pastoralist activities filled up the gap. This can be seen through their settlement sizes. In late Harappan times most of the sites are small camp sites which were probably inhabited by small groups of herdsmen rather than by settled agriculturists and by prosporous traders.

To understand the settlement pattern of Gujarat we can observe the comprehensive list provided by Possehl (1980:89). The number of sites in the sub-period IIa (of Rangpur sequence), is 18, in IIb-c 120 and in III 32. In the sub-period IIb-c the mean size of the total sites is 5'3 ha.

and in period III 3'1 ha. If we compare the number of sites between sub period IIa and IIb-c it is clear that the number of sites increased seven times in period IIb-c. Similarly a comparative study of number of sites between period IIb-c and period III can point out that in period III the number of sites decreased remarkably (see Chart XVII).

In the areas of eastern Punjab and Haryana situations were slightly better. Climatically, Punjab and Haryana belong to semi–arid monsoon zone, but failing to receive the full benefits of monsoon because of its great distance from the sea. A high degree of seasonal variability exists in temperature and rainfall. There is deficiency of rainfall throughout most of the region. But still this region has better precipitation in comparison to north–western areas of the Indian subcontinent. Perennial rivers were probably the predominant ecological factor in selection of sites in pre–and proto–historic periods. This region was effected by the Harappan culture not before the mature Harappan phase. V.N. Misra noted down that Punjab has 34 mature Harappan sites and Haryana has 24. In late Harappan times the number of sites increased in both the regions. Punjab has 85 and Haryana 30 late Harappan settlements. (V.N. Misra 1984 : 473). Our comparative study of various lists provided by Fentress, V. Tripathi, Joshi, Madhubala and *ASIR* has revealed the picture quite clearly. (see Chart XVIII).

A survey has been conducted in the region between the Yamuna and the Sutlej by the Indo–French Archaeological Mission. It is interesting to observe that here the distribution of sites in parts follow the ancient dry courses of the rivers but are also found outside the old beds. This indicates that rains were sufficient for dry farming and thus people could survive away from the limited river banks. But even here the over exploitation of the land resources, which brought at least temporary evacuation of the zone, can be noticed. In above specified area of Haryana, Francfort (1985:260) notices that after the pre–Harappan phases there was a definite contraction of the distribution of mature Harappan sites. Of course, after this period the region was again reactivated in late Harappan and PGW period. Then once again it was abandoned and reactivated during Rangmahal and mediaeval periods. Thus this study also proves that bearing capacity of land had limitations and whenever too much exploitation of its resources took place, the region got depleted of its fertility, and the civilization faced a natural demise (see Chart XIX).

In Punjab and Haryana rivers were providing ample opportunities for cultivation. There was no major upheavals in drainage system, climate was wetter and therefore, drought menaces were fewer. These regions were colonized late. They were not practically populated till early Neolithic times. Therefore, upper regions of Saraswati, Drisadwati, and Yamuna rivers, which pass through Haryana, could endure population pressure till PGW periods at least. Even the upper Sutlej valley which flows through Amritsar, Jullundhar, Ludhiana and Ropar districts continuously supported the people of different cultural levels. These areas remained thickly populated in late Harappan, PGW and even later till NBPW periods (Bisht : 1976, 1978 : Dikshit : 1968, 1977, 1979; Ghosh : 1952; Pande : 1977; Fentress : 1982). Continuity of site occupation can be checked on the basis of single culture and multi culture sites. The multi-culture sites indicate that the area remained populated for a longer duration. A number of multi-culture sites can be traced in these regions.

Though the multiplicity of sites show that the population was increasing considerably, but with the enlargement of the sites, the population escalation reached to its maximum capacity. Approximate suggestions have been forwarded by many historians about the estimated population in various pre-historic centres. Different historians have given rough estimations of different important settlements. According to Lambrick 35,000 residents were probably living in Mohenjodaro (1964 : 71), whereas Fairservis (1967 : 33) puts the total population of Mohenjodaro at 41,240. D. K. Chakrabarti (1979, a : 205-212) feels that the settlements having an area of 12.5 hectares or more were likely to possess 5000 or more people each. The sites which seem to belong to this group are Mohenjodaro, Harappa, Naru-waro-dharo, Judeir-jo-dharo, Dabarkot, Rahman-Dheri, Dewliana Ther, Lurewala, Trekoe, Kalibangan, Devaliyo, Kotadi etc. The above mentioned lists of different settlements in different regions can give us an approximate idea, how the concentration of population was happening in some particular regions in particular times. If Baluchistan had numerous small settlements in pre-Harappan stage, it faced an ecological degradation in mature Harappan phase when comparatively fewer settlements survived. Similarly, Sindh Hakra valley, and Punjab had large population concentration in the mature Harappan phase and the ecological degradation probably effected in its later cultural levels, when the number of sites decreased. Gujarat also had maximum utilization of land during mature Harappan time. In the later period sites became significantly small and show the adverse effects on its ecology.

This problem, of over exploitation of land resources, due to population concentration on a limited area, became a non–issue, once the agriculturists expanded their cultivable lands. With the use of iron on a major scale in agricultural activities, people were shifting away from restricted riverine tracks. Other irrigational provisions became available. Therefore, the problems which arose due to over exploitation of narrow riverine belts did not remain acute.

To conclude this issue of discussion we may now say that famine situations arose in pre–historic times when a limited area got depleted due to over exploitation of its land resources. The problem mainly effected in those days when people were forced to remain in limited river side tracks. Famines occurred as people failed to procure enough surplus from depleted soil and there was hardly any safety provisions against natural hazards.

5

ECOLOGICAL DEGRADATION DUE TO DEFORESTATION AND DENUDATION OF GRASS COVER

Climatically not much difference can be noticed between pre– and proto–historic India and the present times. But a significant ecological degradation occurred due to denudation of grasslands and deforestation. Ecological imbalance causes many natural hazards in the environment, which ultimately effects the agricultural pattern. When a land loses its natural grass cover it increases the aridity and makes the area less fertile. If the forest land gradually vanishes it effects the rain fall pattern and thus it creates the situation where the farmer becomes more dependent on artificial irrigation. Artificial irrigation can only be complimentary to the natural water resources. It cannot solely substitute it. Therefore, clearing up the forest lands from the surrounding areas brings a major set back for the cultivators, who may face the drought years quite often. It can be noticed that as long as there remained enough forest areas in ancient times, drought references are comparatively less. But with the expansion of agriculture from 600 B.C. onwards clearing up of the forest land became such a regular feature that by the time we reach to the beginning of the Christian era, numerous drought incidents, which led to famines are referred to in various literary sources.

In pre– and proto–historic India pastoralism took a major part in subsistence economy. The skeletal remains of the domesticated animals are found from various pre– and proto–historical sites. In the north–western regions, where our earliest cultures originated, maximum number of bones belong to cattle and those of other grass grazing animals. In arid climatic zones, where the scarcity of rain persisted and recurrence of drought years were probably a common feature, cattle were denuding the surrounding grass land areas intensively. It must have affected its ecology.

The special feature of this whole north–western region is the predominance of aridity. Mehrgarh was one of the earliest sites where prehistoric culture developed. It is located at the northern end of Kacchi Sibi plains, and at the foot of Brahui hills. This area falls within a transitional zone, paralleling the margins of Kacchi plains. The rain fall varies here between 100 and 200 mm per annum. Mehrgarh falls under semi–desertic climatic zone. Presently, there are two growing seasons in Mehrgarh area, with one crop planted if there are enough winter rains, and another to use the water from the summer storms. Irrigation is considered essential to ensure a harvest.

On the Quetta plateau rainfall is between 200 and 500 mm per annum. Quetta and Kalat regions have climates with thermo-Mediterranean tendencies, while at Sibi and Jacobabad semi–deserted and tropical desert climates with rainfall less than 100 mm per year persist. Similarly, most of the Sarawan sites lie in the intermontane valleys at about 5000 ft. above sea level (Raikes 1968 : b : 103-171). The meagre winter rainfall is supplemented by quite heavy snowfalls and majority of the inhabitants move down to the plains of Sindh, until the spring, when they return to deal with their crops. The climate of Bannu district too is semi–arid, rainfall has a markedly seasonal pattern. In the south Baluchistan, where sites like Balakot is situated, lies the Khurkhera alluvial plains on the southern side of the Las Bella Valley. Climatically, Las Bella Valley falls under the arid region with generally 100 to 200 mm of summer precipitation. Sudden summer storms are quite frequent. The Swat Valley is situated in the north Pakistan, on a high altitude and dry climate. Most likely a temperate dry forest existed here in pre-historic times, as the remains of wild animals from pre- and proto-historic sites of Swat valley indicate (Compagnoni 1979 :697-700). This whole region, where arid climate persists, ecological degradation was quite prompt and animals played a devastating role.

In Mehrgarh, Quetta Kacchi region, in aceramic neolithic period cattle bone consisted of 4% of total bone assemblage. In its upper level of the same period, cattle bone consisted of 38% in the ceramic neolithic period it consisted of 65%. And only in the last phase of prehistoric phase, when agriculture had substituted the pastoral economic base, cattle bone consisted of 35% of total bone assemblage, (Shashi Asthana : 1985:191; Jarrige, Meadow : 1980:124; Meadow : 1981:34). Many pre-Harappan and mature Harappan sites have been excavated in Baluchistan, western Punjab, Sindh and Rajasthan. The faunal remains as found in these areas indicate that they mainly belonged to grass grazing domesticated animals (see Chart XX).

It is clear from the chart that cattle—sheep and goats, which form an important basis of the economy of Baluchistan even in modern times, must have played a devastating role in prehistoric times. The husk of single yield cultivated crops were not sufficient to fulfil their fodder requirements. The demand for more fodder for their growing numbers of grass grazing animals, must have forced them to move out of these hilly Baluchi tracks. Even in present times, in the lean season, the Baluchis move out of their hilly regions and come to the plains of Sindh and Punjab. Looking for the pasture grounds for their flocks. Some sort of similar situation seems to have existed in prehistoric times. Due to increased population of men and grass grazing animals they deserted their villages and gradually settled down in the riverine plains of Sindh and Punjab. This did not happen in one particular incidence of drought year, but might have taken numerous years of experiences. Grass grazing animals who were foraging in the surrounding grass lands may have brought ecological degradation permanently which affected their rains. In many successive lean years they may have had deserted their villages and again gone back to their Baluchi villages during better times. Until they became exhausted by this process of evacuation and reoccupation, year after year, and then ultimately abandoned the Baluchi uplands.

Similar situation can be observed in other arid regions of India. Sindh and Punjab comprised of vast alluvial tracks where cultivable fields and pasture grounds were more easily available in comparison to Baluchistan. But here too ecological degradation can be noticed due to biotic interference (see Chart XXI). The faunal remains of Sindh and Punjab prove that grass grazing animals were predominant. Along with a heavy population concentration, the sheep and goats became instrumental to denude the surrounding grass lands. Fairservis (1967 : 39) has calculated that "only 1/4 of the total needs of cattle could be met by growing fodder and the rest of 3/4 had to be obtained from foraging in the surrounding forests and grass lands". This formidable assault on the indigenous flora most certainly effected ecology. This must have induced them to cultivate *bajra* which could be grown in less productive fields and in the conditions of aridity. Soil degradation can be noticed in surroundings of Harappan sites. Here the land has become completely infertile due to waterlogging, which may have resulted as the biotic pressure denuded the land from its natural grass covers. Gujarat was another zone where Harappan and late Harappan cultural settlements flourished. A similar study of faunal remains of Gujarat points out the role of animals in degrading the ecology. Husks of cultivated rice could not have been sufficient in Gujarat, as the millet was a late introduction and wheat cultivation lacks any direct proof. In such a case cattle grazed natural grass and low-lying shrubs in the surrounding forests. That brought ecological degradations (see Chart XXII).

Denudation of grass covers from arid and semi-arid zones must have damaged the ecology of the area badly. This must have resulted into soil erosion and must have had effected drainage pattern. Degradation of land profile turned the soil infertile and barren. In such conditions whenever droughts occurred or due to scanty rains in the catchment areas, the rivers did not have a full flow, the agriculture suffered immensely. The chemical properties of the soil consequently declined and many times it resulted into salination of the land, which converted the lands infertile.

Discovery of gypsum crystals from a potsherd at Kalibangan (Rajasthan), is of special significance. Vishnu Mittre (1982 : 205-21) has suggested that ground gypsum is used in agriculture as a surface plaster for conserving moisture in the soil and for aiding nitrogen absorption from manures. It is also used to reduce salinity and alkalinity of soil. Rajasthan water and soil are saline at present. Therefore, it looks like that similar soil conditions prevailed in Harappan period Kalibangan. Possibly due to heavy soil degradation the farmers of Kalibangan were in desperate need to preserve moisture in the fields and there fore, utilized ground gypsum as a surface plaster or as a manure. In the chalcolithic times, when settlements were confined in the riverine belts, the degradation of land profile, due to overgrazing by the domesticated animals, were more pronounced. In later period, when the Rig Vedic Aryans led a nomadic life, they need not have to cling around the ecologically degraded areas though they kept and breeded grass grazing animals.

The subsistence economy of the Rig Vedic people was based on pastoral activities. (R. S. Sharma 1983 : 24). Cow was regarded as the chief source of wealth and were repeatedly referred to in the *Rig Veda.* (I.83.1 : 138.5.; II. 23.18.). Large herds of cattle are mentioned in the *Danastutis* (VIII.5.37). The importance attached to the possession of cattle is shown in the hymns (I.43.2; 162.22; V.4.1.; IX.9.9). The early Aryans were mobile tribal bands, looking for pasture lands for their herds of cattle, sheep and goats, hence the forays for cattle (*gavisti*) were well known. Bharat tribe was called *gavyamgrāmacḥ*, as it desires to hoard the cows (III.33.11) *Vraja* denotes primarily in the *Rig Veda* the cattle resort (II.38.8; X.26.3; 97.101.8) and secondarily it denotes the herd itself (VII.27.1; 32.10; VIII.46.9; 51.5). Oxen were employed for drawing carts and were therefore named *anadvāḥ* (*RV*.X.59.10; III.53.18).

The domesticated animals played major roles in later Vedic economy too. *Go* or cow was considered as the standard of wealth (*AV.* III.11.8; *Vāj. Saṁ.* XX.1.20; XXI.19; *Śat. Br.* II.4.3.13; III.1.2.13; IV. 5.5.10;). Cows provided them with milk products like *Kṣīra* (milk), *Ghrta* (clarified butter), *dadhi* (curds). The cows were milked thrice a day (*Tait. Saṁ.* VIII.5.3.1). Large herds of cattle are referred to in the *dānastutis* (*Y.V.* XXIV). The importance attached to the possession of cattle is shown in the later Vedic literature (*A.V.* I.4.; II. 26.4; V. 29.2.; VI. 68.3.; VIII. 7.11.; X.1.17-20; XI.2.9.21; *Tait. Saṁ.* III.2.3.1; V. 5.5.1; VI. 5.10.1; *Vāj. Saṁ.* III. 59). Oxen were regularly used for ploughing (*Tait. Saṁ.* I.2.8). Oxen were used drawing the carts too (*AV* III.11.5; IV.11.1; *Ait. Br.* I.14; *Śat. Br.* II. 1.4.17, etc.). the flesh of cows and bulls were sometimes eaten (*Śat. Br.* III. 4.1.2; *Sānkh Gr. Su* II.15.2). Beef was needed for sacrifice (Tait. Br. II. 3.; III.8). Though of course the reverse attitude was strengthening gradually (*Śat. Br.* III.1.2.21). The cow was on the road to acquire special sanctity in the *Rig Veda* (VIII.101.15. 16; *Vāj. Saṁ.* IV.19.20; *AV.* X.10; XII.4.5) as is shown in the name *aghnya*, found 16 times in the *Rig Veda* (*Śat. Br.* III.1.2.21). They were used as a form of exchange (*kraya*). Thus we see that grass grazing cattle formed an important part of economy till at least Vedic period. Till this period agricultural fields were not much expanded as paucity of iron tools restricted their advance in the thick forest areas. Besides till Vedic times Aryans were mainly living in the areas of western U.P., Punjab, Haryana and Rajasthan. All these areas fall under semi-arid zone. Therefore, it can be presumed that cattle were degrading the ecology of this newly acquired areas. The biotic interference on the ecology was reduced with the introduction of iron in agricultural sector, when the extension of the agricultural area and multicropping provided enough fodder to the domesticated grass grazing animals and thus reduced their role in ecological degradation.

Ecological imbalances occurred notonly due to the denudation of grass land but by deforestation too. It effected the rain pattern quite heavily. Deforestation on a major scale could only took place with the beginning of ample utilization of iron tools in clearing the forests. It took comparatively longer period to denude the land of its forest covers. At present most of the Indo-Gangetic plains are devoid of big forests. Present forest zone in India is unevenly distributed. Madhya pradesh, Kerala and Andaman and Nicobar islands occupy major portions of forest lands. U.P. and Bihar have 6.7%, Punjab 3% and Rajasthan 2.5% of total forests (R. L. Singh, 1971 : 15). But this was not the situation in the past. North India had vast forest reserves in the proto-historic and even in early historic times. Paleobotanical evidence of proto-historic period provided us with evidences of varieties of trees—the types of which are found in similar zones even at present; though in a very scattered way and do not form any thick forest. They must have existed in protohistoric times in abundance. Our literary sources also suggest that plenty of forest areas lasted till quite late.

Panini mentions several names of forests in his *Sūtras* (VIII. 4.4-5). According to his information there was a forest named *Puragarana* near Pataliputra. He refers to a forest called *Miśrakavana*, which was probably situated in present Sitapur district. Other forests enumerated by Panini were *Sidhrakavana, Śaravana, Ikṣūvana, Plakṣavana, Āmravana* and *Khâdirvana*. But the locations are not specified.

In the north-western India forests were less in comparison to eastern India. But even as late as the time of Hsuan-Tsang a forest of Pilu trees existed near the town of Sakala (Cunningham, 1963 (Reprint) : 162). In Punjab and Haryana, Probably another big forest existed, as *Kamyaka* forest is named in the north of Kuru land in the Puranic literature (Ali, S.M., 1966 : 135). *Naimiṣa* forest was situated according to Varāhamihira on the left bank of the Gomati. (*Br. Sam.* XI.60). This implies that it existed somewhere in the north-west of Lucknow in Sitapur district (Shastri, 1969 : 64). Varāhamihira (*Br. Sam.* XIV.3) locates

Dharmāraṇya in the *Madhyadeśa* i.e. in the middle country. In the sub Himalayan zone, north of the Gangetic plains thick forests are mentioned. (Tamaskar, 1989 : 20). In the western India near Avanti woods are mentioned in *Indriya Jātaka* (No. 423, para 463) and *Sarabhanga Jāt* (No. 522, para 133). South India had plenty of forest lands. *Danḍaka* forest comprised of the territory between the Vindhyas and Saivala mountain (Varāhamihira *Br. Sam.* VI.11). *Mahāṭava* (*Ibid.* XIV. 13) was also situated in the South.

In the central Gangetic region and in the lower Gangetic region forests were more numerous, as these areas come under the moist climatic zone. A forest is mentioned near Kasi (*Jat* No. 59 para 284; No. 94 Para 390; No. 6 para 128; No. 41 para 240). Other were near Kosala (*Jat* No. 17 para 165; No. 36 Para 215), around Ayodhya, near Rajgriha (*Jat* No. 544 para 229; No. 485 para 282), near Avanti (*Jat* No. 522 para 133) near Vaisali (*Jat* No. 108 para 420; No. 149 para 505; No. 152 para 7), etc.

Quite often forests were named after the most common trees of the area. A chart of tree types mentioned in different sources show that most common trees were *Śāl, Āmra, Añjana, Āmalakī, Pippalī, Simśapa, Ambaṭaka, Plakṣa, Khādir.* If we compare these vegetable types with present varieties of natural tree growths, we can see that similar types of trees grew in similar regions, but at present the sample types have survived and the thick forests have vanished due to human interferences (see Chart XXIII, XXIV).

The denudation of forests was a slow but continuous process. It started as early as Rigvedic period (I.10.23). Clearance of forests for acquiring more habitable lands continued (*RAM.* II.80; *MBH.* I.230; *Jat* No. 272 para 358). Forest clearance degraded the ecological balance. *Mahabharata* even says that the famines broke out due to ecological degradation which resulted from forest clearance. (*MBH.* IX. 41.14; X.10.5; I.71.31).

Ancient environmentalists realized the menace and conscious efforts were made to preserve the forests. Kautalya (IV.11) lays down the rule that the people should not harm the trees. Severe punishments were prescribed by him to those who set fire to forests (*AŚ* II.17; VII.12). Same consciousness can be observed in the Jain and Buddhist works (*Cullavagga*, V.32.1; *Mahāvagga*, III.1.3; Jacobi, 1964 II.357 etc). King Asoka also realized the bad effects of forest clearance. In his pillar edict V, he says that "forests must not be burnt either uselessly or in order to destroy living animals". Manu (Xi65) prescribed punishment for those who cut green trees. It was considered a great sin in the *Mahābhārata* (XII.32.13-14; xxix). there are many references of protection of forests in the *Rāmāyaṇa* (IV. 41.41; V. 61.63). But instead of all these efforts denudation of forest lands continued as more cultivable land was required and the old forests gave way to numerous settlements, villages towns and cities.

To conclude this discussion of deforestation it can simply be said that denudation of land, especially in the arid zones, increased the drought possibilities more. We find that wherever land surface was degraded, drought occurred and famines could not be averted.

But we do accept that the process of deforestation was so slow that it could not have created an immediate cause of famine. The effects of deforestation was slow and gradual but its ultimate effects were devastating.

SECTION III

INADEQUATE COMMUNITY RESOURCES

Famine conditions arose when the bearing capacity of a social group was not strong. If the community had enough economic resources to bear the pressure of natural calamities, then it could have averted the famine situations. Economic resources consisted of some primary facilities, such as enough surplus production through advanced agricultural methods, proper irrigation facilities, adequate knowledge of agricultural technology, storage and rationing facilities, and infrastructure for transporting grain to the needy zones. But in pre- and proto-historic India all these facilities were not sufficiently developed, which resulted in inadequate supporting economy. Lack of resources aggravated famine situations.

6

CROPPING PATTERN IN AGRICULTURE

Agricultural prosperity is regarded as the basis for a sound economy. There were some inadequacies prevalent in pre-historic Indian agroeconomy, which aggravated economic depression in times of natural calamities. In the early stages of neolithic chalcolithic periods single crop a year hampered economic self-sufficiency. As long as chalcolithic cultures depended on single crop a year they could not save sufficient surplus to fight against the natural menaces and whenever droughts or floods affected their settlements they were pushed to the brink of famine.

Organized agriculture was introduced into the Indian subcontinent as early as the aceramic neolithic period. Hunters and gatherers of earlier Stone Age, compelled by demographic pressures and the realization of the comforts of settled life, adopted cultivation in regions where environmental constraints could easily be overcome. The earliest agriculturalists developed food habits based on the availability of natural products. The natural growth of wild wheat and barley in some areas were gradually cultivated. In the same way, rice gradually became a cultivated cereal in areas suited to its natural wild growth. The adoption and diffusion of a variety of crops by society could only begin with the extension of contacts between different cultures. That could have been possible only in the advanced stage of human mobility. Settlements could be sustained for longer periods of time only where the environment was suitable for agriculture.

The earliest evidence of cultivated crops is found in Mehrgarh. M. Lechavallier and G. Quivron have shown that the northern Kachi Plain of Baluchistan, where the site of Mehrgarh is located, was occupied by farming communities as early as the 7th or 6th millennium BC (1979 : 71-72). The neolithic site of MR 3 at Mehrgarh presents evidence of the oldest habitational area in the region. Ecologically, the Kacchi Plain is the transitional area between two different ecozones. On one side was the arid inland plateau of inner Baluchistan, Afghanistan and Iran, and on the other side was the alluvial Indus Plain. Besides this geographic mixture, which might have inspired the early agriculturalists of Mehrgarh, there were other favourable environment factors which made Kacchi Plain especially attractive. The valley consisted of fertile alluvial soil deposited there by the drainage system of the surrounding hills. The Bolan River continually flows, providing irrigation water. However, the area faces severe winters, making it difficult to raise a late winter crop. It is basically suited to a single-yield crop per year. The area remained occupied for a considerably long period of time, with a slight movement in occupation sites from the north to the south (see Chart XXV). In the earliest phase six row hulled barley predominated. Next in preference was naked wheat.

But as time passed and agricultural activities in Mehrgarh were extended, this modest farming village became incorporated into a large zone of cultural interaction by 3000 BC. A complex socio-economic structure arose due to demographic pressures. New cultivars were introduced, although ecological constraints forced their scope to be limited. Multiple varieties of wheat and barley were introduced. Even oats became a familiar cereal for the people of Mehrgarh in Period III; however, the environment was not suited to the proper cultivation of rice.

Two other important sites which give us palaeobotanical evidence from the same ecozone of Baluchistan are Naushare and Pirak. (see chart II) Naushare lies 7 kilometres south of Sector MR-1 or Mehrgarh. Therefore, it had a similar environment. The first archaeological evidence found at Naushare indicates a parallel existence with the sites of Mehrgarh during periods VII and VIII—thus giving it a comparatively late start (Jarrige 1986). The Indo-French Archaeological Mission, under the supervision of Jarrige, conducted excavations at Naushare from 1985 to 1986 and collected a variety of seeds, mainly cereal grains. A significant number of fruit stones and a few legume seeds were also found. The evidence indicates that cereal grains, wheat and barley, were the main cultivar. Wheat is represented by three hexaploid, free-thrashing species. Morphobiometric studies have confirmed the predominance of small-sized wheat, similar to *Triticum compactum* and *Triticum sphaerococcum* (Constantini and Biasini 1986 : 354-355). *T. sphaerococcum* is a highly drought-resistant variety, which developed in the north-western part of the Indian subcontinent through mutation and deletion of small blocks of genes of *T. aestivum*. This signifies that the climatic condition of this region was dry and drought prone, even in earlier days and continued to be the same up to the present day. Three species of barley have been identified in Naushare : *Hordeum vulgare, Hordeum vulgare nodum* and *Hordeum sphaerococcum*. Six-row hulled barley seems to have been the predominant over the other two species. However, it cannot be said at this stage which crop, barley or wheat, was more favoured, as the number of available samples is more or less equal. Legume seeds were comparatively rare. The discovery of the seeds of another important cultivar, *Linum usitatissimum*, should indicate that even a textile plant was probably used for extracting oil from the seed. The Naushare samples thus further support the agricultural pattern of Baluchistan, where six-row hulled barley and naked wheat were predominant over other cultivars. The conclusion also supports the picture drawn with respect to Mehrgarh resources (Constantini and Biasini 1985 : 160).

Pirak is the third important site which belongs to this ecozone. This site lies 40 kilometres east of Mehrgarh and was excavated under the direction of J. M. Casal for the Indo-French Archaeological Mission. Jarrige had directed its last excavations in 1976 and 1979. Constantini (1979:c: 326-333) conducted the study of its plant remains. Chronologically, the site corresponds to a later period. The availability of a few Harappan wares—mostly late Harappan wares—puts the chronology of the site between 1000 and 800 BC. The presence of wheat and barley, the common grains of the region, was of course expected. But the occurrence of sorghum and rice was of immense significance. Sorghum or *jwar* was a novel introduction in this ecozone. Sorghum has recently been identified at Hill B in the Oman peninsula in an earlier context, i.e. 2500 BC (Cleuzion and Constantini 1979). In the Indian context, the earliest record of sorghum is found in Mohenjodaro in the Harappan period.

Sorghum is probably of African origin and must have spread into Indian agriculture through cultural interaction. Rice in this north-western part of the Indian subcontinent is the most striking innovation. In Pirak, *Oryza sativa* (rice) grains were found densely packed in a massive deposit, indicating that they were stored there. Sorghum and rice are both summer crops, whereas the previously known crops of the area—wheat, barley, chick-peas—were winter crops. The introduction of summer crops along with winter crops indicates that a multicropping system had begun here. Pirak had provides the proof of their acquaintance with iron as early as 800 BC (Casal 1973 : 171-179), which may have enhanced their capability of intensive agriculture. Pirak is situated in an advantageous geographical position, within the terminal reaches of the piedmont delta of Sibi. This accounts for the availability of irrigation water which was very much needed for rice cultivation. The introduction of sorghum and rice demonstrates the expansion of the cultural contact zone for the people of Pirak. They succeeded in developing cultural contact with southeastern Arabia, where they learnt sorghum production, and with the eastern zones of India, where they borrowed the methods of rice cultivation. Multicropping, or at least doublecropping, also indicates an increase in population, which could not be fed on a single crop per year. Thus rice and sorghum could be introduced into the northwestern part of the Indian subcontinent only in a later period, when cultural exchange with distant areas was common. This can be further substantiated by other sources.

In the pre-Harappan context, palaeobotanical evidence is available from Balakot (in southwestern Las Bella Valley and Sonmiani Bay (Baluchistan), Shahr-i-Sokhta (in Iranian Seistan), Mundigak (in southern Afghanistan), Rahman-Dheri (in Baluchistan), Tarakai-Qila (in Bannu Basin), Leobanr and Aligrama (in Swat Valley). Balakot is situated on the coastal side of Baluchistan, where wheat and barley cultivation dominated (Dales 1977 : 257). Shahr-i-Sokhta is situated on the Iranian part of the southern Seistan where the Helmund River split up into its deltaic network. The cultural sequence can be dated between 3200 and 1800 BC (Tosi 1969). The site was abandoned in the early part of the 2nd millennium BC, possibly because of lapses in the socio-economic system and continual drying of southern Seistan (Biscione *et al.* 1977 : 79-102). Four varieties of barley and four varieties of wheat are traced in this site (Constantini 1979, b: 125). Shahr-i-Sokhta, however, declined and was abandoned before reaching the advanced stage of multicropping.

Another geographically similar site, Mundigak is situated on the Helmund river system in southern Afghanistan. Mundigak must have had an interlinking ecosystem with Shahr-i-Sokhta. The site subsisted on similar cultivars. The identified crops are *Triticum compactum*, *Ziziphus vulgaris* and *Salvadora persica* (Casal 1961 : 260 ; Poulain 1966). No evidence is yet available about summer crops such as rice and sorghum. From Rahman Dheri, in the pre-Harappan context, evidence of similar crops like barley and wheat is available (Durrani 1977 : 2). In Bannu Basin, botanical evidence was available from Tarkai in the form of a large number of charred grains—wheat (*Triticum sp.*), naked six-row barley (*Hordeum vulgare var. nudum*), lentils (*Lens culinaris*), and field pea (*Pisum aravense*). Here also barley was the predominant crop (Thomas 1979 : 230-231). The site is located on the Tochi river which must have provided the irrigation water. Chronologically, it is a pre-Harappan Kotdijian settlement. No new evidence of crops such as rice or millet have been found in the products of this agro-based economy.

In contrast with already specified zones, Swat Valley provided a spectrum of diversity. The two sites in this valley which provide palaeobotanical evidence are Leobanr and Aligrama. At least three types of barley are reported from Leobanr III—hulled barley (*Hordeum vulgare*), naked barley (*Hordeum vulgare var. nudum*) and *Hordeum distichum*. A few grains of wheat (*Triticum compactum-sphaerococcum*) are available. Rice (*Oryza sativa*) is represented by a single whole grain and three fragmented grains. Other cultivars include *Lens esculenta*, *Pisum aravense*, and *Galium*. Aligrama provides similar graminaceous species. Wheat (*Triticum sphaerococcum*), hulled barley (*Hordeum vulgare*) and rice (*Oryza sativa*) were found here. Leguminous remains were abundant in Aligrama. The two sites thus provide a similar picture. They were only four kilometres apart. This valley can be dated to the 2nd millennium BC. Thus, evidence of multicropping in both winter and summer crops existed in Swat Valley. This area provides proof of cultural exchange previous to that of Pirak. (see Chart II).

To sum it up, it can be said that in the northwestern part of the Indian subcontinent, wheat and barley were natural products. Wheat and barley occurred in the western part of the Indian subcontinent earlier than it occurred in the eastern and southern regions. Cultivated varieties of barley can be traced back as early 8000 BC in western Asia, from where it originally spreaded to Iran and then south into the northwestern parts of India. Wheat may, on the other hand be an original cultivar of the northwestern part of the Indian sucontinent. The region between the Hindu Kush mountains and the Himalayas is believed to be the original home of wheat. The wheat and barley culture spread into the Ganges river valley and later into central and southern India as a result of cultural diffusion. In the chalcolithic period, barley and wheat were found in Inamgaon and Navdatoli, and during the OCW period, in Atranjikhera, U.P.

Rice is basically a natural product of the eastern and southern India. It is predominantly an Asian crop. There seems to be general agreement that the cultivated species of rice evolved out of wild perennials. The three species—*Oryza sativa var. fatua, O. perennis and O. breviligulata*—are recognized as closely related to cultivated rice. *O. sativa var. fatua* is the common wild rice of India. Chang (1976 : 143-155) limits the area of origin of domesticated rice to a broad belt roughly between 20 and 23 degrees north, stretching from the central Ganges Valley to the South China Sea. It is further believed that the first varieties of rice to be cultivated were marshy xerophytic species and development of hill rice was secondary. Rice crops require high temperatures and humidity with an abundance of water during its lifetime. Therefore, weather conditions, rainfall and its distribution, temperature and humidity, and length of daylight have a marked influence on the growth and yield of rice, and consequently these factors determine its areas of cultivation. In eastern regions like Assam, West Bengal, Orissa, South Bihar where rainfall is high, rice is dominant crop. In south Indian states of Andhra Pradesh, Tamil Nadu and Kerala, where rainfall is sufficient along the coasts, rice is a very popular product. In northern and central India rice is grown only in those areas where rainfall is favorable.

The earliest palaeobotanical evidence of cultivated rice come from Koldihwa, dt. Allahabad (Sharma, G. R. *et al.* 1980 : 22.-23). On the basis of carbon–14 dating of the neolithic deposits of Koldihwa, rice was cultivated there from the 7th to the 5th millennium BC (Sahi and Ara 1985).

Rice can be classified, on the photo-periodical basis, in two broad groups : (a) long duration varieties taking 140 to 160 days, and (b) short duration varieties taking 90 to 110 days per yield. They are at present harvested thrice a year—*aus* (autumn), *aman* (winter), and *boro* (spring and summer). The winter crop is, of course, the most common. Alluvial soil is considered fertile for rice cultivation, whereas alkaline soil is either totally unfit for rice cultivation or gives a poor crop yield due to the accumulation of soluble salts. The failure of rice cultivation is mainly due to the erratic distribution of rain or non-availability of water.

We have already made observations in our preliminary survey of the northwestern regions of the Indian subcontinent—Afghanistan, Baluchistan, and northwestern Pakistan (Bannu and Swat Valleys). This region remained beyond the natural zones for the production of rice due to scanty rainfall, extreme cold climate during winters, and less humidity. It is possible in a later period, when the Harappan culture was at its peak or even later with the coming of the iron age when communication with the eastern zones became more common that rice may have been introduced as a new crop. But this was not a major crop and thus could not affect the economy of the zone in a substantial way.

With the beginning of the mature Harappan culture, knowledge of agriculture expanded. Their contacts expanded and they were occupying more attractive zones in the river valleys of Punjab and Sindh. The archaeological remains of these regions indicate a society where innumerable small settlements cropped up and were united through a few big urban centres. Such a large human concentration in itself proves that the crop output had immensely increased. Their ecozone spread as far as Bahawalpur state in Pakistan, northwestern Rajasthan, Kathiawar, and Gujarat. Palaeo-botanical data available from the Indus and Punjab river valleys demonstrate that the western food habits, based on wheat and barley cultivation, was dominant. Harappa, Mohenjodaro, Chanhudaro, and all the important cities of western Punjab and Sindh, demonstrated a barley-wheat culture, primarily due to climatic constraints. Dependency on rain was erratic. Most of the sites were on the river's alluvial zone, which meant that they depended on flood irrigation. Naturally, it was quite often that the sowing season of the crops got delayed. After the flood water receded and left enough silt, the sowing could begin. As a result, not more than one harvest could be expected per year. In such a case barley and wheat would be the only crops as indicated by floral evidence from Mohenjodaro and Harappa. Rice cultivation could not come up extensively, probably due to the saline properties in the surrounding soil of Harappa. Presently, land surrounding ancient Harappa has become barren, due to salinity in its soil. But sorghum (*jwar*) was introduced in Mohenjodaro possibly because the hardy crop suited the soil requirements and could provide an alternative cultivar in the years of scarce rain.

In Bahawalpur state and in northwestern Rajasthan, climatic and soil conditions were very much the same. Scarcity of rain and desert like soil conditions were the prevalent ecological features. Barley was the predominant crop of Kalibangan. Even these were of small-size variety, probably signifying the existence of sandy soil. They produced wheat as well, but the existence of rice is quite doubtful. In the Harappan cultural context, two sites of eastern Punjab have palaeo-botanical evidence : Rohira and Maharana. They were not rice-growing regions yet, and cultivated a single crop of barley and wheat annually.

The situation is different when we come to Gujarat, Kathiawar, and the eastern and southern parts of Rajasthan. The climate varies in these regions. They were in close contact with the rice growing cultivators of the east and south and could depend on rain water and perennial rivers for water. Winter there was also comparatively less severe. Humidity was a natural phenomenon-hence, crops like millet and rice could be cultivated.

In the Harappan cultural context, specimens of rice cultivation were found in Lothal, Rangpur and Jokha (in Gujarat). The earliest rice cultivation started in the eastern and southern parts of India. Its earliest evidence was discovered in Chirand (carbon–14 dating gives it an extremely early origin), Koldihwa (carbon–14 date : 7390-7240 B.P), Kakoria, Barunha, Mahagara, Manigara, Sohgaura, and Oriup in the Neolithic period. In chalcolithic background, rice is found in Ahar, Hulas, Un, Mahisdal, and Navdatoli. In the first half of the 1st millennium BC, its existence can be proven from evidence available of Inamgaon, Noh, Ambari, Ruper and Sonpur. Therefore, barley and wheat culture was migrating from west to east and south whereas rice culture was moving in the opposite direction—from east to south and west, simultaneously.

Jwar was a cultivar which was introduced in India quite later. This was probably an alien crop. It was introduced in India through contacts with the Arabian Gulf countries, as this cultivar was known there since the 3rd millennium BC. It was found in the 3rd millennium BC sites of Central Asia, as well as in southern Iran at Polatabad near Tepe Yahya as early as the 6th millennium BC. In India its earliest occurrence comes in Mohenjodaro in the Harappan context. In the post Harappan context, it is discovered in the archaeological site of Shortughai (eastern Bactria) and Pirak (in Baluchistan), in Rohira (Sangrur district, Punjab) and Ahar (Rajasthan), indicating a widely scattered zone. This is basically a hardy crop and can be grown in a slightly moist environment. It is a *kharif* crop, indicating that intensive agriculture had been developed within the society. Whenever the failure of rain adversely affected *rabi* crop, cultivation of *jwar* could provide a suitable alternative. *Jwar* was an alien cultivar and could not win the taste and food habits of the barley-wheat consuming population on a major scale. It is not unlikely that *jwar* was introduced essentially as a fodder because the pastoral communities of Harappan and late Harappan periods must be in need of sufficient fodder for their cattle, and stalks of a single winter crop may not have been enough to fulfil the fodder requirements. Another theory that may be postulated is that *jwar* was a crop for the poorer elements of the society as even presently it is consumed by low income groups. In case of failure of winter crops when barley and wheat became rare, *jwar* could provide a substitute. But it never became vastly popular.

In the areas of Gujarat, Haryana and Uttar Pradesh, where rice could provide an alternative, *jwar* was not at all introduced. To conclude, it may be said that in northwestern India-Punjab, Sindh, and northern Rajasthan wheat-barley culture dominated the late Harappan and the post-Harappan periods and the other cultivars, even if introduced in a few areas, did not occupy the role of a major cereal. This archaeological data can be supplemented from evidence in literary sources. Early Vedic Aryans or Rigvedic Aryans can be fixed approximately in this post-Harappan period, i.e., before the advent of the PGW people, who are usually connected with the later Vedic people.

In the Rig Vedic literature, *yava* is considered as the principal crop. It occurs many times in the text (e.g. *RV* I. 532, IV. 24.7; V. 85. 3; VIII 81.4; X. 27. 9; X. 131. 2). We have seen that *yava* or barley was the main crop of Sindh and Punjab valleys, which was the cradleland of Rig Vedic Aryans. Vishnu Mitter has pointed out (1969-79 : 1-2) that in pre-PGW level the archaeological records of barley are scarce but are represented only by a few grains. It is known from Mohenjodaro, Harappa and Kalibangan. The last named site is the only place from where this grain was found in abundance. These sites belong to Harappan cultural zone. Much after this period barley again appears in Atranjikhera in U.P. dated around 1000 B.C., which can be attributed to OCP level. It is also found in Banawali in Haryana, in approximately same period. But the archaeological evidence of this crop in between 1500 B.C. and 1000 B.C. is practically nil. It is interesting to note that the other principal crop, wheat which was so decidedly proven by the archaeological remains, is conspicuously absent in Rig Vedic sources. *Godhum* (wheat) is not referred to at all in the Rig Vedic *Samhitas*. Its earliest references came in late Vedic literature, when the geographical horizon had much expanded (e.g. *Mait. Saṁ.* 1.2.8; *Vāj. Saṁ.* XVIII 12; XIX. 22. 89; XXXI. 29; *Sat. Br. XII. 7. 1. 2; 29; Bṛhadāraṇyaka Up.* VI. 3.22). Vrīhī was the common name for rice in later Vedic literature. This word is absolutely omitted in the *Rig Veda*. There is a word *odana* which occurs a number of times in the *Rig Veda* (VIII. 66. 10;

VIII. 58. 69. 14). Pāṇinī (V.S. Agarwal : 1953 : 107) in his exposition has equalled *odana* with *taṇḍulaḥ*. Ghurye thinks (1979 : 229) that Rig Vedic Aryans probably were aware of rice products, and named it as *odana*. To prove that *odana* meant rice, a word *kṣīraudana* (rice cooked in milk) can further be quoted from *Śatapatha Brāhmaṇa* (II. 5. 3. 4; XI. 5. 7. 5). Even the wild rice *nivara* was not mentioned in the *Rig Veda*, it occurs for the first time in later vedic literature (e.g. *Kāthak saṁ.* XII.4; *Mait. Saṁ. III. 4. 10; Vāj. Saṁ.* XVIII. 12 and *Śat. Br.* V. 1.4.14; 3.3.5; *Tait. Br.* I.3.6.7). Wild rice, which became a necessary part of the later Vedic rituals, was not at all required in early Vedic rituals. Therefore, the absence of rice in *the Rig Veda* is quite in accordance with the paleobotanical data available to us. But we have seen that barley was not the only cultivar in pre-PGW period. They knew of other crops too, especially wheat. Perhaps the reference to *dhānā* in the plural form is of significance (*RV.* I. 16. 2; III. 35. 3; *RV.* V. 53. 13 VI. 29. 4). It is the generic term for crops and indicates that besides the principle crop of *yava* the people cultivated other crops, too. Rice, though introduced in the pre-PGW period, remained mostly outside the area of the Rig Vedic Aryans, i.e. away from the western Punjab and Indus regions. Therefore, it is not unlikely that *dhana* denoted barley and wheat both, if not rice.

With the later Vedic people, who had expanded up to riverine belt of the Ganges river system, the perspective changed completely. The later Vedic people were an iron-using community and can be identified with PGW-using people. Their geographical horizon had now shifted from western Punjab, Sindh, northwestern Rajasthan and Gujarat to more easterly provinces like Haryana and Uttar Pradesh. They came in closer contact with the rice-growing people and palaeobotanical evidences from these areas convincingly prove it. Atranjikhera, which provides the floral remains as early as OCP and BRW periods, rice is discovered along with the husk and embedded in mud; while in the PGW period, it was found in heaps, and over 50 percent of the rice was without the husk. Chowdhury *et al* (1977: 63) thought that this indicates that rice was produced in large quantities and was even saved as a surplus product. Besides this, rice was plentifully cultivated in most of the areas. Though, we do not possess sufficient palaeobotanical records, whatever floral remains are available indicate that rice was predominant over other cereals, wheat and barley, whereas, earlier we notice that barley occupied the predominant position until the early Vedic age. Proof of rice or paddy grain are available from Atrajikhera in Uttar Pradesh and Rupar, Daulatpura, Khokrakot in Haryana. On the other hand, barley was found in Atranjikhera and Radhan in Uttar Pradesh and Banawali in Haryana. Millet was found at the Purana Qila, although identification of this cereal is still in doubt. Wheat was discovered in Atranjikhera, Rupar, Radhan and Daulatpura. This informative data is not yet complete, we need much more palaeobotanical study material to reach any conclusive decisions. Still, it may be useful to indicate two significant points:

(1) The PGW people had adopted intensive agriculture. At least two crops a year were raised. Wheat and barley were grown as *rabi* crop and millet, cotton and rice were grown as *Kharif* crop.

(2) It may be noted, based on 20th century records, that cultivable areas fluctuate during different years for various reasons. For example, due to insufficient rain in a previous year, there would be a drop in the cultivated hectorage in the following year.

Therefore, it is quite likely that while the *rabi* area remains more or less constant, the area of *Kharif* keeps fluctuating with the late rainy seasons in the later Vedic period too. For rice cultivation, moist soil or low lying damp areas are needed. Dry and elevated lands are suitable for sowing millet.

We notice that most of PGW sites in Haryana are located in the area which received between 500 and 600 mm annual rainfall—38 sites in the 600 mm zone and 142 sites in the 500 mm zone (Breham Datta 1980. Table 4). A maximum number of PGW sites (152) have been discovered in the area where at present rice is grown as a major crop.

Similarly, nearly 252 PGW site have been found in U.P. having alluvial soil. In Uttar Pradesh the main concentration of PGW sites are in the districts of Mainpuri, Meerut, Saharanpur and Bulandshahr, which at present produce abundant rice. PGW people were thus mainly rice-eating communities, though this does not mean that other crops were not grown by them.

Literary sources of the later Vedic period clarify the position in a better way. Wheat (*godhūm*), which was an unknown cultivar in Rig Vedic literature, is quite common in later Vedic literature. *Godhum* is referred to in the *Śatapatha Brāhmaṇa* (V. 2. 160; 13; XII. 7. 1. 2; 29; XIV. p. 3. 22; XII. 9. 15) and in *Taittiriÿa Saṁhitā* (I. 3. 7. 2; II. 6. 4. 4; 11). But *vrīhī* or *tanḍula* (rice) was much more commonly used. It is referred to innumerable times in the *Atharva Veda* (e.g. X. 9. 26; XI. 1. 18; XII. 3. 18) and *Chhandogya Upanisad* (III. 14. 3). Husked and unhusked rice and wild rice (*nivara*) were equally prevalent. Besides these two major crops, the *Yajurveda Saṁhitā* (XVIII. 12) gives a list of agricultural products commonly in use. It includes : (1) rice (*vrīhī*), (2) millet (*priyangu*), (3) kidney peas (*mudga*), (4) beans (*māsa*), (5) *panicum frumentaccum* (*śyāmaka*), (6) wheat (*godhūm*), (7) sesamum (*tila*), (8) barley (*yava*), (9) *panicum millianccum* (*anuh*), (10) vetche (*khalva*), (11) wild rice (*nīvara*), and (12) lentil (*masūra*).

This list is ample justification that by the later Vedic period a variety of crops were commonly used and intensive cropping was done. Later Vedic farmers knew the method of improving the fertility of the soil by the system of rotation (*Tait. Saṁ.* V. 1. 7. 3; IV. 2: VII. 2. 18). Rice was probably sown in summer and pulses in winter on the same field (*Śat. Br.* I. 4. 1. 15-16). The *Atharva Veda* (III. 14. 3. 4; XIX. 31.3) shows that the value of the natural manure of animals in the field was appreciated. *Karisa* denoted the dry cowdungs (*Sat. Br.* II.1.1.7). The society had by now become completely agriculture-based. People were not dependent on one single crop a year. They were able to save plenty of surplus. They had an alternative cropping system. They were well prepared to take further steps toward urbanization. This had resulted due to their expansion in wider geographical horizon and their cultural contacts, which brought the two distant communities with two different food habits into a close relationship. The wheat and barley eating people of Afghanistan, Baluchistan, Sindh and western Punjab had moved toward Gujarat, eastern Punjab, Haryana, western U.P., southern Rajasthan, and the southern provinces of India and started adopting a new rice-eating culture. By the time wheat eaters and rice eaters merged, they developed a new culture in Haryana and U.P. who were known to us in literary sources as the later Vedic people who, through their combined food habits, built up a society based on multi-cropping and thus prepared that solid economic base which was essential for urbanisation in 600 BC.

Diffusion of cultivation trends has some economic significance. It implies that the social group has increased its communication potential with distant lands, from where it has acquired novel food habits. It signifies that a single-crop yield was not sufficient to hold constant surplus product and, therefore, when the population growth reached a maximum, where the bearing capacity of the soil could not fulfill the social demand, the people were forced to migrate or introduced a new cropping system so that the balance could be maintained between the cultivation of products and its consumption. If the introduction of a new crop was sustained for a long period of time, and in fact became a part of the food habit of the community, then that helped to stabilize the settlement. But, if the new crop was just an experimental introduction and had not succeeded in becoming a regular cultivar of the area, then it did not have any permanent effect and lost its importance.

Study has shown that rice, though it was introduced in the northwestern part of the Indian subcontinent as early as the 2nd millennium BC in Loebarn III and Aligrama and in the post-Harappan context in Pirak, it could not remain there as a constant permanent cultivar. The climate did not suit the growth of this cereal. As a result, rice did not bring any basic changes to the economy of the area.

Sorghum was also introduced in Mohenjodaro, Pirak, Ahar and Rohira. But this did not occupy the position of a major cultivar of the whole area. Only a few settlements, due to their specific needs, may have introduced this crop to suit their temporary requirements. Whether this new cereal changed the economic status is doubtful. In the same way, rice was the major crop of eastern India. As long as the communities depended on the sole cultivation of rice, they could not expand. As soon as they came in contact with barley-wheat producing people, their cultural communication system developed. They accepted wheat and barley as another permanent substitute—and only then did they become fit for the beginning of urbanisation. Urbanisation can only become possible with a broad-based economy which is an essential part of broadbased food habits coming from broad-based cultural contacts.

Another important thing to consider is the relationship between man, water and land ownership. We should keep in mind that rice cultivation needs a constant source of irrigation. The rice crop needs water to be stagnant for a required period of time. Therefore, it is not possible where only flood water irrigates the field. In the Indus valley and Punjab valleys, rice could not be sown until farmers remained dependent on flood water irrigation alone. Receding flood waters spoils its growth. Moreover, a mobile pastoral tribal society, depending on flood irrigation, would sow a single crop of wheat and barley soon after the rainy season. They too will not depend much on rice cultivation. Thus, in the post-Harappan Rig Vedic period, rice cultivation could not become popular. For the proper yield of rice other sources of irrigation were also necessary, e.g. canals, wells, tanks, plentiful rains. Farmers would be interested in developing the land by improving irrigation facilities, which was so necessary for rice cultivation, only if they had the ownership rights over the land. Therefore, improved rice yields mean to some extent that the concept of ownership of land had also emerged in the society. This development can thus be conjectured in the later Vedic period or the PGW period when rice cultivation was well established.

Multi cropping started in the real sense with the ample use of iron in cultivation in NBPW period. This period is roughly divided into two phases 600 to 300 B.C. and 300 to 100 B.C. The first period can be equated with the period of Gautam Buddha and Mahavira. We know from the Buddhist and Jaina literary sources, the pattern of agriculture as practised by them. Fields were frequently known after the crop cultivated into it, as is clear by the references in the *Vinaya*, where *Śālikhetta* (field of *Śāli* rice), *Ucchukhetta* (sugarcane field) (*Cullavagga:* 377), *Yavakhetta* (barley field) (*Pācittiya:* 71; 362), and *Tinakhetta* (grass field) (*Pārājika:* 80), are mentioned. Panini also mentions the fields after the crops grown into it (such as *Vraiheya* (field of *vrihi* rice) *Saleya* (field of *sali* rice) *Yavya* (barley field) etc. (*Astadhyāyī.* V. 2. 2). Three yields in a year were mentioned in the *Arthaśāstra*. *Pūrvavāpa* according to Kautalya includes all the crops that are sown in the commencement of the rainy season, e.g. paddy, sesamum, *priyangu; madhyavāpa* comprises green gram and black gram, which are cultivated in the middle of the same season; *masūra*, *kulattha*, barley, pea, linseed and mustard which are sown in autumn came under the category of *pascādavāpa* (*AS.* II. 24. 16).

The extension of cultivation in the middle Ganga plains can be estimated on the basis of a large number of crops enumerated in the Buddhist sources. G. S. P. Misra (1972) has tabulated the varieties. of grains referred in the Buddhist literature. It is evident, that with eastern U.P. and Bihar coming to prominence, rice cultivation had gathered an impetus. *Vrīhī* and *Tandula* are the common terms used in Pali *Nikayas* (*Majjh.* I. 57; III. 90) and the *Jatakas* (I. 429; 484: II. 110; 135; 378; IV. 276; V. 367) for rice. Similarly in the Jain canonical literature *kalmasali* (*Uva* 1.8), *raktaśāli* and *gandhaśāli* have been mentioned as different varieties of rice. *Godhuma* (wheat), *yava* (barley) and *kangu* (millet) were also commonly known. Among the cultivated pulses were grams *kalaya* (Jāt. II. 74), beans (*mooga*), (*māsa*) (*Majjh.* I. 57; III. 90; Angu. IV. 108) and *kolatthi* (*K. S.* I. 189). Late Jain canonical texts mention seventeen varieties of grains, whereas the *Nisītha Sūtra*

Bhāṣya (II. sl. 1029-30; 109) refers to twenty four varieties of grains produced on those days.

The extension of cultivation in NBPW period can be proved through archaeological evidences. The discovery of rice, wheat and pulses in the excavated sites of Ter and Nevasa in NBPW levels testify the authenticity of the literary sources. The NBPW sites multiplied considerably in comparison to earlier BRW and PGW sites. This indicates that the population was growing and new areas came under the ploughs of the cultivator. With the introduction of iron in the fields, artificial irrigation methods had developed, and multicropping could become a common phenomenon. The custom of frequently feeding large numbers of ascetics, supplemented with liberal alms by the householders, point out that the country was abundont in grains. It can be corroborated by the accounts of the foreign writers too, whose writings illuminate the Mauryan and post-Mauryan periods. According to classical writers, 'in addition to cereals, there grows throughout India much millet and much pulses of different sorts and rice also, and what is called *bosporum*, as well as many other plants, useful for food, of which most grow spontaneously'. (Diod. II. 36; Strabo XV. 1. 13. 20; Arrian *Indica*. V). Appolonius remarks that the Gangetic plains were very productive. Its wheat stalks were like reeds and its beans three times as large as Egyptian ones. Its sesame and millet are extraordinarily fine (*see*, McCrindle, J. W., 1893 and R. C. Majumdar : 1960:395).

With the extension of agricultural activities and with the widespread multicropping, failure of one crop did not matter much. The enough surplus production in normal times gave the opportunity for storing. Therefore, in time of natural calamities stored grains could support the economy for some duration. After the regular introduction of multicropping the maladies of famines were to some extent reduced.

7

IRRIGATION AND WATER SUPPLY

Success in crops depends in India, not only on quantity of rain, but on its timely occurrence. If rain fell in continuous manner for a long period, it destroyed the standing crops. Timely pulsation of rains was very much essential. Indian farmers depended on rains on large scale. Artificial irrigation system was always inadequate in comparison to the length and breadth of the cultivable land. Egypt and Mesopotamia had developed canal and basin irrigation system in the proto-historic times. But how far the chalcolithic or even the early iron using people of north India had appropriate irrigation technology is a matter of present discussion. Early cultures flourished on the river banks. Cultivators of Indus valley civilization mainly depended on *sailabi* method of irrigation, where the floods in the rivers automatically provided with sufficient water for cultivation. Scarcity of rain in the catchment areas resulted insufficient supply of water in the rivers, which affected the river courses and many times rivers were dried up, at least partially. Therefore, artificial methods of irrigation was very much needed. Early agriculturists were aware of that. some measures were adopted too.

Wells were of course known to the Harappan people. The wells made in the *'bet'* land of Punjab were shallow in nature. They were simply scooped in the earth, because the water table in the vicinity of the river valley remained quite high and wells were only needed during drought periods. The wells in the *'kadir'* lands were of permanent nature and were seldom even lined with bricks. Wells are found with or without lining, in Harappan period from Mohenjodarao, Harappa, Kalibangan and Lothal. They probably provided potable water, to the citizens of the towns, as all of them are situated in the habitation areas of these sites. It is doubtful whether they were utilized for irrigation purposes or not. Of course, nothing with finality can be said about this at present stage of our knowledge, as archaeological explorations in the village sites of the Harappan period are till now inadequately reported.

In the late Harappan period, posterior to the Harappan culture, no wells have so far been reported from any site. Nor is there much of evidence about the presence of wells at the sites of early iron age, OCP and BRW cultures of the last quarter of the second millennium and early half of the first millennium B.C. From the middle of the first millennium B.C., with the emergence of NBPW period, a number of wells, along with ringwells, can be traced in Ujjain, Rajghat, Prahladpur, Sahet-Mahet, Kusinagar, Kumrahar, Vaisali, Nasik, etc. But all these wells were situated in the residential complexes of the sites, signifying their utility only as potable water. Literary sources provide a different picture, as can be glanced through the *Rig Veda*. The mobile, pastoral Aryan community showed little interest in the matters of agricultural activities on the whole. Therefore, in the irrigation sector too not much improved methods can be expected. Still *Rig Veda* (X. 101.5-7) informs us that they were acquainted with well irrigation. Water was raised by a wheel of stone (*cakra*), to which was fastened a strap (*varatra*), with a pail (*koṣa*), attached to it. Reference to *kupa* (pit on the earth) occurred in the *Rig Veda* (I. 105. 17). Another synonym word was *avata* (*Rig Veda* X. 131. 2). But I and X Mandalas of the *Rig Veda* are considered of later origin.

Some references of artificial irrigation technology are available from the later Vedic literature. *Kūpa* is referred to in the *Artharva Veda* (V. 2. 160; *Śatapatha Brāhmaṇa* III. 5. 4. 1; IV. 4. 5. 3, *Jaiminīya Brāhmaṇa* I.184), etc. By this time Aryans were acquainted with multicropping system and they needed water for their cultivable fields round the year. Water was drawn from wells by means of levers, bullock team, or axle (*Cullavagga*, V.16.2). With the expansion of agriculture since the time of the Buddha, wells became a common part of the rural scene. It is mentioned in the *Arthasastra* that usually the wells were situated on the vicinity of the *khetta* land. Asoka considered diggings of wells, a duty of the king (J. Burgess 1971:99). This situation continued in later periods, as can be seen through the epigraphical sources. Ara inscription of Kanishka (year 41), refers about a well dug by a certain ordinary citizen for the benefit of the society (Sircar; 1963; 154-55; Fleet: 1916: 97). Wells are often referred to in the inscriptions of later period. (E.I. VII. 46; Gadre: 1943: 7). These inscriptions show that in later period the wells were dug both by the state agencies and philanthropist citizens.

Well irrigation could never be sufficient for a dependable agriculture and therefore, the utility of canal irrigation was always felt. The earliest archaeological evidence of a channel can be traced in the Harappan site of Lothal. An inlet channel of 7m width has been found here, connecting a large water reservoir, but its use for agricultural purposes are not conclusively proved.

Another channel can be traced in Inamagaon (dt. Pune, Maharashtra) (Dhavlikar *et.al* 1988: 241, 248), which can be dated in between 1400-1000 B.C., and belonged to the early Jorwe cultural levels. A diversionary embankment wall, 240m. long and 2.25m wide, is traced in this site. A channel 4m. wide and 3.50m deep runs almost parallel to the wall. The water thus diverted could be stored in the channel and was probably used to irrigate the neighbouring fields. This is the only irrigational channel, so far known, which can be dated in the 2nd millennium BC. But our literary sources supply us with ample references of the uses of canals.

Kulya is mentioned in the passages of the *Rig Veda* (III. 45.3; V. 83. 8; X. 43. 7). Muir (1884: V. 464-66) thinks the *Kulya* meant 'artificial water channel flowing into a reservoir'. *Khanitrima* (artificial water channel) is mentioned in the *Rig Veda* (VII. 49. 2). But so far no archaeological evidences, supporting the above claim of Rig Vedic people have come to light. Therefore, we cannot be assured of whether these developments actually appeared in the early Vedic times or these references are the postscripts of the Rig Vedic literature. Besides even if we presume that they acquired the knowledge of these technologies, there is no doubt that these methods were not elaborately developed. Therefore, the lands of Punjab and north Rajasthan, where the early Vedic settlements were situated, remained inadequately irrigated.

Gradually the use of canal irrigation became more common in later Vedic times. *The Atharva Veda* (III. 13) categorically says that they were used for carrying water in the fields. Special hymns were recited on the occasion of cutting the channel for irrigation. Archaeological evidences can be gathered from the PGW sites of Jakhera, where a moat was constructed to divert the excess of river water during monsoons.

With the beginning of NBPW period, when agriculture became the mainstay of economy, cultivation spreaded beyond the riverine tracks. The findspots of the NBPW sites indicate that they no longer remained confined to river beds. Iron was used for agricultural implements and more cultivable lands were acquired, by clearing thick forests of eastern U.P. and Bihar. As they were now occupying the lands even away from the riverine tracks, which did not always have perennial sources of water, they had to develop artificial irrigation systems. Therefore, after 600 B.C., more attention was paid to artificial irrigation methods. Besides, well irrigation (*Jat.* nos. 174, 259) much stress was paid on canal irrigation (*Mahavamsa* VIII. 12.1-2; *Cullavagga* VII. 1. 2. 5. 17. 2). *Nettikas* referred to in the *Dhammapadas* (80.14.5) were not simply water carriers, but builders of canals and aqueducts, 'who forced the water to go where it would not go by itself' (Max Muller's notes on *Dhammapada. SBE* series). Sometimes it led to feuds among the neighbouring tribal communities. For example, we see that the Koliyas and Sakyas clashed frequently for the sake of water of the river Rohini (*Dhammapada* XV.1). Canals are referred to in the *Thera Gatha* (19.877).

Irrigation became a matter of importance with the beginning of the Mauryan period. The classical writers threw enough light on this aspect. Megasthenes (McCrindle 1877 reprint 1960:29) says that 'the greater part of the soil is under irrigation and consequently bears two crops in the course of a year'. He further says that 'a band of officers, who supervised the rivers, measure the land, and inspect the sluices, by which water was let out from the main canal into their branches, as a result of which famines never visit India' (McCrindle. 1877 reprint 1960:31). Since the time of the state controlled economy of the Mauryas, the state took up the responsibility to provide irrigation facilities. *Arthasastra* of Kautalya supports this view. He stresses upon the necessity of irrigation (*AS*. II. 34; VII. 4). Not only wells and canals but tanks were built by the state support. *Arthaśāstra* categorically says that the kings should construct reservoir and provide irrigation facilities (II. 1. 42; II. 24; IV. 3; II. 26; III. 9; VI. I). It refers that cultivable lands (*khettas*) overflowed with water. For the preservation of tanks and dams some rules were formulated in the *Arthaśāstra*. It says "when a person breaks the dam of a tank full of water, he shall be drowned in the very tank; of a tank without water he shall be punished with highest punishment; and of a tank which is in ruins owing to neglect, he shall be punished with the middle-most punishment: (*AŚ*. IV. II).

The inscriptional evidence about the state supported irrigational projects in the Mauryan period come from Junagarh inscription (*E. I.* VIII. 6). Giving a detailed history of Sudarsana lake and the canals attached to it, this inscription refers back the original construction of this lake to the Mauryan period. It says that it was first built by Pusyagupta, a local Governor, who was on the rolls of Chandragupta Maurya's administrative staff. This lake and its dam were again reconstructed during the time of Asoka, by the local Governor Tusaspa, as due to some natural hazards the dam was damaged. Junagarh is situated in the western parts of India, which falls under dry climatic zone. Mauryan kings, therefore, took special interest to save the agriculture of these dry lands, by supporting it by a huge irrigation project. The same ideology was pursued by the writer of the *Mahābhārata*. In a well known verse (II. 5. 67) sage Narada advises Yudhisthira "I hope that in your domain the tanks are full and increasing (in numbers) and (the water) is divided proportionately".

Agriculture should not depend on rainfall. Guards were employed to check the ruptures in the embankments (*MBH*. I. 3; XII. 120-8). The *Mahābharāta* (II.5.77) and the *Ramayana* (II.100.46) emphasise that the canals should be dug by the kings. Manu's references of "*satam udakagama*" and "*prasara vāhinī*" possibly indicate channels for irrigation (VIII. 248. 252).

Hathigumpha inscription of Kalinga king Kharavela, provides us with an epigraphical record to support the above literary evidences. It is said in this inscription that Kharavela reconstructed and extended an old canal which was originally built three hundred years earlier than his times (*Tivasasta-purve*) (Sircar 1963:213).

The archaeological evidences of the canals are very few. In the NBPW period the remains of a canal can be traced in Besnagar (dt. Vidisa M.P.), Kumrahar (Patna, Bihar) and Ujjain (M.P.). But how far they were utilized for irrigating the cultivable fields, cannot be decidedly said. Besnagar is situated on the rivers Betwa and Bes. The site is protected by a fortification wall with a moat on the west. D. R. Bhandarkar (1914-15:69) traced a storage canal, 2.13m high and 56m long with brick walls serving as embankments. At Kumrahar the site is situated on the river Ganga. A canal with a width of 13m and depth of 3m is located by the side of the Mauryan "pillared hall". It is conjectured that the canal served to bring huge chunar pillars to the doors of the hall and thus was used as a supply route rather than an irrigational canal (Altekar, Misra: 1959: 24). In Ujjain a brick lined channel of 11m wide and 2.59m deep has been traced to a length of 45m.

The site is situated on the river Sipra. But how far it was utilized for irrigating the fields cannot be ascertained.

Not only the state but other sources were employed too to construct irrigational facilities. According to *Jatakas* (No. 31; No. 536) canals and tanks were dug by corporate efforts and for cooperative irrigation. It reflects a later stage when the state's control over economy was slackened. Gradually the public consciousness towards the need cf artificial irrigation was improved and public started contributing in building irrigation projects. Collective responsibility for irrigation became a common feature in post Mauryan period. (*AS*. III, 10; *Yaj Sm. II. 1919-93; Viṣṇu Sm. V, 73; II. 1; Manu Sṁ. VIII, 221; Brhaspati Sṁ. VIII. 9; XVII.* 5. etc.). *Visnu Dharma Śāstra* (XLI. 1) and *Vāśiṣṭa Dharma Sutra* (XVII. 8) refer that the king and people both construct tanks and canals alike. Tanks ponds and channels were built to demarcate the boundaries between two villages (*Manu*. VIII. 248). Stringent punishments were prescribed by Manu (IX. 279) for those who caused any harm to water reservoir. He says that the offenders who break the dam of a tank full of water shall be drowned in that very tank. *Yajñavalkya Smriti* (II.150) refer about *kheya* (dyke) which served the purpose of irrigation and *bandhya* which served to keep the water off. It says that the erection of dykes in the middle of another man's field is not prohibited act, as it may be productive and of considerable advantage. The land which was provided with an efficient system of man made irrigation was known as a *devamātrika*.

Many interesting laws were formulated by Manu for preserving the purity of water in the tanks. He says in IV. 56 "let him not throw urine or faeces into the water, nor saliva, nor (clothes) defiled by impure substances, nor any other impurity, nor blood, nor poisonous things". (This rule was repeated in IV. 46-47; XI. 174). Demand for water was quite acute. Manu observed the practice of stealing and diverting the water (III. 163; XI. 174, 281) and condemns them. But in the enemy country he recommends that one should destroy the tanks, ramparts and ditches to bring foes to their knees. Tanks, fountains, cisterns and wells were recommended to be built where boundaries meet to demarcate the different fields. (VIII. 248). *Visnu Smriti* propounds the law that the king should give capital punishment to those who destroy the embankments (*setubhedaka*).

The evidences from Buddhist literary sources, belonging to post-Maurya period are also not lacking. *Milindapañho* (*SBE*. XXXV. VI. 416) informs that fields were well provided with conduits for bringing water into them and embankments (*maryada*) to keep the water in. *Mahāvastu* (III. 303) refers to *udakavaha*. In the time of Aśvaghosa (1st-2nd century AD.) numerous irrigation methods were quite commonly known. In his compositions references of dams, tanks, wells are available frequently (*Saundarananda* 24:53; 26:65; 27:58; 13:6; 0:5; 11:61; *Budhacarita:* 2:12). Ceylonese chronicals also refer about ponds (*Dīpavaṁśa* XX.9.10; *Mahāvaṁśa* XXXV. 86), tanks and canals (*Mahāvaṁśa* XXXV: 96-98; XXXVII: 47-50). From the *Amarakoṣa* we know (IX. 36: 67) that canals and tanks were constructed profusely in the Gupta period. In the *Harivaṁśa Purāṇa* of Jinasena (ch. 102), it is said that the Yamuna was diverted to Brindavan by Balarama, apparently for irrigation purposes.

The existences of irrigation tax '*udaka bhāga*' in the *Arthasastra* (II.34), suggests that this tax was levied on the cultivators who utilised state controlled tanks and channels. But if the farmers utilized the irrigation facilities build by themselves, they were on the contrary, exempted from the tax altogether (*AŚ*. III. 7.9). In the Gupta inscriptions a tax is named *udranga*. This may be, as Maity (1957:62) suggests, a water tax. But Niyogi (1962:187) on the other hand thinks that it has nothing to do with irrigation, but was a police tax. The absence of irrigation tax in post Mauryan period, might have been due to the fact that the state generally ceased to bear the responsibility of irrigation and consequently had no moral ground to claim any cess for the reason'. (R. S. Sharma: 1965:00). Thus the literary sources clearly indicated that from the Mauryan period onwards artificial irrigation facilities had considerably improved. We can confirm this analysis with the help of archaeological remains too.

Construction of tanks and reservoirs had started on an organised manner from NBPW period onwards. Ujjain, which was situated on the river Sipra, provides us with a massive tank, which can be dated to NBPW period. It measures 10.30m.x 7.92m, built of burnt brick, presumably for storage of water. It is connected with a long channel traced to a length of 25.9m. with a right angled bend (Banerji, N.R.1965:). In the late phase of NBPW period a baked brick wall 3.6m. wide and exposed to the length of 75m. at Ropar, (district Rupnagar, formally district Ambala), has turned out to be the retaining wall of a large tank, fed by rain water, through a brick built inlet (Y. D. Sharma 1955-56). Similarly from Tamluk, a burnt brick stepped tank is exposed and a burnt brick wall running for nearly 8m. at Hastinapur, which may have been retaining wall of a tank, reveal the same analysis (Roy, T.N. 1983: 128-140). At Kankali Tila (Mathura) an impressive baked brick tank complex 35x35m., belonging to its period IV (i.e. between A.D. 100-300) has come to light. The tank is cut into the natural soil to a depth of about 3.96m. from the original ground surface. On the top of the north wall of the tank a stone channel has been fixed for the purpose of filling it up with the water. Near the outer end of the ramp leading to the tank a well was also dug.

Besides the available remains of tanks there are numerous epigraphical records which inform the construction of tanks and reservoirs. An irrigation tank was built by Greek Theodoros, the Datiaputra, in Swat valley, in A.D. 29 (Konow, Sten. 1929.1.:24. Line 1-3). A *puskarini* (tank) and a *udapāna* (reservoir) is referred to in the Mathura stone inscription of the time of Mahaksatrapa Somdasa (*Luder's List : 82; E.I. IX. 246)*. A pond (*puskarinī*) made by Sonaka (Saunaka), the son of Hariti, is referred to in the Kevali Kunda cave inscription (*Luder's List* : 107). Kanheri (district Bombay) record of 2nd century AD., refers to the construction of reservoir by one *setthi*

Punaka, which shows public consciousness. Junnar cave inscription of the time of Nahapana (Sircar: 1963:172-73), refers to the construction of a tank by Mahakastrapa Ayam, who was a subordinate officer of Nahapana.

In the Gupta and post-Gupta periods when the rural economy came to the forefront, kings and subjects both paid more attention to cultivation through artificial irrigation methods. All over India, whether it was dry lands of Rajasthan, semi arid areas of Haryana, or the wet climatic zone of Bengal and Orissa, we know from numerous epigraphic references that wells, ponds and canals became a common part of the rural scenario. In Rajasthan, cultivation could only prosper, provided it had irrigation facilities. It seems that lakes, wells or any other water facility was provided along with donated cultivable land to donee. Whether the land was donated to a religious institution or to an individual, the purpose of a land gift was to accrue some income by encouraging the cultivation. Therefore, some sort of water facility, near the donated land was a basic requirement and donors usually kept this in their minds, while donating a piece of land, especially in Rajasthan. Late charters like Belera land grant charter of Mularaja (V.S. 1051) (*E.I.*X.78), Jodhpur copper plate inscription of the time of Durlabharaja (V.S.1069) (*E.I.*XIII: 206) and Hathal copper plate inscription of Paramara king Dharavarsa (V.S.1237) (*I.A.*;45;193) etc are a few records which further prove the above statement.

In Bengal which comes under wetter climatic region, and where dependency on artificial irrigation was not that acute, even there it was usually kept in mind that the donated land should have provisions for water supply. While demarcating the boundary line of the donated fields, a lake, a pond or a well are often mentioned by scribes. This means that these were regarded as essential requirements, while assessing the utility of the donatable land. (for example Damodarpur copper plate inscription of Budha Gupta-Sircar 1963:61-64; Gunaighar copper plate inscription of Vaniya Gupta-*Ibid.*: 33). Damodarpur copper plate inscription of the time of Kumar Gupta I (448 A.D.)

refers about the provincial viceroy Ciratdatta of Pundravardhana and Kumaramatya Vetravarman, who were the administrators of the district of Kotivarsa, as jointly donating a land with the right of using canals excavated for watering the fields, lying in the west of village (*E.I.* XV: 133; E.I.XVII: 193).

Rivulets, embankments, artificial water courses and lakes are mentioned in Khalimpur copper plate inscription of Dharmapala, while depicting the boundaries of a particular village named Madhasalmali (*E.I.* IV: 243). The presence of these water resources itself prove that the value of the land was definitely increased due to presence of so many types of water resources. Sometimes the tanks or lakes were excavated by individual citizens, not kings or high officials [for example, an ordinary person like a son of a scribe, constructed a tank for religious benefit (Bodhgaya stone inscription: *ASIR*: 1908-9: 150).

Rains in Orissa had never been very dependable. In the Buddhist sources many droughts had been referred to in the country of Kalinga. Therefore, artificial irrigation was a primary necessity in this region. From Gupta period onwards tanks often demarcated the boundaries of donated land in Orissa. Urlam plate of Hastivarman (G.E. 80) (*E.I.* XVII: 330-34), Achyutapura plates of Indravarman (G.E. 79) (*E.I.* III: 127-30) and Puri plates of Dharmaraja refer the construction of tanks in their respective donated fields. Storm water channel of a tank is mentioned in Santabommali plates of Indravarman (G.E. 87) (*E.I.* XXV: 194-98), which encircled the donated land. Tekkali plates of Indravarman (G.E. 154) (*E.I.* XVIII: 307-11) also mentions *a tadaga* and rivulet Vidyut Ganga on the boundary of the donated land. Chicacole plate of Devendravarman (G.E. 183) refers to a donated field which was surrounded by trenches. The trench in the western side of the field had the supply of water from the nearby hills. All these references point out that primarily those agricultural lands were in demands for donation which had irrigational facilities.

Above description now leads us to conceptualize the

developments. Agricultural limitations which brought famines time to time in ancient period, was mainly due to lack of enough irrigation facilities. Vast land were available in India to fulfil its staple, food demands, provided the artificial irrigation was adequately developed. Geographical constraints were constant. Many areas of India had dry and arid climate where dependency on rains was an absurdity. Even in the wet areas, middle and eastern Gangetic zones inconsistency in rain pattern was conspicuous. India is drained by numerous rivers and rivulets. It is profusely gifted with lakes and natural water sheds. But in spite of all these natural bounties extensive cultivable land lay in between, where nothing but artificial irrigation was needed for survival.

The earliest agriculturists depended on the natural resources of water for irrigation. Primitive agriculturists procured limited production. Surplus was not sufficient to provide for the non-food-producing community to survive round the year, and develop other modes of economic activities. Gradually the agriculturists learnt to utilize the maximum benefits of river-valley cultivation and thus enabling society to sustain non-food-producers. The secondary producers emerged as significant social force. They depended for their food requirements on the agriculturists, who on their part depended on the secondary producers for fulfilling their other needs. This interdependence of the various social groups, their interactions and coordination, could only evolve for the benefit of society when mobility intermixing and concentration of population in geographically significant zones could take place. To maintain a social group coherent, a controlling machinery was required, which ultimately paved the way for the state formation. Artificial irrigation projects could only be carried out where the social mobility had led to population concentration. More mouths needed to be fed. As long as the settlements were situated near the area of natural water source, they could manage without an artificial irrigation. But when the population concentration reached the peak levels, a single crop in a year failed as a subsistence economy. They required to procure two or three crops a year, and thus artificial irrigation became a prerequisite. In prehistoric times the awareness for such needs were manifested but large irrigation works were a rarity. Therefore, in the drought and flood afflicted years population reeled under famines. In the absence of reserve water facilities in the rural areas, a second crop could not be procured after preliminary devastation. This resulted in frequent famines. After first millennium BC. Proto-historic Indians improved the agricultural methods. Double cropping pattern emerged. When the mobile Rig Vedic tribesmen matured as settled agriculturists in the later Vedic times, then onwards, which can be equated with PGW and NBPW periods of the archaeologists, the necessity of artificial irrigation was realized and proper devices were developed, as we have already seen in our survey of PGW and NBPW sites.

Major irrigation works could be constructed with the state help alone. Under the Mauryas when the state controlled the economic life, big lakes and sluices for irrigation were made by the provincial governors. State provided the facilities and reaped its benefits. Not only two or three crops in a year were procured, but through direct and indirect taxation, royal treasury was filled. Still during Mauryan period too we hear of famines. This indicates that even if the state paid attentions to develop irrigation, the size of the country and its variety of natural hazards were so immeasurable, that no security from famine could be guaranteed.

After disintegration of Mauryan empire, theoreticians realized that due to the vast nature of the agricultural problems, no government could ever provide a security from famine. It was now considered not only the duty of a king, but also duty of the society, specially the rich community, to provide the irrigation facilities to fight the famine menace. Donation of land was eulogized along with the donations of wells, tanks, canals, which were considered as meritorious. Religious benefits could be accrued by these philanthropist constructions and to this path both kings and subjects were encouraged alike. An agriculturist society which came into prominence with the Gupta period, provided a religious garb to the economic requirements. Law givers sanctioned punishments for those who harmed water reservoirs. Scribes praised those who donated wells, tank or any other irrigation constructions. Now the main economic activity was land based and land could only be beneficial with added artificial irrigation facilities. Royal and public consciousness towards this sector of agriculture minimized the occurrence of famines. Though complete remedy of this affliction could not be reached but the gap between periodic recurrence could be extended.

8

AGRICULTURAL TOOLS AND TECHNOLOGY

Agriculturists are universal conservatives. Progress in agriculture had always been slow all over the world. Agriculturists belong to the lower levels of society. The higher intellectual properties belonged to the upper classes, who tend to become the exploiters and oppressors. They thrive on the toils of simple agriculturists. Therefore, innovative methods are introduced last of all in agricultural sector. In India too early farmers were satisfied with their meagre tools, till increased population pressure brought the impetus to improve the agricultural technology. This need could only be made with the introduction of iron, which brought basic changes in agricultural technology. But no constant efforts were made to improve the structure, shape, design and function of agricultural tools and implements. Once a tool reached a required standard, stagnation in this field could be perceived.

Agricultural implements used by the pre-historic people were not of advanced nature. The chalocolithic men kept their agricultural tracks confined to the river banks. Therefore, not much necessity was felt for improved mode of agriculture. The soft alluvial lands of the river banks provided sufficient production. No deep furrowing was needed as the land was utilized after the receding floods left silty clay on the shores, which were naturally very fertile, but gradually they learnt the method of deep furrowing, especially in the areas, which were more arid and where drought possibilities were larger than the possibilities of yearly floods. Therefore, the earliest occurrence of a furrowed plot of land can be traced in the site of Kalibangan (Rajasthan). With the decline of the mature Harappan civilization, agricultural advancement was hampered. Whatever progress was achieved in the mature Harappan period in the field of agricultural activities, were now gradually lost in the dark ages represented by late Harappan, OCP and BRW periods.

The OCP deposits are of shallow nature. Excavations at Ambkheri (*IAR* 1963-64: 53-55), Baheria (*IAR* 1966-67: 43-44), Bahadarabad (*IAR* 1971-72: 54) in Saharanpur district, Jhinjhana (*IAR* 1962-63: 70) in Muzaffarnagar district; Lal-Quila (*IAR* 1969-70: 380) in Bulandashahr district; Atranjikhera (Gaur: 1967) in Etah district and Saipai (*IAR* 1971-72: 46-47) in Etawah district show that the depth of OCP deposits vary between 0.5m and 1.5m. The material culture of OCP people are found sporadically. No habitational deposits are found in OCP levels. Evidence for structural activities comes from only Lal-Quila, but is very limited in nature. In Ambkheri (Deshpande 1967: 1) a hearth and brick klin have noticed along with OCP deposits. OCP is found along with the 'copper hoards' in Bahadarabad, Nasirpur, Rajpur Parasu, Baheria, Kirtarpur and Bisauli. The types of copper implements found in these 'copper hoards' show the absence of agricultural tools.

Another ceramic industry which comes to light is that of Black and Red Ware (BRW). The late find spots of BRW show that it is widely distributed and belonged to different cultural horizon. It is not feasible to associate this type of pottery with any specific period. BRW was the earliest pottery during which period we find the earliest iron tools.

In pre-PGW and pre-NBPW periods, introduction of iron varied from region to region. In some places we find that the iron can be traced along with the microliths or megaliths; in some other regions it can be traced along with BRW (*see* chart XXVI). Iron was introduced in pre-PGW and pre-NBPW levels in different chronological sequence. Pre-PGW times can be regarded as the Rig Vedic times. Neighbours of the Rig Vedic people, who were called *anaryas*, were cultivators and traders. Rig Vedic Aryans attacked their settlement and usurped their agricultural products, together with their kine, as their war booties. *Loptr* or loot was one of their main source of economy. Early Aryans despised agriculture as it was regarded as the occupation of the conquered people. Therefore, Aryans themselves were relieved to a great extent from the cultivation work load. Their agricultural activities remained minimal. The references of agriculture in the *Rig Veda* are very few. Out of 10462 verse of the *Rig Veda* only 24 refers to it.

The early Aryans were basically pastoral warrior community. But still they had some knowledge of agriculture. Axe and sickle are mentioned in the *Rig Veda* (Griffiths Tr. p. 107, 108,160, 616, 39, 214; I.58.4). Even plough cultivation with the help of oxen/cows was known to them (1,23.5;1.33.15;1.176.2; IV. 57.8; VIII. 20.19; X 34.13; X 146.6, etc.) *Phala* (ploughshare) occurs in the *Rig Veda* (IV. 57. 8: X.117.7). The furrowed land is referred to in the *Rig Veda* (IV. 57. 6-8). Special respect was shown to the agricultural implements. *Śūṇa, Sīra* and *Sītā* were regarded as minor goddess. (IV. 57.6; X 101.3). Ploughing is mainly referred to in the *mandala* I and X of the *Rig Veda*. Which are considered as of later composition. Twin gods Aswins were specially remembered in connection with the ploughing procedures (VIII. 22.6). The authors of *Vedic Index* observes that *urvara* and *ksetra* are the regular expressions in the *Rig Veda*. *Khanitra* (shovel or spade) for digging is mentioned in it (1.179.6). It seems that the Aryans learnt the method of ploughing from the aboriginal tribes as the Vedic words *langala* (plough), *kuddala* (hoe), *khala* (threshing), *śūrpa* (winnowing etc.) seem etymological more connected with Dravidian languages than with the Sanskrit (H.P. Chakrawarty 1986:197). The more common word for plough, *hala*, do not occur in the *Rig Veda* (R. S. Sharma 1983; 25). It has been pointed out by some scholars that in the Vedas non-Aryans have been depicted as *akrsnah*, (or one who does not know ploughing). Randhava

(1980: 297) has suggested that probably the procedure of ploughing of the Aryans and non Aryans differed in their details. Rig Vedic ploughs were made of wood as the reference of iron plough is lacking. In archaeological remains of pre-PGW times no iron plough is recovered.

PGW period is considered contemporary to that of late Vedic period. The literature of this period shows that the people had definite knowledge of iron. But archaeological remains of PGW levels indicate that the iron was mostly used in the non agricultural tools.

Ploughing (*krisi*) is repeatedly referred to in the later *Saṁhitās* and the *Brahmanas* (*AV.* II. 4. 5; III. 12. 4; VIII. 2. 19; VIII. 10. 24; VIII. 13. 11-12; X. 6. 12; X 5. XII 2. 27; *Tait. Saṁ.* VII. 1. 11; *Mait. Sam.* 1. 2. 2; III. 6. 8; *Vāj. Saṁ.* IV. 10; IX. 22; XIV. 19, 21; *Śat. Br.* VII. 2. 2. 7; VIII. 6. 2. 2; *Tait. Br.* III. 1. 2. 5; III. 7. 7. 8). *Śatapatha Brāhmaṇa* in fact devotes a whole chapter (VII. 2. 2) torites in connection with ploughing. *Phala* (ploughshare) was a commonly known agricultural implement referred to in the later Vedic literature (*Kathaka Sam.* XIX. 1; *AV.* III. 17. 5; *Mait. Sam.* II. 7. 12; *Kausitaki Br.* XXV. 15). The ploughed land was called *urvara* and *ksetra*. Manure (*śakan, sakrta, karisa*) was known to them. The plough (*langala* or *sira*) was drawn by oxen. Sometimes teams of six, eight or even twelve oxen were employed (*AV.* VI. 91.1; *Kāt. Saṁ.* XV. 2). D.K. Chakrabarty thinks (1976: 114-24) that as this text is decidedly known to have acquainted with iron, the aforesaid ploughs were heavy ploughs that had iron ploughshares. In the *Atharva Veda* (X.62-3) an amulet born of a plough-share is referred to. The amulet is described as not being smitten by the skilful hands of the smith. The reference of 'smith' in this connection suggests that the plough share concerned was made of some metal—most likely iron as that would have been of much utility. *Satapatha Brahmana* (XII, 2.2.16; XIII. 3.4.5) mentions 'a ploughshare that has got hot during the day, and when thrown into the water, splashes, hisses and smokes in volumes'. Thus it seems that introduction of iron for cultivation purposes had started by later Vedic times, though it is not unlikely that its use was yet on a limited scale.

Revolutionary changes in the field of agricultural implements occurred with the beginning of NBPW period. Many NBPW sites provide us with the iron agricultural tools. Iron hoe specimens are found from Nagda, Navdatoli, Chirand and Atrajikhera in levels associated with NBPW. Hoes dated in the early centuries of the Christian era, found at Sisupal garh have a long tang, with a circular section, unlike the socketed ones with ring fasteners from Navdatoli and Brahmagiri. Iron spades have been found in Ujjain in levels dated between 750-500 B.C. The iron plough shares are found from Timbarva in NBPW period. Other historical sites that have yielded the iron ploughshares are Nevasa, Saradkhel, Kausambi, Rairh and Somnath. (Ist to 6th centuries A.D.). Insufficient archaeological remains of the iron and agricultural tool are because of fewer excavations in rural areas and possible recycling of the metal itself.

The NBPW period is reflected in the Buddhist and Jain literary sources. Many Brahmanical religious and secular literatures were also composed in this period. Iron became available in plenty as the concentration of population shifted towards eastern U.P. and Bihar. Iron rich mines were available in Bihar, which ushered in a period of dramatic changes in the matters of agriculture. Hence onwards multicropping and intensive agriculture could start on a regular basis. This brought self sufficiency and plenty of agricultural surplus. But it does not mean that after 600 B.C. references of famines are absent. In fact there had been many occurrence of famines even after agricultural technologies were ushered in. After this period no further revolutionary changes can be perceived in technology. A stagnation set in and a gradual increase of population continued. In the absence of further improvement in this sector, possible shortage in subsistence economy cannot be ruled out.

9

STORAGE AND DISTRIBUTION OF AGRICULTURAL PRODUCE

Natural calamities were unavoidable. To fight against these maladies a strong socio-economic support was an essential prerequisite. As long as social groups remained small and scattered they could move out of the area which were affected due to floods or drought. But when a social group settled down on a favourite land, their movements were restricted. Due to their stable positions, concentration of population reached its maximum capacity. Now it needed to have some sort of supporting system, which should safeguard its interests during the time of natural emergencies. If any settlement had capacity to store its surplus agricultural products properly and help its inhabitants in the time of dire calamities, through a public distribution system, which in modern terminology can be called a rationing system, then famines could be averted during droughts or flood situations. But in ancient times it seems that this supporting system was very much inadequate.

Some archaeologists, of course, try to focus that 'storing' was known to Indians from very ancient times. Beginning of agriculture can be traced in Mehragarh (Baluchistan) as early as 6000 B.C., Mehragarh farmers cultivated besides *emmer*, *eincorn* and two-row-barley. Mehragarh became a large settlement. Though, it is considered as a part of Baluchistan but in fact is very much a part of the Indus river system. Jarrige's (1982: 79-84) excavation of this area reveal that this site had a continuity of occupation for more than three millennia prior to the rise of Harappan culture. The last phase corresponds to 4000-3000 BC. The distribution of the potteries of this period cover some 40 hectares. This is an ample proof that Mehragarh had quite a large concentration of population and therefore, definitely needed a supporting economy, which could save its population in the years of scarcity. It is interesting to note that such a necessity was realized by its early occupants and they constructed a storehouse or granary.

South of the neolithic site of Mehragarh are the remains of settlement belonging to 5000 BC. In this cultural horizon a large rectangular building has been exposed, which is divided into ten narrow corridors. The building is preserved in some places to a height of one metre. It has no doors. Jarrige (op. cit.) suggests that it was probably 'a store-house' or 'granary', as large number of barley and wheat imprints are noticed in the compartments. Thus, Mehragarh represents a well settled cultivator's society doing not only rudimentary farming, but even surplus production to save a part of it in the store house.

In the mature Harappan period concentration of population in big towns was more evident. The society became more complex. New classes emerged in the society like those of administrators, priests, scribes, seal cutters, engineers, stone workers, potters, weavers, brick makers, brick layers, traders, sweepers, etc. Wheat and barley were the main crops. Probably, *bajra* i.e. sorghum and *jwar*, i.e. millet were not widely used, even if nominally introduced. Therefore, it was much more needed to store the surplus food production, whenever they reaped an abundant crop yield. The storing of gains was necessary for the maintenance of town folks, who were gathering social importance through trade and commerce. Some scholars have identified some building as 'granaries' of Mohenjodaro and Harappa. To the west of the Great Bath in Mohenjodaro a remarkable group of 27 blocks of brick-work have been revealed, which are criss-crossed by narrow ventilation channels. Wheeler has interpreted this structure as the podium of a great 'granary'. Similar to this, a 'granary' has been identified in Harappa too. But doubts have been raised on the identification of these structures. Fentress (1976: 133-83) has pointed out that in Mohenjodaro the 'granary' would have needed a huge wooden superstructure to give it a shape of a store house, for which there is no archaeological evidence. Shaffer (1982: 41-50) has pointed out that the so-called 'loading dock' at the Mohenjodaro structure faces a narrow congested street, making very unlikely that it could have functioned as a grain transfer and distribution centre (see also Jansen 1979: 251-59). This type of granaries or storehouses are not found in other big city centres of the mature Harappan period. The Lothal structure has been designated by its excavator as 'warehouse' and may not thus be 'granary'. To summarize, it may be said that enough doubts has been raised about the purpose of the structure generally known as 'granary'. Besides that, even if we presume that they were 'granaries', they could not have stored enough grains to supply to the surrounding satellite settlements through a centralised public distribution system. It needed a state controlled economy, and how far this stage was attained by the Harappan people, is yet a matter of conjecture. Further it can be argued that Harappan cultural horizon was much extensive and it cannot be imagined that from the granaries of Harappa and Mohenjodaro any help could have reached to the far off settlements, if any famine situations had developed in those areas.

In the succeeding periods very few archaeological evidences are available to prove the existence of granaries or store houses. The necessity of storing had always been realized. People of various cultural background built big store jars and storing pits where they accumulated grains for their personal security. In the chalcolithic cultural background storage jars can be traced in Ahar, Bahal, Banwali, Eran, Kakoria, Kotla Nihang Khan, Maheswar Navdatoli, Nevasa, Sonpur. In the Malwaware-Jorweware cultural background, storage jars are found in sites like Apegaon, Chandoli and Inamgaon. In the Bara ware cultural stage, they are traced in Bara and Daulatpura. In the

OCW context from Ambkheri and Lal Qila. Storage jars remained in common use in succeeding PGW and NBPW periods. Storage jars can be traced in sites like–Ropar, Rajgir, Sarnath and Sirpat Baram. Sometimes storage pits were also built, for example, in Ahar (chalcolithic period), Chandoli (Malwa-Jorwe cultural level), Gilund (chalcolithic BRW context), Inamgaon- (Jorwe cultural level), and Nevasa (chalcolithic context).

Proper 'storehouses' were rarely built. The only granaries so far traceable are from Inamgaon (Pune district), which is traced with the Malwa ware culture context (1600-1400 B.C.). Later on in the NBPW period a storehouse has been traced in Rajgir (2nd-1st century BC.) and in Sirpat Baram (Varanasi), the latter one attached to a monastery (See chart XXVIII).

Literary sources provide us with a fairly good knowledge about the storing provisions of our ancient people. Whether there was any systematic storing known to the Rig Vedic Aryans or not, cannot be ascertained at present stage of our knowledge. The '*urdara*' occurs in the *Rig Veda* (III.14.11)., where it is mentioned that '*urdara*' was filled with the grains (*yava*). Sayana renders it 'granary' (Monier Williams—*Dictionary*), but Roth (*St. Petersburg Dictionary*) seem to be more correct in simply making it 'a measure for holding grain' or 'garner'. In the Rig Vedic period agriculture based social stratification had not crystallized. The tribal community was still mobile pastoral groups. Therefore, no question arose about a settled *janapada*, which could support any, storage, or granary. In the absence of proper 'storing' facilities Rig Vedic people must have suffered whenever floods or droughts brought calamities. This may be the reason that even though they had a floating economy, they became acquainted with hunger and famines. Griffitih in his translation of the *Rig Vedà* refers to famines six times. The nearest synonym we could trace in these *slokas* is *amati*, which does not exactly signify 'famine' but carries the meaning 'hunger', 'poverty' or 'economic depravity'.

Gradually with the emergence of settled villages (or *janapadas*) the kings realized that storing of grains are essential for their stability. In *Chhándogya Upanisad* (IV.I.1) a reference occurs about a king Mahavrsas Jnanasruti Pautrayana, who was very much anxious for the welfare of his people. He built *avasthas* everywhere in his realm so that people throughout his kingdom can be provided with staple food. Rice and barley seems to have been the main items of food supplied by the king. *Aasthas* meant not exactly store houses. *Nilagalasala* or, *Nilakalasala* was an officer, meant according to the commentator of the *Atharva* Veda as 'grain keeper'. (Whitney:1905: 292-93; Bloomsfield: 1908: 466). Does it mean that they keep the surplus grains in some sort of granary? Probably rice was properly dried up and then preserved as we get the reference of *parivapa* in later *samhitas* which denotes dried grains of rice (*Tait. Sam. II. 1.10.1; VI. 5.11.4;* VII. 2.10.4; *Kat. Sam.* XXXIV. 11; *Vāj. Sam.* XIX, 21. 22; *Ait. Br.* II. 24; *Tait. Br.* I. 5. 11. 2). But even if they learnt to store their personal accumulation of grains in the form of dried rice in their private possessions, how far state controlled granaries or store houses had emerged in the later Vedic period, is doubtful. In the PGW cultural context, or in the later Vedic period, no archaeological evidence of any granary has yet been found.

Concept of proper storing and rationing of food products developed with the Buddhist period. In the *Majjhima Nikāya* (II. 50) a reference comes about a town called Thullakotthika, which belonged in the kingdom of the Kurus, but the exact identification of the place is not yet certain. At this station Gautam Buddha spent some time. The place received its name from the fact of its granaries always being full and its crops plenteous. Soon the state realized its duty to store the food products for the times of scarcity. Ancient thinkers regarded it the duty of a king to preserve enough crops as a safeguard against calamities (*Dīgha Nikāya.*11). In fact with the beginning of the Early Historic period (late NBPW period or with the beginning of the Christian era) the corresponding literary sources start providing us with the references of granaries or store houses. Sanskrit Buddhist text *Divyāvadāna* (p. 293. line 11) mentions that the state made special efforts for the collection of foodstuffs (*annadyam samhritya*) and after counting and weighing it (*ganayitvā, māpayitvā*) used to place them in the granary (*kosthāgāram*) in every village, city and town, etc. (*Sarvagrama, nagaranigamaparvata rājadhanisu*).

Arthaśāstra (II. 1-15) mentions a superintendent of storehouse. Whatever was collected for the storehouse, half of it was reserved to ward off the calamities. Old collection of grains was replaced by the new supply.

The *Rāmāyaṇa (Kiskindha Kanda*, 28) and the *Mahabharata (Śaṇti Parva*, 69. 35) urge the rulers to deposit all sorts of grains and other provision in the royal granaries, probably with the intention to help the sufferers during the time of famines. In the period of the *Ramayana*, the king was specially enjoined to look after the welfare of those engaged in agriculture and cattle rearing to relieve their distress and secure their prosperity (II. 100. 47-47). The state maintained its own granary (*dhānyakosa*) (II.36.7). The *Mahābhārata (Śaṇti Parva*, 243. 2-3) refers the keeping of grains in storage by the people.

In the description of Manu, cities were portrait as centres of activities. The capital cities possessed royal storehouse *(kosthāgāra)* (IX,280). They were guarded by palissade, walls (*prākara*) intercepted with gates (*dvāra*) and by a ditch (IX.289). This shows that the security of capital city was a matter of much concern. Any person guilty of harming the store houses was meted severe punishment (IX. 280).

In Patanjali's *Mahābhaṣya* (I.2.45) we are told that the granary was known as '*koṣṭha*' and '*kuśala*'. The person who stores the grains in jars was known as '*kumbhidhanya*'. (I.3.7).

Two inscriptional references are found which shows that in the Mauryan period the storing of the grains was regarded the state responsibility. Sohgaura copper plate discovered from Gorakhpur U.P. Contains short Brahmi inscription of Ashoka's time. It refers to two storehouses with the provision of fodder and wheat in the province of Kosala to ameliorate the suffering of cattle and the men in times of distress (*I.A.* XXV: 261; *E.I.* XXII: 192; *JRAS.*; 1907:91). The other one is the Mahasthan fragmentary store plaque inscription of the time of the Mauryas and refers about the storehouses, from where grains were distributed to famine-hit populace (*JASB*, XXVIII. 1932: 123).

Besides the state run granaries, rich individuals also showed a consciousness for storing. But whether this stored grain was utilized for distribution amongst the needy and poors or whether this accumulated foodstuff was really hoarded for the purpose of making profits in the days of scarcity, depended on the personal characteristics of the rich man who had collected the stuff. We possess examples of both types of individuals. In *Dhammapada* (IV.3.340. *Har. Or.Ser. II. 32)* it is said that during the time of Pasendi, who was a contemporary of the Buddha, rich people were in the habit of keeping large quantities of grains for the purpose of distribution amongst the mendicants and the poors. *Sresthis* (males and females alike), for example Anathapindaka, Culla Anathapindaka, Visakha and Suppavasa served the society by distributing food to the poors and *Bhikkhus*. This may show that a social awareness had developed by the Buddhist period.

Buddhist source *Mahāvastu* (III, 379, 374, 382, 402) while describing the wealth of the heads of the guilds at Markata, Mathura, Benaras, and Kosala include granaries. These granaries were probably a part of the hoarding by the rich patriarchs. But it cannot be ascertainel whether they helped the needy from these hoards or not. *Arthasastra* categorically says that 'hoarded wealth of the subjects could be confiscated for feeding the hungry'. This may have practically materialized in the days of 'state controlled economy', but otherwise the personal storing and hoarding was a social menace. In the *Milindapañho (SBE.* XXXV. 161) a reference occurs about the stores of a wealthy man. He has stores of all kinds of wheat, rice paddy, barley and dry grains, oilseeds, beans, peas and also has stores of ghee, oil, buttermilk, curds, honey, sugar and molasses kept in jars, pots, pans and other sorts of containers. The tone of the description indicates that this storing was in fact a hoarding meant probably to gain profit during the time of economic emergencies.

The practice of storing by private individuals became more and more common in the post Christian era. Jain sources refer about '*saṁvāha*', which were situated on hill tops or any other place of safety, where farmers could store their corn (*Bṛh. Sam.* I. 1092). Many types of storing jars and storing provisions are referred to in the Buddhist and Jain literature, like *kumbhi, karabhi, idura, alinda* and *muttoli. Ocara.* was a type of storing house. Jain sources give us a detail description of the method of storing. Harvested corn were stored in granaries (*kotthagaras*), made of straw, grass etc. on an elevated platform or on the upper story of the house. It was covered with cowdung and sealed up with mud from all sides, so that the corn could be preserved with all its food value for longer period (see Jain. 1947).

In the inscriptions of the early Christian era *sattra (satta* in Prakrit) has been referred again and again. They meant 'feeding houses', usually built by the kings, state officers, or even guilds of rich traders for the religious benefit, with the purpose of feeding the poors. Gadha (Jasdan) pillar inscription of the time of Rajan Mahaksatrapa Svami Rudrasena records the erection of a '*sattra*' by a private individual (Luder's *List 967*). *Punyśālā* pillar inscription of Huviska's reign, dated in the year of 28, mentions two guilds, the name of the first is broken and the second is flour makers guilds. A permanent deposit of 550 *puranas* was made to these guilds by some Vakanapati, probably a foreigner, so that from the interest of the total sum of money a *punyasala* (free feeding house) can be run to feed 100 Brahmins every month and to distribute every day some necessary articles of food to the hungry and thirsty (Sircar. 1963: I.151-152). *Sattras* were quite often built along with a temple (*devakula*), for example it is referred to in Mandara Hill Narasimha cave inscription or G.E.30 (*E.I.* XXXVI: 303-5); Damodarpur copper plate inscription of the time of Buddha Gupta (*E.I.* XV. 142;

Sircar 1963: I. 337); and Paharpur copper plate inscription of G.E. 159 (*E.I.* XX: 59; Sircar 1963: I: 359). In the post Gupta period state officers or small tribal chiefs quite often built *sattras* for helping the poors (e.g. Kuluha hill inscription of Visnugupta 11th century A.D., *E.I.* XXX. 84-85). Inscriptions from Bihar refer about *sattra*, which were usually attached with a *devakula* (shrine). Shrines and *sattras* were donated by pious donors for the benefit of the mendicants (Sahai: 1983: 34-35). In Madhya Pradesh we find a king granting a village for the benefit of *sattra* (Baloda plates of Tivardev 8th century A.D., *E.I.* VII: 102-3). But these *sattras* were not actual 'store houses'. They may have helped to mitigate the problems of the mendicants and poors during normal times, but they could not have substituted the state run proper store houses which are utilized to support to poor populace during the times of scarcity.

Just storing the grains is not sufficient to mitigate the evils of famine. What needed more was a proper distribution. This may be called in modern terms 'rationing'. The best example of distribution of grains to famine hit populace, has been supplied by the Mauryan inscriptions referred above. In the Kautalya's *Arthaśāstra* (Tr. Sham Shastri p.208) the equitable distribution of food stuffs (*bhakta samvibhagam*) has been mentioned. With the state controlled economy of the Mauryas storing and rationing during the time of scarcity could be visualized. Similarly the *Divyavadana* mentioned census of the population for rationing, so that they could get an equal amount of grain (*samam bhaktam*). The persons who took the census was supposed to be an expert in statistics (*ganita kusala*) and one in charge of granary was known as *kostagarika purusa*. The *Divyāvadāna* mentions one *manika* per unit for equitable distribution of food stuff. In the *Anguttara Nikāya* (IV. 69-70, 84) a reference occurs about mode of rationing during war. It has been suggested in the text that a city, especially one situated on the frontiers was required to have strong defensive systems and was required to provide with four kinds of the supplies: (a) stores of grass, wood and water, (b) rice and corn, (c) sesame, beans, vetches and cereals, (d) medicaments consisting of ghee, fresh butter, oil, honey, sugar and salt, to tide over the evil machination of the enemy. It can be presumed that some sort of controlled distributive measures were also known to them, in order to conserve the limited supply.

The *Arthaśāstra* (Sham Shastri pt. 11: 131) refers that during the time of natural calamities, especially during droughts, the state controlled the distribution system. Sometimes it forced the people to migrate from the drought-hit areas to neighbouring lands where agriculture is not hampered due to climatic hazards and sometimes the hoarded wealth of the subjects were confiscated for feeding the hungry (V.2.35). Kautalya recommends that the king during a famine should provide seeds and foodstuffs to his subjects or share his provisions with them or institute the building of forts or waterworks with grant of food (hard manual labour scheme of today) for future good and present relief. He advises the king to take help from the foreign countries. The steps as envisaged in the *Artha Satra* could have been realized in practice as the state was maintaining strong control over all sorts of economic activities during Mauryan period. But in the post-Mauryan times how far state controlled rationing could be continued, is doubtful.

Another equation which needed to be discussed in relation with the storing of the foodstuff, is connected with the movements of the grains. It seems that with the rise of urban population, it became essential for the political authority to control the food movement. Food has to be brought from villages for the survival of the townsfolk. Villagers would not surrender their surplus for the urban social groups voluntarily. Their meagre demands, tool, clothes etc., could be fulfilled in their own village society by internal exchange system. Therefore, the state had to enforce the food movement from villages to towns with coercion. Collection of tax in kind was most common method of transferring grains from rural areas to urban centres. It seems that the king's share (*bhāga*, possibly 1/6 or 1/8 of the gross product), was handed over to the tax collecting agencies and this was stored in the royal granaries. From this collection of grains the state provided relief in times of need to the poor people. But besides this the food movement was not a very common thing. Trade in foodstuffs could hardly have entered in the items of trade between distant places as it was too bulky to carry and had little margin of profit, though its complete absence was not possible either. A late work *Nisitha Sutram* (Vol. IV. sl. 56-64) provides us with a reference that traders went out for trade with carts loaded with wheat. But usually the food wagons carried by the far distant traders were for their own consumptions. In *Jataka* (I. 429) we hear of rice, beans, and other grains dropped by passing wagons, as they were not items of trade but were meant for their personal use. Food trade was not carried out on a large scale. Thus in the absence of large scale food trade urban population relied on local supplies for their food demands. In such situations if drought, flood or any other natural menace hit any particular area, people could not hope for relief through distant traders bringing them grains.

To sum it up, it can be said that in comparison to rising urban population the storing facilities remained inadequate in most periods of ancient Indian history. Voluntary food movement through vast trading network was not a common practice. Though, the conception about the utility of storing was realized from the very beginning of our history, but it was not practice much elaborately by the state, except in a few periods, like that of the Mauryan times. There were very few voluntary agencies helping in storing the grains with the purpose of mitigating the calamities. The *avasthas* or *sattras* were hardly a substitute. It could hardly face the challenge during famine situations. In a country like India, natural menaces had always been a constant occurrence and famines broke out because the state and social organizations had hardly ever taken adequate precautions by storing the grains sufficiently in big granaries. The infrastructure, which could have prevented the famines was not adequately developed, and therefore, the occurrence of famines were regularly reported throughout the ancient history.

SECTION IV
IMPACT ON SOCIETY

10

SOCIO-ECONOMIC DIMENSIONS

Occurrence of famines depends on the bearing capacity of the society. It means the capability of a social group to sustain its economic strength against a natural catastrophe. If a particular social group possessed enough surplus, and if the surplus is more or less equally distributed, if most of the people in a society has enough stores, or has enough purchasing power to buy the foodstuff during the times of scarcity, then the bearing power of that society is strong, and even if any natural disaster occur, it cannot create famine situations. But, if it is otherwise, and there are large numbers of social groups living under the poverty line, then the bearing capacity of that society cannot sustain its economic balance during natural calamities and it causes famine. Thus inadequate bearing capacity of any society is a major cause which brought famines in the past.

From the very beginning of economic evolution, the concept of personal property had divided the society between 'haves' and 'have nots'. Even in the primitive tribal society there always remained a few who possessed more than the majority of the people. But, a tribal society shared their production, through a more democratic mode of distributive system, than a settled community, where a marked distinction arose due to the ownership of land becoming the prime factor.

Crafts and industries fulfilled the primary demands of any society. These non-agriculturist social groups needed to be fed. And hence arose the demand for enough surplus food production. A class of people controlled the sources of production, though, they may not be the primary producers themselves. They formed the basis of governing class and religious sector. Thus the class distinction was formalized with the rise of a settled agricultural life.

The mature Harappan phase was the first urban civilization of Indian history. It developed a planned town, network of roads, fortifications, brick buildings, raised platforms, systematic drainage, seals and amulets, and art objects, etc. The urbanization occurred in the centres of administration or in the places of industrial production, trade-commerce, and religio-cultural activities. Many mature Harappan cities had acropolis-lower town division. Some settlements were constructed on artificially built hills, which usually rose to the heights of about 25 metres above its surrounding plains. Of course, these 'hills' varied in size. The public buildings of social importance were usually located on this portion of the settlement. In the lower town area of the site, the remains of numerous foundation walls of domestic structures can be found. Acropolises were probably inhabited by the privileged class, who held the reigns of political, religious and economic powers, whereas the lower town was populated by ordinary citizens, who supplied the commodities—food or craft products to the privileged sections. Thus the urbanization during mature Harappan phase definitely depicts a class based society—a consumer group and a producer group. Urbanization was possible because there was enough surplus production, which could be exploited by the elite manipulators for their own luxury and benefit. The surplus production in agriculture could only have materialized when the population moved towards the fertile alluvial soil of the river valleys.

A developed communication system was also an essential prerequisite for the cities to flourish. The food products needed to be transported from villages to towns-either through river routes or by pack animals and loaded carts. The agriculturists would never give up their surplus products voluntarily. The state was required as a coercing agency. Religion made the whole procedure smoother by introducing fear of the God and the king amongst the ordinary producers. Now the agriculturists produced not only for himself or his family but for the larger society as well. The state and religion became the exploitative agencies.

The accumulation of wealth in the cities is quite evident, as sophisticated articles are found mainly from the urban centres. The state and religion provided security to the moneyed class of the society. Therefore, the cities were often fortified. In short, one thing is clear that the urbanization could only be sustained as long as there is enough surplus production of agriculture. When due to some reason the agriculture suffered, the super structure of urbanization collapsed. Therefore, the decline in rural output caused deurbanization. The decline of food production could be due to many reasons—drought, flood changing of river courses, depletion of soil fertility, etc. This could bring famine situations in towns and villages alike, but the poor suffered most. Bearing capability of the Harappan society declined gradually. In the late Harappan times their economic stability was on the wane. Reused brick structures, badly executed art objects, squatter type settlements, absence of imported goods, and sites of smaller size all indicate their poor standards. Such a society could not have enough food surplus and economic strength to fight against the natural hazards.

The early Aryans were mobile warrior tribes, who could get rid of the situations of scarcity by moving out of the depleted region. But still as they had already started some agricultural activities they stuck to their lands till the excesses of calamity forced them to evacuate it. In early Vedic period the unit of production and the unit of consumption was not strictly demarcated, as they were yet basically pastoral cum militant tribal groups (Sharma, R. S. 1977: 1-12). The absence of abundant surplus production created less social tensions. Generally war booties were distributed through the institutions like *sabha*, *samiti* and *vidatha* amongst all the members of the tribal community.

But gradually as they became more and more settled, the class division became a distinct social phenomenon. The terms like *rayi, raya, bhaga, riktha, pana, dhana,* and *magha* indicated the idea of their wealth. As soon as the concept of property materialized in Rig Vedic societies, it made automatic subdivisions between 'haves' and 'have nots'. The people below the poverty line could fall prey to criminal activities. The references of anti-social elements in the Rig Vedic literature definitely provides us with the proof that a number of people were surviving under the economic deprivity. They were forced to adopt the unfair means to fulfil their needs, specially during the time of scarcity. *Musivan* (*RV.* I. 42. 3), *taskara* (*RV.* I. 191. 5; VIII. 29. 6), *paripanthin* (*RV.* I. 42. 3; 103. 6; X. 85. 32) were the common robbers and thiefs. The cattle thief was especially named *tayu* (*RV.* 1. 65. 1), he is also alluded as stealer of clothes (IV. 38. 5). In the days of difficulties the people were forced to take loans. *Rina* or debt is repeatedly mentioned in the *Rig Veda* (II. 27. 4; VII. 12. 5; X. 34. 10 etc.). Debtors were frequently bound by their creditors to posts (X. 34. 4). The amount of interest payable is difficult to make out. The wealthy people thus prospered. *Sri* is the regular word for prosperity which occurs in the *Rig Veda* (VIII. 2. 19). The wealthy people kept *dasis* (VIII. 19. 36) and *dasas*. *Dasas* generally meant hostile and alien tribes (X. 54. 1; X. 69. 6; VIII. 85. 18, etc.). But in some cases it is referred that the *dasas* were meant to serve (X. 62. 10). *Dasas* were not utilized in the productive works. The cultivation which was in its infancy did not need to be supported by forced labourers. The single yield in a year was just sufficient to fulfil their local demands.

As there are no references of big towns or cities which needed to be supported by the surplus products of the village folks, there may not have been much requirement to transport the agricultural products to distant urban centres. Yet the Rig Vedic people knew the use of carts (*śakaṭa*) (X. 146. 3). Oxen were used to draw the carts, they were called *anadvāh* (X. 59. 10; III. 53. 18).

Stratified society became more pronounced with the beginning of later Vedic period. In later Vedic times we find the consolidation of property in a few hands. A definite class of rich people emerged and as a consequence a large number of poor persisted on the verge of scarcity. On one side was an affluent class, capable of huge donation and supporting the priestly class, spending profuse money for *yajnas* and sacrificing large number of animals, which could have otherwise, been used as productive force. On the other side poor people were quite numerous. They were sometimes too poor to support themselves with fair means, and, therefore, became involved in criminal activities. The increase of crime in later Vedic society gives a significant note. A number of allusions come about people who took up petty theft as their livelihood. *Taskara* or robbers are referred to many times (*AV*.IV.3.2; XIX.47; 50.5; *Vāj. Saṁ. XI. 77. 78;* XII. 62, XVI. 21; Nirukta. III. 14). *Stena* were cattle and horse thieves. Rudra is called lord of assailants (*avyadhin*). *Stayu* were pickpockets. *Mūṣnant* were another name of stealers. *Vikranta* were cutters. *Vājasaneyī Saṁhitā* (XVI. 25) and *Atharva Veda* (XX. 47-50) devotes several hymns to night, chiefly for protection against the evil doings of thieves and robbers. *Paripanthin* (*AV*.1.27.1; III. 15. 1; XII. 1. 32; *Vāj.Saṁ*. IV. 34. etc) and *parimosin* (*Sat.Br.* XI. 6.3.11; XIII.2.4.2) meant robbers and thieves respectively. The reference of criminals was not completely a new phenomenon in later Vedic period. It existed in the early Vedic society too. But it seems that by the later Vedic period there was a definite increase in the cases of theft and robbery. This reflects the unequal distribution of wealth in society and indicates that a large portion of society was living on the margins of scarcity. They were the people who could get afflicted with famines if any natural calamity occurred. They had no capacity to bear the brunt of famines.

With the beginning of the period of second urbanization, wealth was confined into the hands of a few. Amongst higher castes, a limited number of *gahapatis* hoarded huge wealth. The hoarded property was immense, but confined to very few. Rich trading community are often mentioned in the Buddhist sources. Traders travelled to distant places with their caravans of five hundred carts (*Dh. Pada Com.* Bk. I. story 6). Treasurers were quite often referred to as extremely rich persons (*Dh. Pada Com.* Bk. IX. story 8; Bk IV. story 8). The brahmana *gahapatis* frequently appear in the *Jatakas* as owner of huge properties. Ksatriyas were not agriculturists (Wagle: 1966: 152). In the republic kingdoms of eastern India, which were predominantly occupied by the Ksatriyas, cultivation was managed by them, but the actual work of tilling the land was done by *dasas* and *kammakāras*. (*Cullavagga*:279; *Books of Discipline* V:253). In the monarchical states of Buddha's time the distinction between the rich and poor was much pronounced. In Ekanala in Dakkhinagiri a brahmana of the Bharadwaj clan is mentioned, who was a rich agriculturist. Five hundred ploughs were needed to cultivate the fields owned by him. On the day of festive sowing he used to distribute food to a large gathering. (*Sutta Nipata Comm. Paramatthajotikā* 1.4, *Kāsi Bharadwāj Sutta*) Canonical texts speak of *khattiya mahasalas* or wealthy Ksatriyas, but they mostly acquired their wealth through trade and no reference is found of a rich Ksatriya agriculturist. The rich merchants mostly of Vaisya origin, hoarded huge cash. The best example of that was the banker Anathapindaka of Savatthi, who could easily spend crores of gold coins for the purchase of Jetavana (*Vinaya. Cullavagga.* VI. 4.9; *Apannaka Jat,* No. 1 and *Palayi Jat,* No. 229). Similarly in *Mahasutasoma Jātaka* (No. 537) we find a wealthy brahmana, who owned so much of wealth through trading activities that he transported his goods from east to west in five hundred wagons. There was another rich banker Dhanajaya Setthi, who presented as dowry to his daughter Visakha, five hundred carts full of money, five hundred carts full of vessels of gold, along with other materials like ghee, rice, ploughshares, cattle, slaves, etc. (*Dham. Pada. Com.* Bk. IV. story 8). The rich *kutumbika* (house holder) is mentioned as going on a journey in a cart to collect debt (*Kakkata Jāt.*No. 267, *Takkala Jāt.* No. 446). Probably wealthy farmers carried on a lucrative profession of money lending in the villages.

Similar allusions are found in the Jain canons. Ananda a rich landowner of Vaniyagama, possessed a large number of ploughs, cattle and carts. Parasara was another *gahapati*, who prospered in agriculture and hence was known as *Krisiparāśara*. He possessed six hundred ploughs (J. C. Jain. 1947: 143).

Side by side with the wealthy *gahapatis* we find the poor cultivators, struggling against starvation. The poor farmers in times of scarcity sold their plots under extortion, fell into debts, and were reduced to the status of hired labourers. They were sometimes even forced to sell their independence and accept slavery as a respite from hunger. Some *Jataka* stories throw light on the relations between wealthy and poor farmers. Amongst the poors of the society, there existed different grades. *Kammakāra* and *bhaṭakas*, i.e. hirelings or wage earners belonged to that group of society who could barely survive. They were called *duggatas* (poor) in contrast to *sugatas* (rich). The term *dalidda kammakara* occurs many times in the Buddhist canons (*Pacittiya*.108; *Cullvagga*: 254). *Dalidda tunavaya* occurs in *Majjhima Nikaya* (II:89) and *Anguttara Nikāya* (III:84). An ordinary labourer earned not more than a *masaka* or even half a *masaka* and in almost in all the instances of hired labour, it is inevitably mentioned that the wages he got were hardly sufficient for his maintenance (*Suvanna Hamsa Jat*. No. 136, *Sutano Jat*. No. 398, *Gangamāla Jāt*. No. 421). It is often mentioned with regard to day labourers that he or she 'lived a hard life'(*bhatim krtwā kicchena jivati*) (*Bahiya Jat*.No. 108, *Suvanna Hamsa Jāt*. No. 136, *Bandhanagara Jāt* No. 201, *Sutano Jat*. No. 398, *Culla Dhammapala Jāt*. No. 358, *Kummasapinda Jāt*. No. 415, *Gangamāla Jat*. No. 421).

These landless labourers, who worked as hired labourers in farms were clothed in ragged loin cloths and were living in miserable conditions (*Dhamma Pada Com*. Bk. XXV. story. 10). Even the farmers who owned a small plot of land, were not in much happier situations. They not only ploughed their own land themselves (*Somadatta Jat*. No. 211), but sometimes they borrowed oxen to plough their fields, as they had no capital to buy a pair of oxen themselves (*Gamanicanda Jāt* No. 257). There were two types of labourers—slaves and wage earners.

The poorest of poors were the *sudras* or the people belonging to the lowest status of caste division. In *Jātaka* stories we hear of *pukkasas* or *chandalas*, (*Amba Jāt.* No. 474) as poor, unfortunates, who were economically oppressed and socially hated. Dhamma Pada (Bk. 2. Story 27) specially comments that '*chandalas*' made their living by working for hire, but received not enough wages to buy morsel of rice to sustain themselves. Probably never in ancient times the *sudras* could fetch social and economic justice. In the *Dharma Sutras* of the post-Mauryan period, the condition of the *sudras* became worse. Manu specifically says that even the name of *sudra* denoted contempt and meekness (II. 31). They were generally very poor and could not have any savings (X. 129) (*saktenapi hi sudrena na karyo dhanasancayah*). The purpose of the existence of the *sudras* was to serve the upper castes (VIII.413). They were given old discarded clothes, rejected household things, straw and husk left after winnowing corn (X. 125).

Social inequality had become sharper by the time the *Mahabharata* was composed. In the *Mahabharata* quite often the poor parents lamented for the birth of their children, as it was difficult for them to provide them food (XII. 28.24; XIII. 318.17; III. 132. 11/12). Poor men were often discarded by their relatives (*MBH.* V. 70.20). Poverty was considered the greatest sorrow of life, even worse than the loss of a husband or a son (*MBH.* V. 132.12-13; V. 70.22). In one particular context Bhisma says "the wretched sinful poor suffer during famines, in calamities and are always exposed to dangers, they are more dead than alive. The rich who are respectful, content and who are engaged in pious work take delight in festivities, enjoy heavenly bliss and the delight of luxury" (XII. 171.34). The *Ramayana* (III.12.5) too refers about the wretched conditions of the poor. Thus the bearing capacity of the poor was totally nil. Any unfortunate economic upheaval would effect them worst.

Sudras were not necessarily slaves. There were *sudra* slaves and other slaves too. In the early Buddhist texts four types of slaves are mentioned. They are: (1) those who were born of slave parents or begotten of slave women;

(2) those purchased of money; (3) those who were reduced to slavery under coercion by bandits; and (4) those who took slavery of their own accord.

In post-Buddhist era the types of slaves increased. The *Arthaśāstra* (III.13) mentions five kinds of slaves: (1) *dhvajahrta* were those captured in battle; (2) *ātmavikrayin* were those who sold themselves; (3) *udaradāsa* were those born to slave parents; (4) *ahitaka* were those who had to adopt slavery for the non-payment of debt; and (5) *daṇḍapranīta* were those enslaved under legal orders. Manu (VIII.15) refers seven kinds of slaves, viz. *dhvajahrta* (captives of war), *bhaktadasa* (those serving for subsistence), *gṛhaja* (offspring of slave parents), *kreeta* (purchased by masters), *datta* (given as gift), *paitraka* (inherited), and *daṇḍadāsa* (enslaved under legal punishment). The number of *dāsas* continued to increase, as more and more slave workers were needed for production purposes. By the time of Nārada (V.26.28) fifteen types of slaves are mentioned. If we see the kinds of slaves it is quite clear that amongst them there were many who were forced to become slaves due to their economic conditions. Whenever crops failed in a particular region, food became scarce, poor people could not survive unless they sold themselves as slaves. The existence of slavery in itself is a proof that the bearing capacity of the ancient society became gradually lesser as the complexities of social injustice increased.

The economic condition of the slaves were very tragic. Though they were provided with food, clothes and a place to live in their master's home but they generally had no property rights. Sometimes they were sent by their masters to work in other places but whatever they earned was taken away from them by their masters (*Nāmasuddha Jāt.* No. 97). Many references occur which depict how miserably slaves were treated (*Dhamma Pada Com.* Bk. XVII. Story 6). They had to work hard till late and had no social security. Buddhist sources tell us the story of how a slave revolted against his *Sakyan* mistress (*Pācittīya* : 241). But we should not confine ourselves into one sided picture of the slaves. Master slave relationship depended on human factors. Many stories tell that the relation between a master and his slave was cordial. Manu says that "slaves are one's own shadow" (IV.185), their sentiments should be kept and needs attended to (IV. 180). One should arrange for their upkeep in a measure competent to supply their wants (X. 124).

As far as property rights of slaves were concerned, views differed from authority to authority. In the Mauryan period most humanly attitudes can be noticed. They were allowed to possess property and accumulate wealth. Kautalya prohibited Aryans to become slaves. He recommends that an Aryan whose life was mortgaged due to economic grounds, was subject to redemption from slavery, by his kinsmen (III. 13). He guards the chastity of women slaves. He made it a punishable act on the part of a slave owner if he employs a slave for menial jobs. But this sympathetic attitude of *Artha Śāstra* vanishes with the *Smriti* literature. Manu in the clearest terms forbade a slave to possess property, his earnings and hoardings belonged to his master (VIII.299-300). The slave was expected to perform all kinds of menial jobs, debased or impure works for his master according to the authority of Nārada (I.107; V.41). But still the treatment towards slaves was not so harsh in compare to those of the Roman Empire. As a result when classical writers commented on slaves in India they even thought that slavery did not exist here altogether. There is an allusion of prosperity of the slaves (*dāsa parivriddhi*) (*Br. Sam.* IX. 12). Therefore, no general statement should be made about the conditions of the slaves. It differed from time to time and family to family. But still there is no doubt that during scarcities, this social group definitely suffered worst. They would come under the grip of the famine, whenever the food will be insufficient.

In Buddhist India a large number of religious recluse had emerged, who did not produce anything but were chronic consumers. The number of these religious mendicants were fairly large. Quite often in the *Dhammapada* stories bands of five hundred *bhikkhus* are referred to (Bk. VI. Story 8. Bk. III. Story 6). Sometimes the number of monks are enumerated as several thousands (*Dhamma Pada. Com.* Bk. IV. Story 3. Bk. V. Story 1). And in one place their number is counted as that of crores (*Dhamma Pada. Com.* Bk. II. Story 3. 257). These Buddhist and Jain *dasa kammakaras*. The *Samyukta Nikaya* (I. 91) indicates that the alms given to *Samanas* and monks needed to be fed by the society. An interesting point emerges in the early Pali text that there existed a tension of relationship between *samana brahmanas* and *dasa kammakaras*. The *Samyukea Nikeya* (I.91) indicates that the alms given to *Samanas* and *brahmanas* could be utilized for some gain, if given to *dasas* and *kammakaras*. Which means that there was only 'a limited surplus' available in a common household. That was the reason that the ideology of *dana* was so much encouraged by all the monastic organization. For the laymen *dana* was considered as the only way to ensure higher status of rebirth. (U. Cakravarty: 1987: 58-59). This tension in society arose because there was not abundant surplus in the society. Whenever the scarcity of food afflicted the people, they considered slaves and mendicants as extra burden on them. During famines monasteries suffered a lot. Monks could not get enough alms. The meaning of the word '*durbhiksa*' (i.e. famine) is very significant. It means that during famines, *bhiksa* (alms) became hard to get. Sometimes during famines mendicants had no other choice but to commit suicide (*Vyavahara Bhasya*: X. 557-60). Concentration and hoarding of the property by a few magnates of higher castes was the real cause of suffering of the poor. In Buddhist times this was practised mainly in Kosala and Magadha states, not in the Republican states. In the Republics the distribution of wealth did not have much disparity. In the monarchical states and in the capitalist society, where competitive economy prevailed, social distinctions became more pronounced. The hoarding became so troublesome for the society, that Kautalya recommends that during famines the rich people should be forced to 'vomit out' (*vamana*) their riches. Money earned by the mercantile community by unfair means, was a known factor. In *Mahābhārata* (V. 39-52) Vidur says about the "illegally earned money" (*adharma-oparjitair-arthaih*). In another context, the *Mahābhārata* refers that greedy men adopt illegal means to acquire wealth because their social status depends on their affluence (XII. 284. 7-9; XII. 283-24; XII. 281. 4-5). In the *Milindapanho* (*SBE*. XXXV. p. 161) a reference occurs about the stores of a wealthy man. He has stores of all kinds of wheat, rice, paddy, barley, oilseeds, beans, and had also stores of ghee, oil, buttermilk, sugar etc. Thus all these allusions from different periods of ancient Indian history makes it vividly clear that the society was widely divided between the rich and the poor. The gulf between them was very vast.

If the landed property of a rich brahmana *gahapati* is a donation from a king as a remuneration for his religious function, then it was exempt from the taxes too. These rent-free land of the brahmana *gahapati* was a loss for the treasury. The burden of the taxes thus fell more on the ordinary farmers. In the *Dīgha Nikāya* it is especially said that *gahapati* is a free man, one who cultivates his land, one who pays taxes, and thus increases the king's wealth' (1.53)

The *Artha Śāstra* says that excess collection of taxes by officers was punishable (*AS.II.IX.* 68-70). But how far constraints were followed by the tax collectors seems doubtful. The tax collectors were named *balipatiggahaka, niggahaka, balisadhaka* etc. They even used force to fill the coffers of the king (*Mahapingala Jat* No. 240; *Mahā Assāroha Jāt.* No. 302; *Dūta Jat* 478). Expressions like 'oppressed with taxes' (*balipidita*) occurs in the *Jataka* stories (*Gandatindu Jāt.* No 520). It seems that the ordinary folk, farmers or traders, suffered through tax oppression quite often.

Let us now have a survey of proportional relationship between wages and prices. All labourers did not receive wages. The state had the privilege to extract forced labour (*visti*), whenever it considered it necessary, either for the public welfare works or as a right over the defeated army after his victory over a region, or as a punishment for tax lapses. Besides that, slaves had no right to claim wages.

At the most sometimes a nominal money was paid to them as ex-gratia. Wages were paid only to the independent labourer, skilled or unskilled. The amount of wages were determined by the agreement between the employer and the employee. When the work was performed by a worker without any preagreement between the employer and the employee, then it was fixed on the basis of the wages paid to other workers engaged in similar works (*AS*. III. 13.183). Some authorities give us approximate idea about the wages which were customarily fixed. Kautalya says that a farm labourer, a herdsman, and a mercantile labourer respectively obtain ten per cent of the crop grown, butter clarified, and mercantile sold, if no previous agreement about the ratio of wages had been decided (*AS*. III.13,183 see also *Nar.* Sm. VI.2; *Yaj.* Sm.II.194).

Though the purchasing power of the *pana* was high (Pran Nath 1980:148), the wages were so meagre that price indexes points out a difficult situation (R. Mehta. 1939: 222-28). In early Buddhist literature we find the prices of every vendable commodity mentioned (*JRAS*. 1901: 882). In most case the prices given are fantastic and fabulous. We can explain this with a few examples of actual market prices of certain commodities[1]. It appears that the articles of food were cheap. A small quantity of *ghee* (purified butter) could be bought for a *karsapana* only (*Vin.* VI, 248-50). Meat of a chameleon could be bought for *kakani* or an *ardhamasaka* (*Mahaumagga Jat.* No 546). Fish cost seven *masaka* (*Macchāuddana Jat.* No. 288), a jar of liquor for one *masaka*. It is further commented that a *masaka* was sufficient for an ordinary wage earner to buy a garland, perfume and some strong drink (*Gangamala Jataka.* No 421). Other commodities were comparatively more expensive. A donkey cost eight *kahapans* (*Mahaumagga Jāt.* No. 546), a pair of oxen twenty four *kahapanas* (*Ibid)*, a cow for fifty coins (*Āva. Chu.* 119). The land for a monastic cell (*vihara*) cost five hundred *kahapanas* (*Majjh.* I. 55,3).

Another survey of prices can be derived from the *Artha sastra.* Pran Nath (1980:98) has calculated prices in copper

---

1 *Pana* is copper coin. 1 *pana* = 20 *masas* = 4 *kakani* = 20 *kapardas* or cowries

panas for per maund of articles, in the time of Kautalya. We can quote a few items from his list for perusal—paddy 2 *panas*, *dala* 6 *panas*, pepper 56 panas, spices 29 panas, curd 6 panas, ghee 60 panas, husked rice 5 panas, sugar 48 panas, oil 41 panas. *Artha Sastra* (II. XIV.98) followed the system of state control of prices. Therefore the essential food items for the consumption of average family remained under control. But soon after the decline of the Mauryas this system was no longer in vogue. As is evidenced from *Brhat Samhita* (Shastri: 320), fluctuation of prices was determined by economic factors.

Wages were paid both in cash or in kind. Cash payments were made either daily or after the completion of work. Pātañjalī (I.3.72; V.4.116) especially say that the wages were recommended for labourer engaged in royal services. Patanjali refers about the workers engaged for the five, six or seven coins (V.4.116). A courtesan's fee for the whole night was fifty to hundred *kahapanas* (*Mahāvagga. S.B.E.* Vol. XVIII. p. 171-75, text. VIII. 1: 1-3). A teacher's fee for the whole course was thousand *kahapanas* (*Susima Jāt.* No. 163, *Tilmutthi Jāt.* No. 252, *Nigrodha Jāt.* No. 445, *Sarabhanga Jāt*, No. 522).

But an unskilled labourer earned one and half *masaka* daily (*Sutano Jāt.* 398). In *Gangamāla Jātaka* (No. 421) the wages of the water carrier is referred to. He received half a copper *pana* a day. A grass cutter was paid one *māsaka* a day. This amount was just enough to buy daily food for two persons (*Gangamāla Jāt.* No. 421). The wages of the skilled labourer depended usually on the agreement. But the lowest amount given to them was two *panas* a day (*AS*.p.248). Royal officers like clerks, accountants, writers, astrolergers, story tellers, bards and musicians had their wages fixed on different scales—starting from two hundred and fifty copper *panas* to the maximum of thousand copper *panas*. (*AS*. p. 247-8). To summarize now it can be said that the earnings of the unskilled labourers was far away from being satisfactory. The above survey of prices and wages can at least point out that the labourers were living on the verge of poverty and the ordinary middle class earned just enough to survive in the normal economic situations. They did not earn sufficient to have much savings for the times of scarcity. Therefore, whenever there was any natural calamity, ordinary folks had no provisions to face the difficult times and they fell into the grips of famines.

The scarcities became famines when the population escalation crossed the bearing capacity of the society. Population estimation in any period of ancient Indian history is practically an impossible pursuit, as the source materials are either nill or vague. Still some efforts should be made to get an approximate idea about the density of population. In prehistoric times most of the sites were concentrated on a limited river zone. It became thickly populated in some favourite areas, whereas in other places, away from the river the belts vast areas remained vacant. Baluchistan was thickly populated in chalcolithic period. Excessive population can be noticed in Jhalawan district (see Chart VIII.). In Sindh, sixtyone prehistoric sites can be traced (see Chart X). A thick population concentration can be seen along the Hakra flood plains in Cholistan district (see Chart XIII). Though there had been a slight shifting of population in pre-Harappan, mature Harappan and late Harappan periods, maximum population pressure can be noticed in the mature Harappan period (see Chart VII). North Rajasthan faced the maximum exploitation of its land during the mature Harappan period along the Saraswati and Drisadwati river valleys. Population explosion can be noticed in Hanumangarh Tahsil of Ganganager district in mature Harappan period. Sikar district of north Rajasthan became overpopulated in OCP period (see Chart XV.). In Haryana, the Saraswati, Drisadwati and Yamuna valleys had huge population concentration during late Harappan and PGW times (See Chart XIX). Population explosion in Haryana can be noticed in Ambala, Kuruksetra, Jind, Karnal, Gurgaon and Hissar districts. In the early Harappan period the concentration was only in Jind, Karnal, Gurgaon and Hissar districts. In Indian side of the Punjab, population reached a higher ratio in late Harappan and PGW periods primarily. Excessive population can be noticed in the districts of Gurdaspur, Jullundhar, Ludhiana, Patiala, and Sangrur (see Chart XVIII). Gujarat witnessed population explosition in the mature Harappan period (period II-BC of Rangpur sequence) when hundred and twenty settlements can be located in this region. In south Rajasthan Udaipur and Chittorgarh districts witnessed concentration of population along Berach-Banas group of rivers in the times of Ahar culture and in BRW/PGW periods (see Chart XVI). In Uttar Pradesh a population explosion occurred in Saharanpur district along with tributaries of Yamuna in Harappan period. Kanpur district had a heavy population in PGW and NBPW times.

The barometer to check the increase in population is not only the multiplicity of the settlements but the expansion of the sites too. But as the horizontal excavations are very limited and the whole settlement is rarely revealed, this method remains unsatisfactorily utilized. But there is no doubt that when the number of villages multiplied in a specified period, the settlements quite often became larger. To explain this point let us see a few example. In the early Harappan period when a population increase can be noticed in Baluchistan, some of their sites expanded remarkably. Dabarkot and Rahmandheri acquired quite a big size which indicates that they had a heavy population concentration. In mature Harappan period western Punjab, Sindh and north Rajasthan were witnessing a population explosion. Therefore quite a few settlements of this time also became very large. On the basis of their site size modern historians have tried to give their population estimation.

Site	*Estimated Population*
Mohenjodaro	41250 (Fairservis 1967)
	35000 (Lambrick 1964:71)
Harappa (exclusive of citadel)	23544 (Fairservis 1967)
Harappa (citadel)	35000 (Lambrick 1964:71)
Chanhudaro	495 (Fairservis *op.cit.*)
Ganweriwal	(Mughal 1982: 85-95)
Gumanwala	(Mughal *Ibid.*)
Dewaliana	(Mughal 1970: 15, 158)

Chakrabarti (1979: 205-15) suggests that settlements having an area of 1,25,000 sq.fit. or more, were likely to possess 5,000 or more people each. The sites which he could enumerate in this group are Naruwarodharo, Judeirjodaro, Dabarkot, Rahmandheri, Dewaliana Ther, and Lurewala. In modern standards the number of populations estimated above will not considered as excessive. But we must keep it in mind that in early prehistoric background even these numbers should be considered big enough, because the society did not have capability to bear with larger population. Another point to note is that this increase of population happened only in a few restricted zones not in all parts of the land. Many areas outside the river valley zones remained absolutely empty.

With the beginning of the Aryan period literary sources become available. In several hymns we find the Aryans praying for birth of 'unlimited' (probably meaning any) sons. (*RV.* II. 40. 6; 42. 3; IV. 53.'7; 55. 4; V. 3. 6; 4.10; 24.42). It can be thus, implied that there was no danger of over population in the *Rig Vedic* times. On the other hand, they needed more hands to fight against their enemies, and to expand their habitational areas. If we check it up with the PGW settlement pattern, which are considered as the contemporary of the later Vedic age, it can be seen that the clusters of settlements existed in particular areas, whereas vast empty tracks existed too. No overall population explosions occur in such situations. Though, it is possible that a few riverine belts became overpopulated during later Vedic period too, as it had happened in earlier chalcolithic times.

In Buddhist and post-Buddhist age urbanization became a prominent feature. This signifies increase in population. Buddhist narratives amply speak of 'teeming cities', which were thickly populated. Besides the over crowded urban centres the countryside also had numerous settlements. The kingdom of Magadha is described as consisted of eighty thousand *gramas* (*D.N.* II: 130). This can be substantiated by the archaeological evidences. A large number of NBPW sites can be traced only in the mid Gangetic plains. Their maximum concentration can be seen in Allahabad,

Ghazipur, Kanpur, Lucknow, Mirzapur and Varanasi districts.

Various historians have tried to give a population estimation of Buddhist and post Buddhist India on the basis of literary evidences. Pran Nath (1980: 117-18) has taken up the evidence of the Buddhist books. According to which Vaisali is said to have contained 7707 *rajans* (or state owners). If Vaisali here means Vaisali *janapada*, then Pran Nath guesses that 'ten *janapadas* should constitute a *desa* (country), this would mean that there were about 7707 *rajans* (or state owners) in the whole of the *desa* or country, in which Vaisali was included. If the *desa* again can be regarded as an average size country this would mean that whole of India (with its 84 *desas*) contained 6473880 *rajans* (state owners). Taking from 15 to 20 persons for each estate, the population of whole India would come to between 100 to 130 millions. The total population of Vaisali *janapada* is given in Buddhist books as 16800'. (Jayaswal 1943. p. 51. n. 5).

Another population estimation can be deduced on the basis of the figures given for the strength of the army of small states of Punjab who fought with the Greek invader Alexander. Classical sources give the numerical strength of the armies of various kings thus :

Countries	*Foot Soldiers*	*Cavalr Y*	*Chariots*	*Elep-hants*	*References*
Malloi and Sudracae	90,000	10,000	900		McCrindle p. 252, 234
Aphrikes	20,000	10,000	X	15	(*Ibid* 272)
Porus	50,000	3,000	1,000	130	(p. 278)
Agalassian	40,000	3,000	X	X	(p. 285)
Assekenians	30,000	20,000	X	30	(p. 60)
Kingdom next to Sibi	40,000	X	X	X	(p. 232)
Ambri and Sigambri	80,000	60,000	X	X	(p. 324)
Cuphitas	2,00,000	X	X	X	(p. 323)
Total	5,50,000	96,000	1,900	175	

According to *Mahabharata* 18 *aksauhini* forces were engaged in that great battle (*MBH. Bhisma Parva. Adh.* 16. p. 25). One *aksauhini* army is defined as equivalent to 21,870 elephants, 21,870 chariots, 65,610 horses and 1,09,350 foot soldiers (Monier Williams *Sanskrit dictionary*). But while making any estimation of population on the basis of these military records, one must keep in mind that an exaggerative account is more likely quoted, because the purpose of the storytellers is not to give a historic document but to show the importance of victory by giving a higher scale of figures, so as to escalate the prestige of their heroes.

To conclude this discussion we must admit that no proper hypothesis can be drawn about the population as the source materials are too vague. But one thing is certain that India as a whole was not overpopulated in ancient times. Only a few 'favourite zones' witnessed the population explosions in particular times.

Some social laws had prevented excessive birth rates. For example, monogamy was a general practice; marriages were restricted to some particular time of the year, the early deaths were quite common, many deaths occurred due to the frequent wars, droughts, floods and famines, a large number of ascetics in society maintained celibacy, etc. All these factors restricted the growth of population. As a result, till comparatively recent years large tracts of the country were lying vacant in the form of deserts, waste lands and forests. The housing plans in the cities, as can be traced through archaeological remains or through literary description, indicate that multistoried houses were constructed only in the urban centres, which had comparatively thick population. Usually the houses were single story, small thatchments, which had enough empty space attached to it, used as courtyard, cow-pen, pig-sty, stable, etc. Therefore, it can be roughly concluded that over-population was not a problem for India as a whole. The problem was that the population was not distributed evenly throughout the length and breadth of the country, but was concentrated on few 'favourite zones' and thus the bearing capacity of those particular zones got depleted.

Whenever an overpopulated area was hit by some natural disaster, the bearing capacity of that region came to a collapse. Then people had no choice but to migrate from these areas or face famines. We find in Buddhist sources references of floods, which made the people to desert the area. (*Vin.* I. 149). The villages where people once resided in multitudes became vacant and thus were called '*amanussogama*', or the village without any people (*Vin.*I.149; Majjh.II.97.100). These type of deserted localities are mentioned even in later accounts. For example, we can refer to Huan-tsang's travel records. He (Watters. II. 198) describe certain areas, which were once teeming with people but when he visited the settlements, they were utterly depopulated. These tragic incidents may have happened due to excessive population pressure and over-exploitation of land resources.

To conclude this chapter we may now finally say that the bearing capacity of a society is vulnerable for the resistance against famines. If the society is diagonally divided between the rich and the poors, if the poors of the society were living on the verge of utter poverty, if there was unproportionate hoarding in the hands of the rich, and poor could hardly survive with their meagre wages, if there was no regular control of prices and prices fluctuated depending on the principle of demand and supply, and if there were some areas where population concentration happened unevenly, then the 'bearing capacity' of that society cannot be regarded as strong enough. Scarcity of food would become a common malady. The natural disasters were quite common in Indian geographical conditions. To face these disasters society needed to build up its own resistance. But the bearing capacity of ancient Indian society had many weaknesses and therefore the occurrences of famines were also reported periodically in every epoch of history.

11

BEHAVIOURAL IMPACT OF FAMINE AFFECTED POPULACE

Long persistent abnormal economic conditions during famine shattered the social fabric to a large extent. Behaviour of a famine hit populace showed the intensity of the malady. Duration of the famines, its geographical extension, nature of the scarcity, all were decisive factors for social anomalies.

This study is primarily based on the literary evidences, which were mostly not contemporary official records but survived as ancient stories. Fabled accounts do not provide us the necessary details. The nature of our source material are as such that due concessions has to be made for exaggerations. Even as early as the Vedic times, a few stray references are available about famines. Earliest mention of a long duration famine during the time of Santanu can be traced in the *Rig Veda* (X. 98) and in Yaska's *Nirukta* (ii. 10). The famine in Santanu's time was resulted due to a severe drought. Reference to famines of Santanu's rule, passed over for generation (*Vishnu Purana* IV. 20. 9-30). Similarly, floods had created devastating results, in fact sometimes bringing an end to their whole cultural zone. One such deluge, in which Manu played a leading role was first mentioned in the Vedic literature (*Sat. Br.* I. 8. I. 1; *Kathaka Saṁhitā* II. 2). Some of these devastations were so enormous that their memories lingered till historical ages. The story of Manu had such a universal appeal that it became a legend. *Matsya* (I. 30. 32; II. 10. 15; II. 25) and *Bhagvata Purāṇa* (VIII. 24. 54-55; I. 3. 5) refer the story of this deluge. Another famine of Vedic times, when Vasistha helped people with forest products, was supposed to have occurred in the *Krita Yuga*, soon after the '*devasura* battle'. The mention of this '*devasura* battle' is of course available in the Vedic literature. But the conceptual classification of the *Yugas* is of late origin. In the Vedic literature there are no categorical references of the four ages-*Kali*, *Dvāpara*, *Treta* and *Krta*. The *Puranic* chronology, (*Brahmanda Purāṇa* II.8.88, II. 65. 34; 72. 20-2; and *Matsya Purāṇa* p. 173-78), which refer to this incidence of famine in *Treta Yuga*, cannot be assuredly dated unless we stress on the commentator's remark that the famine occurred 'soon after the *devasura* battle' and thus place it roughly in the Vedic period.

The *Vishnu Purāṇa* which preserved the ancient traditions and stories, narrates another famine, due to heavy flood in the Ganges, during the time of Nicaksu, the son of Adhisima Krsna and father of Usna (IV, 217-9). The Puranic sources referring these early incidents of famines, were composed so much later in period, that they lost their historical significance. It can only be deduced from such references, that intense drought and heavy floods remained prevalent even in the hoary past. The devastations created by such natural menaces were so acute that these legends occupied the memories of people till very late.

Traditions persisted about long duration famines. A long duration famine which lasted for twelve years is referred to in the Jain sources, during the time of Chandragupta Maurya. The Jain tradition as recorded in the *Sthavirvāndi Charita* attributes the period of this famine, some two centuries after the demise of the Master, when Chandragupta was ruling in Magadha.

Similarly various literary records are available belonging to the post Mauryan period, which enumerate long duration famine episodes. The *Rāmāyaṇa* and the *Mahābhārata* provide us with some famine references (*MBH*. I. 230; I. 71. 31; IX. 41. 14; X. 10. 51; X. 175. 38-46; XII. 137.24;

XII, 141. XII. 37.22). Quite often famines were of long duration. Traditionally to express the ferocity of famines, twelve years' period were allotted, which of course, cannot be accepted as literally true. In one of such twelve years famine *Mahabharata* (IX. 71. 31) says that 'forest dwelling seers and their families were affected too'. Another twelve years famine during the time of legendary Kuru king Samvarana is referred to in the epic literature (*MBH.* I. 175. 38-46).

Famines due to heavy excessive rain and flood which destroyed standing crops were often mentioned in the *Jātakas* (*Gahapati Jāt.* No. 199; *Champeyya Jāt.* No. 506). Strabo referred to floods in rivers, overflowing the banks, causing settled areas to be evacuated which looked deserted (Strabo XV. 1. 18.70). Other classical writers informed about the devastating floods too (Arrian,. I VI; Curtius. VIII, IX; Diodorus Bk. 17. Ch. XC. iv.). Floods due to heavy rains which broke the river banks and devastated crops were so frequent that many contemporary literary sources depicted these disasters (*Milindapañho,* II.1.10; *Dhamma Pada.* XVI. 6; IV. 3.338; *Buddhacharita* XIII. 6; IX. 15; *Suttanipāta.* I. 14; *Tevijja Suttanta* I. 24).

But most of the famines were due to failure of rain which resulted due to prolonged droughts. (*Mahāvastu Avadāna.* III: 358; *Mahāsupina Jāt.* No. 77). *Milindapañho* (*SBE.* xxxv. p. 15) referred a place called Kajangala (extreme east of the Middle country), which was afflicted with a long drought. *Maccha Jāt.* (No. 75) referred famine due to drought in Kosala, when 'there fell no rain—the crops withered and everywhere the ponds, lakes and tanks dried up'. Famines were enumerated in Dantapura, in the Kingdom of Kalinga and in the kingdom of Kasi (*Kurudhamma Jāt.* No. 276, *Pannasanipala Jāt.* No. 526; *Kacchapa Jāt.* No. 178, *Vīraka Jāt.* No. 204). In drought struck Kasi, the region became so unbearable that even crows flew away, (*Vīraka Jāt.* No. 204).

Occurrence of famines became more frequent from the early historic period and remained a constant malady throughout the ancient period of Indian history. A few references can be enumerated here to show the gravity of the recurrent calamity.

Drought and famine references are quite numerous in the *Purānas*. The *Vishnu Purāṇa* (IV. 323) refers a long duration (12 years) famine. The *Skanda Purāṇa* (a work of 5th-6th century A.D.), mentions drought as a common incidence (I. 11. 40, 219, 222, 226; II. IX. 9. 8; 9; VI. 37. 7; VI. 1. 129. 9. etc.). *Kali* age is characterized by such eventualities. Droughts destroyed the crops as well as the country and the people, as it brings famines (*Skanda Purāṇa* V (iii). 11. 80; VII (i). 255. 9-10(I).

From fourth century onwards, innumerable references of bad harvest, scarcity of rains, drought and famines are referred to in literature. Most interesting is to observe the contexts of the *Brhat Saṁhitā*. The author Varāhamihira, is usually assigned the period of 4th-5th century A.D. This text makes:

42 forecasts of bad conditions due to disease, want of food;

7 forecasts of bad conditions of farmers;

5 forecasts of scarcity of food;

42 forecasts of famines;

32 forecasts of drought or scarcity of rain;

11 forecasts of heavy rainfall and food;

5 forecasts of earthquakes;

9 forecasts of devastating fires;

14 forecasts of pestilence;

35 forecasts of disease and sickness;

2 forecasts of plague;

2 forecasts of sufferings of the citizens at the hands of their kings;

4 forecasts of decline in population.

And only one forecast of prosperous condition of cultivator (See V.K. Thakur; 1981. 298).

The above list signify the worsening conditions of the

agriculture during his times. He also refers long duration famines (traditionally given 12 years time) (III. 27-8) and sometimes extensive famines covering a vast stretch of land (XI. 33-36).

Floods and famines are referred to in the Jain sources too. Kancanapura flood is mentioned in the *Vyavahara Bhasya* (X. 450). Extensive famines engulfing whole of the Uttarapatha; and another one embracing whole of the Daksinapatha, is referred to in the *Avasyaka Curni* (p. 396; p. 404).

In fact, whole of the Indian subcontinent suffered due to famines in ancient times. The Ceylonese chronicles *Mahāvaṁśa* and *Dīpavaṁśa* (composed in the 5th-6th century A.D.), notice many famine incidents which occurred there. *Ekanalika* famine occurred in Ceylon during the time of king Kancanga (*Mahāvaṁśa*. XXXVI. 20). The *Mahavamsa* (XXXII. 29-30) refers to another famine which effected the mountain region of Kotta in Ceylon, during the reign of Dutthagamini. Another drought is mentioned in the *Mahāvaṁśa* (XV. 94-95) at the time of King Samiddha.

The *Dīpavaṁśa* mentions "a drought among the *Yonakas* (i.e. Greeks), when people suffered from famine, like fish into the shallow water." (Ch. XV. 47-49). All these references of Ceylonese chronicles point out that droughts, pestilence and famines were quite widespread, and affected practically the whole of the subcontinent—much beyond its natural boundaries. Similarly, in the extreme north, the Kashmir region was afflicted with famine many times. Kalhana's *Rajatarangini* (II. 17.54) depicts a long duration famine in the time of Tunjina I, who was the successor of Pratapaditya and Jalauka. The date of this king is uncertain. But as he is described as the successor of Jalauka, son of Asoka, he could be roughly dated in the early Christan era. Another great famine occurred in Kashmir in AD 917-18 (*RT.* V. 270-74). The same source refers some more famines in later period, e.g. in AD. 1099 in the time of Kashmir king Harsa, in AD 1121-28 in the time of Sussala (*RT.* VIII. 1206).

Famine was a major economic malady. The social

implications, therefore, was bound to be of complex nature. Famines were usually of long durations. A short time scarcity of any article—food or water never created a famine. The death toll due to hunger rose to unbearable heights and normal social behaviour were forgotten. Our ancient records provide us the detail description of severities of these unfortunate incidence which had occurred many times.

Remembering the twelve years prolonged drought during the period of Kuru King Samvarana, compilers of the *Mahabharata* comments that during the time of terrible season of drought not even dew fell on the earth and consequently no corn grew, the people being afflicted with hunger and starvation became dead skeletons and the city looked like the land of the king of the dead full of ghostly beings. (*MBH.* I. 175. 40-43).

Death toll during famines in pre-Mauryan context presents a threatening picture. *Samyutta Nikaya* (IV. pp. 323-324) refers famine in Nalanda, when people died in such large numbers that the place turned white with men's bones and its crops grew to mere stubs. *Anguttara Nikaya* (I. p. 160; III. p. 41) also refer a heavy death toll during famines. The *Divyavadana* (X. 132) refers three types of famines, classification stressing on the degree of its severity of deaths.

During prolonged droughts food scarcity reached such a menacing stage that even the fish, tortoise and crows died of hunger. *Maccha Jātaka* (No. 75) refers a famine in Kosala, when "the crops withered and everywhere the ponds, tanks and lakes dried up. Even the pool of Jetavana gave out and the fish and tortoise buried themselves in the mud. Then came the crows and hawks, with their lance like beaks and busily picked them out writhing and wriggling and devoured them." But the *Vīraka Jātaka* (No. 204) speaks of a worst situation, when during a famine in Kasi even the crows were unable to get food to survive and left the famine-stricken land.

The Ceylonese chronicle *Mahavāṁśa* (XXXVI. 20) refers *Ekanālika* famine. *Nali* is a certain measure, equivalent to

4 *prasthas* or handfuls. The people were reduced in this famine only to get a handful of grains, and thus this name was given to this particular famine. The *Mahāvaṁśa* (XXXII. 29-30) refers to *akkhayikā cāṭakam* famine. The famine was so called because the nuts called *akkha* (*Terminalia bellerica*) were eaten, which in normal times were used as dice. In the *Atthakatha*, the famine is called *pasanacataka*. A pestilence on the island is mentioned in the same source (XV. 60).

The graphic references of famine given by Dandin makes one infer that it was the outcome of first hand experience. Narrating the occurrence of famine in Trigarta region he reports "Indra sent no rain for 12 years, the grain production dropped, plants failed to seed, trees bore no seeds, the clouds were barren, rivers dwindled, swamps were mere mudholes, springs were dry, bulbs, fruits and roots grew scarce, story telling declined, robber bands multiplied, thirsty crows migrated... The scarcity of food led the householders to eat in turn the goats, the sheep, the drove of buffaloes, the herd of cows, the servants and even the children and wife (*Daśakumāracharita* tr. by D.C. Ryder: 166).

Famines were quite often followed by epidemics, which worsened the crisis. Malaria was a natural outcome after the stagnant flood water breeded the mosquitoes (*Kacchapa Jataka* No. 178; *Therīgāthā PTS*. 1893:170 line 20; *Mahavagga* VI. 20). Jaundice, due to contaminated water was quite regular occurrence (*Dhamma Pada* Bk. 14 story 5; *Mahavagga* VI. 1; VI. 14, 7; VIII. 123).

Numerous occurrences of famines which were quite often accompanied with plague or some such epidemic, are referred to in various literary sources. *Mahāvastu* (I. 284-88) refers terrible famine in the city of Kampilla and Vaisali, accompanied by severe plague. Two types of plagues were referred to—*mandalaka* and *adhivasa*. While *mandala* plague left none alive in a family, the *adhivasa* plague killed every living being of the district. The city of Vaisali was infested with *adhivasa* type of plague. Cities like Kampilla, Mithila, Videha and Rajgriha seems to have suffered similar fate (*Ibid.*1236-40). Tararath (Fol. 6.B) refers a terrible epidemic in Magadha in the time of king Subahu, son of king Ajatasatru. *Dhamma Pada* (II. 1.231) refers to a plague which broke out at Rajgriha. The commentator remarks that 'when the plague broke out animals from flies to cattle were the first to die and then the slaves and subsequently the masters and mistresses of the household.' Similarly, another devastating famine is recorded in Vaisali, which was followed by plague and intestinal diseases. The plague killed all the townsfolk and ultimately people could only have a respite when the Exalted one visited the town himself (*Dhamma Pada* XXI. 1. HOS. pt. III. p. 168-69). The *Vinaya Pitaka* (Ch. I) refers a famine in the Vajji country during the lifetime of Buddha. A fear of plague is referred to in *Saundarananda* (V. 39) and in the *Buddhacarita* (XVI. 119).

Quite often the famines were accompanied by further maladies like earthquakes and pestilence menaces. The *Mahāparinibbāna Suttanta* (tr. Rhys Davids *SBE* XI) which is usually dated three centuries before the commencement of the Christian era, refers about the earthquake. Later on in the *Milindapañho*, a work of early centuries of the Christian era, another reference occur about the mighty earthquake, which devastated not only the mankind but even the *Asuras*, *Gandharvas*, *Yaksas* and the *Nagas* (IV. 1. 35-38 *SBE. vol.* XXXV)

But pestilence were of worse magnitude. As early as the *Chhāndogya Upaniṣad* (I. 10.1) a reference is made to the Kurus being overwhelmed by *maticis*. The *Sabdakalpadruma* (*St. Petersburg Dictionary*) says that *maticis* means "a kind of small red birds", and Jacob (*JRAS.* 1910: 510) suggest that the "locusts is meant". Later on in the *Cullavagga* (*Vinaya Text* Pt. II. *SBE.* Vol XX: 326) references are available about blight and mildew diseases which affected the crops and spoiled them thoroughly. *Kurudhamma Jātaka* (No. 276) tells a story of famine in Dantapura, in the kingdom of Kalinga, where drought was followed by pestilence. The *Avadanasataka* (I. 78. 14) referred to a pestilence of terrible effect. *Jatāka* stories mention pestilence along with fire, storms, plunder many times. (*Lakkhana Jātaka* No. 11; *Nigrodhamiga Jātaka* No. 12; *Baka Jataka* No. 38; *Tandulanali Jataka* No. 5; *Gahapati Jātaka* No. 199; *Bharu Jātaka* No. 213 *Kurudhamma Jātaka* No. 276; *Sussondi Jātaka* No. 360; *Kumbha Jātaka* No. 512). The *Mahavamsa* (XV. 60) refers to a pestilence in the island of Sri Lanka at the time of Kakusandha a teacher versed in all truth. The *Yuga Purāṇa* gives a description of 12 years famine, which was followed by a pestilence (Tr. Mankad: 20). Thus it is quite vivid after a study of our various source that famines were of common occurrence throughout our ancient period of history.

When a prolonged drought occurred then the rural areas got mutilated and the worst effects were felt in the towns. Towns were worst hit because of concentration of population. The *Mahavagga* (VI. 19.2; VI. 32.2) refers to famines in Vaisali and Rajgriha cities. The *Saṁyutta Nikāya* refers a famine in the city of Nalanda (IV. 323-24). The *Cullavagga* (VI. 21.1) informs that the city of Rajgriha was devastated due to famine. The *Jātaka* stories have innumerable references to, which we have already quoted, where towns and cities were perished due to famines. e.g., Kosala (*Jat.* No. 75), Dantapura (*Jāt.* No. 276), Benaras (*Jat.* No. 178) etc. Kosala and Kalinga were referred to as most common famine effected zones (*Brhat Saṁhitā* X. 26). The *Visnu Purana* refers to droughts and famines which occurred in the towns of Dwaraka (IV. 13.112), Kasi (IV. 13.116) and in Kalinga (VI. 1.24.25). The population concentration in the towns was the main cause for its being worst-affected areas.

From the very beginning of the history of famine people considered the easiest remedy was the migration to distant lands, where the subsistence economy had not collapsed. Remembering the twelve year long famine during the time of Kuru king Samvarana, the compilers of *Mahābhārata* say that, when during that terrible season of droughts, when all the crops perished in the Kuru kingdom, people afflicted with the fear of '*hunger left their homes in despair and fled in all directions*' (*Mahābhārata* I. 175.38-41). The

Dhamma Pada (II. I. 188) refers a plague in the city of Bhaddavati. "When the disease broke out, of the first to die were flies. Afterwards in regular order insects, mice, domestic fowls, swine, cattle, slaves, and last of all members of the household. *Only those who managed to flee saved their lives.* But the tragedy was that while migrating from their home to distant towns, the ordinary folks suffered not only due to troubles of travelling, but they experienced the widespread effects of the famine; because the food was not so easily available even in the neighbouring territories. A story depicts the misfortunes of a treasurer of Bhaddavati who *with his family set out on the road to Kosambi,* while they were still on their way their provisions for the journey gave out and their bodies became exhausted from exposure to wind and sun and from hunger and thirst. They reached Kosambi with difficulty and they took up residence there, on the next day when the meal time was announced and the blind and the poor and the other unfortunate persons went to obtain food. The daughter of the treasurer also went to procure food for the family. There the poor people quarrelled with each other to get some food". This depiction of the story tells the miseries of the famine-hit people, who even after migration were not relieved of their problems. Similar stories are many times over recorded in our ancient literature. The Jain traditions contain many memories of the famine in Chandragupta's time, when a mass migration of the Jain monks took place.

Mauryan period witnessed a few devastating famines. The Jain traditions as recorded in the *Sthavirvadicharita* avers that 'some two centuries after the demise of the Master, a terrible famine 'lasting for twelve years', took place in Magadha, at the time of Chandragupta. Consequently, half the community accompanied by the king, under the leadership of Bhadrabahu *moved off near the sea* in between 299-296 B.C. while the other portion remained in Magadha. Jain traditions vary about the details of this well-preserved story of famine during the time of Chandragupta (see Jain J.C. 1947 : 20). The *Darsanasara* refers 'twelve year famine in Magadha' when Bhadrabahu *migrated with his follwers to Karnataka* and Sthulabhadra remained in Magadha with his disciples. This brought a division between Svetambara and Digambara sects of the Jain community (see Jain J.C. 1947 : 20). According to Harisena, the famine occurred in Ujjain, when Visakhacarya *led the monks to Punnala* in the south Mysore; while his teacher Bhadrababu, along with his disciples *proceeded to Sindhu.* We are told that Visakhacarya was none else but Chandragupta of Ujjain, who was initiated by Bhadrababu (*Brhatkathakosa* 131:38-41). According to Hemacandra the famine had occurred in Magadha when Chandragupta was ruling (*Parsiṣṭaparvana.* VIII. 414. ed. by Jacobi). In the *Āvasayaka Cūrni* (252) as a result of the famine Bhadrababu *migrated to Nepal.* Thus the Jain sources, which were compiled and written much later, after fifth-sixth century A.D., vary in their details. But most of them at least believed that the famine occurred during Chandragupta's time, and a large number of the monks had to migrate. This brought a division in the Jain community and thus was an important event in the history of the Jain sect.

To prevent the destruction by flooded rivers *Artha Sastra* recommends that 'villagers living on the banks of rivers shall during the rainy season, *remove themselves* to upward countries'. The migration to a safer place was considered as the best remedy. The compilers of the *Viṣṇu Purāṇa* recommends this measure when it is said that "oppressed by famine and taxation men *will desert their native lands and go to those countries which are fit for the coaser grains*" (VI. 1. 38).

Eating habits during famines were badly affected. As early as the Vedic time, when famines were of less frequence, it is said that "compelled by starvation men ate dog's flesh" (*RV.* IV. 18.13). Buddhist literary sources, which provide many details of famine incidence, show that how much degraded the food habits became during famines. The *Mahavagga* (VI.23.10) says that "in famine people ate the flesh of animals like horses, dogs and snakes". In the *Atthakatha* the famine is called *Paṣāṇacāṭakaṁ.* In the *Divyāvadāna* (X. 132) the famines are classified on the basis of food available to people. "In the *cancu* famine the people kept alive on the grains which were collected in a box for the pacification of dead; in *svetasthi* type the people boiled bones till they became white and drank the soup (*kvatha*); in the *śalakā vrtti* famine the people collected grains and mollasses collected in holes with sticks and boiling them in good quantity of water drank the soup". This explains that the pangs of hunger goaded them to search out food from every corner without any religious and moral inhibitions. In the *Rupamatī Avadāna* (see Moti Chand 1945:18-30) the story depicts a famine hungry mother who was even driven to eat her own child, when Rupamati intervened and by feeding the hungry mother with her (Rupamati's) own flesh avoided the worst tragedy. Asvaghosa (*Buddhacharita* XIV.13) also says that people ate their children in famine. These stories thus provide pathetic examples of cannibalism.

Famines broke the morale of the people. The god fearing religious minded town folks discarded their normal behaviour of entertaining the guests. The scarcity of food changed their social customs. Whenever any famine struck monks and mendicants were first hit. *Vinaya Pitaka* refers two devastating famines—one in Veranja and another in the Vajji country (I. 211-215). During famines a limited number of *bhikkhus* were invited (*Mahāvagga* VI. 19.2). *Cullavagga* depicts (VI. 21.1) that during a famine in Rajgriha people invited selected monks for meals. Sometimes *bhikkhus* themselves did not accept the invitation (*Mahāvagga* VI. 20.4; VI. 18.9). During famines Buddha prescribed some concessions for *bhikkhu sangha*. Like, they could keep the food indoors, cook indoors, take whatever they can pick up, eat food brought from within, or receive before meal time, eat things found in woods or in pools. But these privileges were forbidden for *bhikkhu sanghas* in normal times (*Mahāvagga* VI. 32. 2). The alms to *bhikkhu* became gradually less if famines lasted for a long duration. In Verañja, the Exalted One was staying with five hundred disciples, when a famine struck the town. Monks went throughout and about Verañja for alms, but received none (*Dhamma Pada*, VI. 8.).

In the *Samantapasādikā*, written by Buddhaghosa Thera (ed. Birbal Sharma 1964: I: 164) this famine in Veranja is described and it is especially mentioned that during the extreme scarcity of food the people lost their respect for the monks as they could not provide them with the alms. In the *Cullavagga* (VI. 4;1 VI. 21) it is said that during a famine in Rajgriha, "when people were unable to provide food for the whole *sangha*, though they were desirous, Buddha appointed an apportioner of ration—who would apportion the food by arranging the food in small heaps and fastening tickets or marks upon them". The *Mahāvagga* (VI. 17. 7-8) refers to a famine in Rajgriha, when Buddha even permitted his brotherhood of monks to eat the unoffered fruits if there is nobody available who can give it to them in alms."

But these mild relaxations in norms were not always sufficient. In the Jain chronicle *Vyavahāra Bhāṣya* (X. 557-60) famine in Kosala is described where *sadhus* were so much affected with famine that they committed suicide.

Relation of kinship and quasi-kinship were insurance against disasters such as famines. Subsistence husbandmen were always threatened by droughts, floods and crop-blights. Max Gluckman (1977:14) rightly observes that "their simple technology made it easier to move people to food, than food to people: in times of shortage tribesmen moved towards those of their relatives who have escaped disasters". Famines were mostly of such intense nature that family tie which had always been traditionally considered as sacred bondage were shattered. Though initially families tried to save their progenies from the disasters of famines and thus send their children away for the sake of safety. One such story of plague is reported in Rajgriha (*Dhamma Pada*. II. 1. 231), when everyone was dying and parents were also struck with disease. They asked their son to leave the town and only come back after a lapse of long period and look for the buried treasure they were leaving for the son. The son came back after twelve years and dug the wealth out. Family linkages played a significant role during famines. Sometimes men were wise enough to leave their homes when famines stuck them and took refuge in their kinsmen's place, much in advance (*Dhamma Pada* VIII. 9). We hear of a poor man who was supported by his daughters, when his hometown was afflicted with famine. He moved from one daughter's house to another daughter's place, to save himself from disaster.

But sometimes bitter family relationship followed due to famine distress. We hear of a man named Kotuhalaka who left his home town during famine and proceeded with his wife and son towards Kosambi, with a hope for job there. His provisions for journey were too meager and it could not last long. As a result they were forced to leave the boy on the way. They reached the destination ultimately. On reaching, the hungry man ate so greedily that he fell sick and died, leaving his wife as a destitute, to serve as a slave woman to sustain herself. (*Dhamma Pada* II. 1.70.). Familiar stories, where family ties were shattered, people abandoned their dear ones in distress and migrated to distant lands to save their own souls can be heard in the *Kathasaritasagara* (ch. III. st. I.b.tr Tawney vol. I. p. 19).

The scarcity of food had driven people to immoral means. As early as the time of the *Śatapatha Brāhmaṇa* it was said that whenever there is drought then the strong seize the weak" (*S,B*, XI. 6. 3. 1). Robbery and theft had been common maladies in a strife-torn society. Vedic literature provide many names for these miscreants, e.g. *paripanthin, taskara, tayu, stena, musivan,* which denotes robbers, thieves, etc. The miscreants in society increased in number whenever the scarcity reached to its climax during famines. The urbanization which commenced from 600 BC, brought famine situations quite often, and robbery during these times were essential part of the malady. The *Vassantara Jātaka* (No. 547) specially tells that during great famines "men being unable to live used robbery". The moral degradation during famines was noticeable in the *Brha Saṁhitā*. Robbery became pretty common (III. 13-14; III. 173). Even noble folks left their families in distress and fled to save their own lives. Scarcity of food affected the health of the people, especially children, who became devoid of flesh and looked like skeletons (III. 12-17).

The famine conditions had forced the people to sell the children for the sake of food. In the times of scarcity people often sold themselves as slaves or even prostitutes. In the *Anguttara Nikāya* (III. 208) we find the allusion of '*satta vannijja*' or 'trade in living beings'. Budhaghosa (Law: 1941: 32) explains the word as meaning '*manussa vikkaya*', or traffic in human beings. This traffic might be taken to imply the trade of women and slave (Law. 1941: 32). In the Jain sources it is said that during famines people sold children or accepted slavery (*Vyavahāra Bhāṣya* 2.207) (J.C. Jain : 1947: 119).

Crafty traders benefited during famines. Rice was usually in great demand in famine-hit villages. A *Dhmma Pada* story (I. 10. 126) tells that a man named Chanda, who made his living by killing pigs, earned a lot by selling his rice, in times of famine, in exchange for shoes. It says that in times of famine he would go to country with his cart filled with rice and return filled with shoes, bought in villages for a mere pot or two of rice apiece. Jain literature provides similar stories. Hoarding during famines, which made the starvation more acute was quite common. The *Vyavahāra Bhāṣya* (X. 557-60) tells the story of Sravaka of Kosala who hoarded grains. During famine when prices rose high he sold the grains at high profits. But he would not give any to monks. This forced the Jain monks to commit suicide. A later writer Ksemendra (See Moti Chand: 1984: 5) gives an interesting description of the grain merchants who are the happiest people during famines, as they could earn a lot of margin in their grain trade.

Scarcity of food created many compulsions in society. Though the caste rules had been usually rigid in ancient times but during famines, when survival was jeopardized, the caste codes were relaxed. Buddhist laws for the monks which were specified in the *Vinaya Pitaka* showed the prescribed concessions during the time of scarcity (*Vinaya: Mahavagya*, VI. 17.7, 18.4; 19.2; 20.4) Even generally forbidden meat could be unsumed during famines (*Ibid* VI. 32. 2). Similarly, Brahmanical laws were moulded accordingly during the time of famine. Profession of the brahmanas which had many restrictions during normal times were relaxed during emergencies like famines. A brahmana who had fallen into distress could accept gift from anybody (Manu VIII. 339; X. 102; 114). Manu tells that during famines a brahmana was allowed to save his body and soul by consuming even dog's meat (X 106; X. 1080) and if situation worsened he was not even prohibited to accept cow's meat from low caste people (X. 107) as at crisis the main objective was to avoid the death of a brahmana. Brahamana and Ksatriyas could adopt lower caste occupations during distress (X. 98, VIII. 411-412 X. 83, 95). Lending money, which was considered an unworthy profession during normal times, was permitted to brahmanas and ksatriyas during famines (X. 117; X. 118). The basic belief behind these relaxation of caste rules was that the brahmanas should be protected by all means. Manu categorically says (VIII. 134) that "a kingdom of that king in whose dominion a *srotriya* pines with hunger will be afflicted with famine". The society which since time immemorial was dominated by the religious sector, had given its most sympathetic consideration for them. It was considered the prime duty of a king to safeguard the interest of the brahmanas, who were on their part providing the religious sanction for their temporal authority. Thus, deliberating on the causes of famines brahmana thinkers had considered the wrath of unhappy brahmans and their curse as the main cause of earthly distress of a king.

In early stage of Brahmanic literature composers believed that the prayers to various gods can bring relief against natural disasters. As early as the *Rig Veda*, prayers were composed for the gods like Aditya and Indra (BK. III. 18. 10-11; VIII. 55. 14; X. 42. 10) who could save them from distress and famines. In the *Rig Veda* there are some prayers specially composed to ward off famines. (*RV.* I. 112. 11, III. 8.2; III. 53. 15). in the *Atharva Veda* many such prayers against all types of calamities can be traced e.g. prayers for counteracting drought (VII. 18); charm for hastening of rains and fair weather (IV. 15; VU. 128); prayers against injury to the grains by lightning (VII. 11. 1). It was also believed in the Vedic times that if any king offended any brahmana sage his curse would bring disasters to his kingdom. Vitihavyas, who seem to be *Sriñjaya* offshoot, were perished due to the curse of sage Bhrigu (*AV.* V. 19. 1; V. 18. 10). If any major mistakes were done by any king during sacrificial ceremony then also he incurred wrath of the gods and natural disasters brought reverses to his kingdom. Such a story is available about a king Vrddhadyumna Abhipratarina of Kuru dynasty, who made an error during a sacrifice and the brahmanas cursed him for that. (*Rig Veda Brāhamaṇas* tr. Keith *Intro.* p. 41). This belief persisted throughout our ancient history. A belief existed that if an innocent brahmana is killed by a king 12 years drought would follow (*Kathāsāritsagar* ch. V st. Ic. Tr. Tawney 1. 52-53). The kings were blamed for famines. It was usually believed that due to negligence of duty, or due to some sin incurred by the king, his kingdom got depleted by natural disasters like famines. The situation could only be ameliorated by the king himself or if he could bring a saintly person in his kingdom. Many stories can be cited which support this age old conception. The cause of famine during Santanu's time was his unlawful accession to the throne of his elder brother Devapi. The famine could only be stopped when Devapi performed a *yajna* for expelling the drought (*Visnu Purana* IV. 20. 9-30). Non Brahamanical literary sources shared the same belief. In the *Rajovada Jātaka* (No. 334) it is said that "When the rulers are unjust everything beginning with the wild fruits in the wood lose their sweetness and flavour". The *Nalika Jātaka* (No. 526) blamed the king of Kasi for his unrighteous activities which brought drought and famine there. The *Gandatindy Jātaka* (No. 520) considered that for famine and droughts kings were to be blamed. The same ideas were repeated in *Manichor Jātaka* (No. 194).

Two types of conceptions existed as far as kings duty towards famine was concerned. One, that the king should procure all help for famine affected people. Two, he should take precautionary measures to prevent famines. King's active support to fight against the famine menace are depicted in the *Dhamma Pada* (Bk. 18. story 10) and in the *Divyāvadāna* (XX: 291-93). In the *Dhamma Pada* story it is told that "when the king's house priest made forecast of famine in three years' time the treasurer caused more abundant crops to be sown than even earlier, spent all the wealth he possessed buying grains, caused twelve hundred and fifty granaries to be erected, filled all the granaries with rice, and when all the granaries were filled to overflowing capacity, filled *chatties* and other vessels and dumped the rest on the ground and buried them in the pits. What remained, he mixed with clay and used to plaster wall. When famine arrived he made use of the grains which had been stored and then he asked his retinue to go into the mountains and obtain sustenance from there."

The *Divyāvadāna* story is of a king named Kanakavarna, whose treasury were full and whose subjects enjoyed a degree of prosperity. But even in his reign due to "inauspicious planetary conjunctions a drought of 12 years was foretold. To save his people from starvation he decided to collect grains from all over India. After taking a census (*gaṇanā*) of all people and surveying the position he decided to start a granary (*koṣāgāra*) in every village, city, town-let, which was to provide equal amount of grain to everyone (*samam bhaktam*). To give his resolution a practical shape he summoned his accountant general (*gaṇaka mahāmātra*), ministers (*āmatyas*), chamberlain (*dauvārika*) and members of the council (*pariṣedaya*) and ordered them to collect grain from all over the country, take census of the people and after starting granaries—everywhere to bring rationing into full force. They carried out the king's order faithfully. Eleven years of famine thus passed. But in the 12th year the accumulated grain was exhausted and people began dying of hunger. Such was the condition of the country that not a grain was to be had, only the king had a measure of his share. The king offered his share to Bodhisatta, with the result that Bodhisatta caused the prosperity of the country to return". In the *Avadāna Śataka* (I:1.75), similar dutiful king Brahmadatta of Kasi had been referred to. He considered that "whatever eatables and drinks are stored for the royal household rightfully belonged to the people" and therefore, ordered his officials to distribute them to the masses. Very adequate and responsible steps were taken by the state to ameliorate famine. The measures adopted were: (a) taking stock of existing food condition; (b) taking census of the people; (c) acquisition of food grains and stocks from the area with a view to its equitable distribution; (d) establishing state granaries in villages, cities, etc.; (e) importing food from plentiful areas; (f) recruiting the services of the entire state machinery from the highest to the lowest staff in a coordinated effort to combat famines; (g) treating every citizen equally for relief measure; (h) transferring the population from the deficit area to surplus area.

In the *Arthaśāstra* where welfare functions of the state had been stressed upon, the details of the duties of the king in this regard was alluded to. To fight the pestilence it recommends that 'remedial measures shall be taken against pestilence. Physicians with their medicines shall overcome pestilence', 'the same remedial measures shall be taken against epidemics'. But probably the menaces were so large that sometimes human efforts were considered insignificant and sacred magic, mystic rites or prayers to special deities were recommended. For example during droughts, the god Indra, the Ganges, and *mahākacchapa* were specially worshipped to pacify the wrath of the Gods, who were believed to be unhappy and thus causing the malady. But Kautalya stressed on the role of the state to ameliorate the famine situations. "During famines the king shall show favour to his people by providing them with seeds and provisions (*bījabhaktopagraham*). He may show favour by distributing either his own collection of provision or the hoarded income of the rich among the people, or seek for help from his friends among kings'. In modern terminology this can be equated with 'state subsidies', and 'foreign aid programme'. He can pursue the policy of 'thinning the rich by exacting excessive revenue (*karsanam*), or causing them to vomit their accumulated wealth (*vamanam*)'. This can mean an 'extra emergency cess'; or 'the king with his subjects may migrate to another kingdom with abundant harvest'. This process can be called 'forced evacuation of the famine affected zone'. Pestilence which destroyed the crops were quite common. The king was advised to carry on remedial measures against pestilence on a war footing. With a view to destroy rats, grains mixed with the milk of the milk-hedge plants, or grains mixed with such ingredients as are treated in Bk. XIV, may be left on the ground, similar measures may also be taken against the danger from locusts, birds and insects.

To protect the higher standard of agriculture production state provided the irrigation facilities and guarded them against any defaulters. The *Arthaśāstra* notes that if any one damaged the irrigation dams, he was duly punished (Bk. IV. Ch. 11). Girnar inscription of Rudradaman, while giving the history of Sudarsana lake and its dam, specify that the lake and its dam was originally constructed during the time of Chandragupta Maurya and later on was reconstructed during the time of Ashoka, when it suffered a damage due to excessive rain and storm (Sircar: 1963). Thus this inscription further proves that the irrigation provisions were accorded to the Mauryan subjects by their kings on regular basis. Inscriptions belonging to the Mauryan period are also available to prove that the sanctions of the *Arthaśāstra* were actually practised. Sohgaura and Mahasthan inscriptions are of immense importance to us (Sircar: 1963:82; *E.I.*XXI. 85; *IA.*1933: 177). Mahasthana stone plaque inscription, of 3rd century BC records a famine, when the people of Samvagiya were affected. To ameliorate the tragedy paddy was supplied from the nearby prosperous city of Pundranagara. The famine seems here not of extensive nature, because the nearby town itself could supply the remedial measures. People needed not to evacuate the entire region. Therefore, it is quite likely that the famine occurred due to some local mishaps, like a sudden flood in a local river, as droughts usually affected a larger area. Another famine is recorded in Sohgaura copper plate inscription (*IA.* XXV. 261). A royal order was issued to *mahamatras* of Sravasti to distribute grains and fodder, preserved in the two grain houses in Usagama, in the time of distress to the nearby villages of Tiyavani, Mathula, and Chanchu. Here too famine seems to be not of far extensive nature. These two references probably did not correspond with the famine episode of the Jain chronicles in the time of Chandragupta Maurya. The

Jain sources refer to a famine which affected a vast area, as they record that a large number of people evacuated during famine.

Similar instances of state subsidy can be traced in other literary references. In the *Sudhabhojana Jātaka* (No. 535) we are told that king Brhamadatta of Kasi built six alms hall for his people and set on foot for alms–giving on a grand scale. The *Rāmāyaṇa* (I. 8. 12) categorically believed that the king could ensure timely rainfall by his righteous conduct. It was the king's duty to provide artificial irrigation during the time of drought (*Ibid.* II. 100. 45; II. 114. 21). King had to save the farmers from the pests (*Ibid.* II. 11422-23). In the *Purāṇas* also king's responsibility to ward off famine was given stress to. In the *Bhagavata Purāṇa* (IV. 16. 8) story of king Prithu is given who provided water to his people when there was no rain. Further on in the same *Purāṇa* (IX. 9. 6-11) Bhagiratha legend occurs, who brought the Ganga from Kailash mountain and made it flow through north India for the sake of the welfare of people, which acccrued religious benefits for his forefather too.

The king's duty to save his subjects from famines was considered essential. A later writer like Bana states (*Kādambarī* tr. Kale 1924) that king Tadapida had laid at rest all calamities over the region by simply performing his duties religiously. In the Kalhana's *Rājataranginī* (I.p.58), during a famine in Kashmir, king Tunjina bought food for the grief–stricken people with his own treasures as well as the accumulated wealth of his queen and his ministers. Even the late inscriptions like that of Dharasena II (Malia copper plate) states that it was the royal responsibility to check calamities affecting people and it declares that the wealth of the king was for the protection and maintenance of the helpless (*CII.* III. 165). In Jain chronicles we find that proper care was to be taken to protect the fields from *itis* or the calamities of season. People were given food at the time of epidemics and famine. (*Nisītha Cūrni* II. 455).

But the natural disasters were so common that the state help were negligible. These efforts to minimize the natural maladies by activising the state's economic functions were not sufficient. Quite often, we see, that the kings surrendered to the extreme disasters as their sheer misfortunes. Even though they accepted their responsibilities but instead of taking any remedial measure themselves they took refuge in the religion. A famine is referred to in the time of Kuru king Samvarana (*MBH.* I. 175. 38-46). Thereupon, the people of the towns, afflicted with hunger, left their houses in despair and fled in all directions. Family ties were torn as under. They abandoned their wives and children. The city looked like a land of ghosts, and the city dwellers were reduced to skeletons, due to starvation. This famine occurred, as the narrator says, due to the negligence of the king, who had left his kingdom unprotected and was himself dwelling in distant country. When the sufferings of the people reached high peak, *they called the king back and with his return the situation became better.* The wickedness of the king of Anga, Lomapada (or Romapada) was considered as the main cause for the famine in his kingdom (*RAM. Bālakāṇḍa.* IX. 7.9). The *drought was overcome, when the king invited young sage Sringa in his domain.* To keep him permanently in his kingdom he gave his daughter Santa in marriage to him. The legend thus impresses upon the belief that the drought was occasioned due to the sins of a king and can be ameliorated by his good deeds and by blessings of holy men.

One interesting point to note in the above stories is the importance given to religious personalities. Drought could only be remedied after a religious person, came to the effected territory. It seems that religious groups were trying to impress upon the society their importance. In the economic sector religious sector had hardly anything to contribute. They were very rarely connected with material production works. Therefore, to maintain their supremacy in the society they floated the ideas that they can prescribe religious remedies even to economic crisis. Their moral strength had such divine power, that just their presence, or some rites performed by them, could bring prosperity to society.

Even non-Brahmanical literary sources project similar expectation from religious persons. The importance of Buddhist monks, virtuous persons, or even sometime, virtuous animals were realized as necessary safeguards against natural menace or famines. *Maccha Jātaka* refers a famine in Kosala, which could *only had its remission after Gautam Buddha visited the town himself.* Mahāvastu (1. 284-88; Tr. Jones, *SBB*. Vol.16) refers a famine in Kampilla. *Sage Raksita, was brought from the Himalayas, to rescue the people by his mere presence in the city.* In Videha and Mithila, when many thousands of city dwellers perished due to a famine and a plague, a *virtuous elephant*, which belonged to the king of Kasi, *was brought for rescue purposes.* The plague and famine of Anga *was stopped due to the arrival of a holy bull.* The famine in the city of Dantapura in Kalinga, could only be *curbed after a holy elephant was brought from Kuru land* (*Dhammapada* Bk. 25. story. 20). A story of a devastating famine which killed "*satasahasra*" lives is referred to in the *Avadanasataka* (II. 8. 5-10). To *ameliorate this disaster monk Ananda was invited.* A late traveller Taranatha, records the memory of an old episode of famine in Jananta and Rajgriha, which were *brought under control through the magical power of Vasubandhu*, disciple of Asanga (Tārānātha. folio. 63.b). Again the same traveller gives the *credit to Arya Avalokitesvara for saving the people of 'Jambudvīpa' from famine, just by his arrival to that region* (*Ibid* fol. 63, b).

King's role to mitigate famine was stressed in the *Mahāvaṁśa* (XXXVI. 75-79). When king Siri Samghabodhi heard about the distress in the island, he lay down on the ground to do the penance and did not raise himself till the downpour flooded the region. It was believed that the drought in Sir Lanka persisted during the time of king Samidha, till *all knowing teacher Konagamana came to rescue the people* (*Mahāvaṁśa* XV. 94-95). In the Jain chronicle *Āvaśyaka Cūrni* (see J.C. Jain 1947: 199) it is recorded that *during a famine in Uttarāpatha Arya Vajra Swami used to get alms by magical practice.*

To conclude this discussion now we can say that famines had been a constant feature of our ancient history.

From the very beginning of the Vedic time, till the end of this ancient period of our history, there is no paucity of literary materials about famines. In the oldest times there were fewer incidents. In the Maurya time, with state controlled economy, the famines were better resolved. With the disintegration of the centralized administration in the post Mauryan epoch, famines became unmanageable. With the rise of feudalistic society in the Gupta period and post Gupta time, the state shed off its responsibilities to save the people of distant provinces from natural disasters and as the plains of north India gradually became thickly populated, dependency on agricultural land increased, thus famines became more frequent. It affected every region of the country. It was quite often of long duration, which brought immense calamities to the ordinary masses.

Chart 1

Name of Province	Assam	Bengal	Orissa	Chhota Nagpur	Bihar	U.P. (East)	U.P. (West)	Punjab	Delhi	Kashmir	NWFP	Baluchi-stan	Sindh	Rajasthan (East)	Rajasthan (West)	Agra	Gujarat	Kutch	Central India
	1	2	3	4	5	6	7	8	9	10	11	12	13	14	15	16	17	18	19
Year (A. D.)																			
1296									D										
1296-1317									D										
1343-45									D										
1351-63										D									
1494									D										
1500									D										
1527												F							
1540-43												D							
1554-55									D						**E.**	D			
1576									D										
1577																		D	
1594-98																			D
1613-15								D											
1623																	D		

Chart 1 (Contd.)

1630									D							D		D/F	
1660									D							D			
1769-70		D/F			D														
1783-84		D					D			D				D	D				
1790-92			D											D			D	D	
1799-1801											D								
1803-04											D			D					D
1812-13														D		D	D	D	D
1819-20											D			D			D		
1820-22													D						
1833-34								D			D			D					
1837		D						D			D				D		D	D	
1853-55														D					
1860-61		D						D			D			D				D	
1865-66		D	D	D															
1856-57			D		D														
1868-70								D			D			D			D		D
1873-74		D/F			D		D				D								
1878-/78-79						D	D	D		D	D								

Chart 1 (Contd.)

1884	D						D												
1888-89		D		D															
1890-92	D			D									D	D					
1896-97	D				D	D	D	D		D				D				D	
1899-1900	D						D						D			D	D	D	F
1901		F		F												D			
1902										F									
1903			F	F															
1904							F		F		F	F				F		F	
1905						F					F		F	F				F	
1907					F	F			F										
1908				F, D			D			D		D	D	D					
1909				D			D		D										
1910										D		D							
1911							F		F	F	F	F	F						
1913						F						D						F	
1914							D			D	D								
1915		F			D		F		F		F	F	F	F		F		F	
1916						D				D	D	D						D	

Chart 1 (Contd.)

1917					D	D	D		D	D	D		D	D					
1918	D			D	F	F	F		F	F	F	F	F	F		F		F	D
1920							F		F	F	F								
1922	D		D	D															
1924		F		D									D	D					
1926													D			D			
1927													D			D			
1929										D		D							
1932				D															
1933		D					D			D				D				D	
1935				D															
1936		D			D	D													
1942			D				D							D				D	
1944						D					D	D	D			D		D	

W.L. Hare's Table of Famines (Sec. Digby 1901 : 135)

Chart 2. North-western India: Botanical Remains

Site	*Location*	*Period*	*Cultivar*	*References*
Mehrgarh	North Kacchi plain	**Pd. I** Aceramic Neolithic	1. Wheat a) *Triticum monococcum* b) *T. dicoccum* c) *T. durum* 2. Barley a) *Hordeum distincum* b) *H. Vulgare* Var. *nudum* 3. *Zizyphus jujuba*	Jarrige 1979: 93-114
		Pd. II Ceramic Neolithic	1. Wheat 2. Barley 3. Cottonseed	
		Pd. III Chalcolithic	In addition to earlier cereals 1. Wheat a) *T. aestivum compactum* b) *T. aestivum sphaerococcum* 2. A new type of barley *H. hexasticum* 3. Oats (*avena*)	
		Pd. IV	All earlier known crops and wine grapes	
Nausharo	Kacchi plains	**Pd.I**	1. Wheat 2. Barley	Constantini, Biasini. 1985 and

Chart 2. (Contd.)

			3. *Vitis vinifera* 4. Legumes 5. *Linum usitatissimum*	1986:354
Pirak	Sibi Kacchi Plain	**Pd. I** Late Harappan	1. Wheat a) *T. vulgare compactum* b) *T. sphalrococcum* c) *T. riticum sphalrococcum* 2. Barley a) *H. vulgare* b) *H. distinctium* c) *H. vulgare* var. nudum 3. Rice (*Oriza sativa*) 4. *Avena* sp., 5. Sorghum 6. *Panicum miliaceum* 7. *Linum usitatissimum* 8. *Zizyphus jujuba* 9. *Vitis* sp.	Constantini, 1979 a: 272-77
Balakot	S.E. of Las Bela and Sonmiani Bay, Baluchistan	Harappan	1. Barley 2. Legume 3. *Stellaria* 4. *Zizyphus* sp.	Dales 1977:257

Chart 2. (Contd.)

Shahr-i-so-khta	Seistan E. Iran	Pre-Harappan	1. Wheat (four varieties) 2. Barley (four varieties) 3. *Pupulus* sp. 4. *Celtis* sp. 5. *Dalbergia sissoo* 6. *Adennanthera ch. pavoniana* 7. *Pistachia ch. vera* 8. *Vitis vinifera* 9. *Tamarix* 10. *Acer* 11. *Fraxinus* 12.˙ *Adinach cordifolia*	Constantini 1979.b:125
Mundigak	S. Afghanistan	Pre-Harappan	1. Wheat (*T. compactum*) 2. *Zizyphus vulgaria* 3. *Salvadora persica*	Casal 1961 :260 Poulain 1966: 119-135
Rehman-Dheri	Bannu basin	Pre-Harappan	1. Barley	Allchin, Allchin 1983:148 Durrani 1981:135
Tarakai-Qila	Bannu basin	Pre-Harappan	1. Wheat (*Triticum sp.*) 2. Barley (*H. vulgare* var. *nudum*) 3. Lentil (*Lens culinaris*) 4. Field pea (*Pisum arvense*)	Thomas 1979:231

Chart 2. (Contd.)

Loebanr III	Swat valley	Pre-Harappan	1. Barley—3 types 2. Wheat—2 types 3. Rice (*Oryza sativa*) 4. Rye seeds 5. *Lens esculenta* 6. *Pisum arvense* 7. *Galium* 8. *Vitis vinifera*	Constantini, 1977:704
Aligrama	Swat valley	Pre-Harappan	1. Wheat (*T. sphareococcum*) 2. Barley (*H. vulgare*) 3. Rice (*O. sativa*) 4. Legumes 5. Celtis	Constantini 1977:706-7
Harappa	Montgomery	Harappan	1. Barley *H. vulgare* 2. Wheat (*T. compactum*) 3. Peas (*Pisum arvense*)	Vats 1940:466
Mohenjo-dare	Larkana Sindh	Harappan	1. Barley (*H. vulgare varnudum*) 2. Wheat a) *T. compactum* b) *T. sphareococcum* 3. Sorghum (*jwar*)	Marshall, 1931: 586
Chanhu-daro	Sindh	Harappan	1. Barley *H. vulgare* var. *hexastichum*	Mackay, 1943

Chart 3. North Western India: Zoological Remains

Site	*Location*	*Period*	*Animal Remains*	*References*
Mehrgarh	N. Kacchi plains	Aceramic Neolithic to Pre-Harappan	**Domestic Animals** 1. Dog (*Canis familiaris* L) 2. Ox *Bos indicus* L. 3. Goat *Capra hireus* L 4. Sheep *Ovis arises* **Wild animals** 1. Jackal *Canis aerous* 2. Fox (*Vulpes* sp.) 3. Wild ass (*Equus hemionus*) 4. *Barasingha Cervus duvauceli* 5. Black buck *antelopecervi capra* 6. *Chinkara Gazelle doreas* L. 7. Wild Ox *Bos numadicus* 8. Wild goat *Capra aegagrus* 9. Urial *Ovis orientalis* 10. Pig *Sus scrofa* L. 11. Water buffalo *Bubalus-bubalis* 12. Nilgai *Boselaphus tragocamelus* 13. Chital (*Axis-axis*) 14. Elephant (*Elephas maximus*)	Meadow 1981: 34-4; Asthana 1985: 191;

Chart 3 (Contd.)

Shahr-i-shokta	Iranian Seistan	3,200-1800 B.C.	1. Domisticated ox (*Bos indicus*) 3. Wild ox (*Bos nomadicus*)	Caloi & Compagnoni 1979: 187
Kili-gul-Mohammed	Quetta valley	Pd. I-III	1. Sheep 2. Goat 3. Cattle 4. *Onager Equus hominoeus*	Fairservis 1956: 382
Rana Ghundai	Lorlai	Pd. I-III	1. Ox (*Bos indicus* L.) 2. Ass (*Equus asinus* L.) 3. Sheep (*Ovis arises*) 4. Horse (*Equus caballus* L.) 5. Onager (*Equus hominoeus*)	Ross 1946: 286
Surjungal	Lorlai valley	Pd. I-III	1. Sheep 2. Goat 3. Cattle 4. Fox 5. Dog	Fairservis 1959: 299
Nal	Baluchistan	Pd. I-III	1. Sheep 2. Goat	Hargreaves 1929
Mundigak Timbo	S. Afghanistan	Pd. I-III	1. Sheep 2. Goat 3. Ibex 4. Gazelle 5. Dog 6. Horse 7. Lynx	Shaffer 1978 a: 149

Chart 3 (Contd.)

Amri	Sindh	Pd. I-III	1. Bull *Bos taurus* 2. Goat 3. Sheep 4. Ass 5. Gazelle	Casal 1964 164-169
Balakot	Baluchistan	Harappan Pd.	1. Sheep 2. Goat 3. *Nilgai* 4. Gazelle 5. Dog 6. Shell 7. Onager 8. Cattle 9. Water buffalo 10. Pig 11. Fishbones	Meadow 1977: 275-316
Tarakai & Lewan	Bannu basin	relatively recent	1. Insects (mostly bees) 2. Molluscs 3. *Enidae (Subzebrinus* sp.) 4. *Bos* sp. 5. *Ovis* 6. *Capra* 7. *Canis* sp.	Thomas 1979: 227
Jalilpur	W. Punjab	Pre-Harappan	1. Cattle 2. Sheep 3. Goat	Mughal, 1972: 119 1974: 110

Chart 4. Floral Remains of Gujarat (Selected Sites)

Site	*Location*	*Period*	*Cultivar & Wood Remains*	*References*
Lothal	Ahmedabad	Harappan Pd.	1. Rice *Oryza sativa* 2. Bajra *Pennisetum typhiodeum* 3. Wheat	*IAR* 1955-56: 6 *IAR* 1959-60: 18 S.R. Rao: 1963: 161 Possehl, 1977: 537
Rangpur 1	Surendranagar	Harappan Pd.	1. Rice *Oryza sativa* 2. Bajra *Pennisetum typhiodeum*	S.R. Rao: 1963: 161 S.S. Ghosh, 1961: 295 S.S. Ghosh & K. Lal: 1963: 161-171 Possehl. *Ibid.*
		Post Harappan Pd.	1. Bajra, wheat: **Wood remains** *Acacia, Albizzia, Soymida, Fabribuga, Tamarix, Petrocarpus sontalinus*	
Surkotada	Kutch	Harappan Pd.	1. Finger millet *ragi* *Eleusine coracana* 2. Italian millet *Sataria italica*	*IAR* 1974-75: 78
Jokha	Surat	Late Harappan	Husks of paddy	Mehta & Choudhury *et.al.*, 1971: 14-15

Chart 4 (Contd.)

Nagara	Kaira	Pd. I. 1000 B.C. to post-Christian era	1. Rice 2. *Kodara* 3. *Matha* 4. *Kansarilu gullu*	Mehta, and Shah 1968: 153
Oriya Timbo	Bhavnagar	Late Harappan	1. Millet	G.E. Wagner 1990: 127
Lothal	Ahmedabad	Harappan Pd.	1. Rice *(Oryza sativa)* 2. Bajra *(Pennisetum typhiodeum)* 3. Wheat:	*IAR* 1955-56: 6 *IAR* 1959-60: 18 S.R. Roa: 1963: 161 Phossehl. 1977: 537
Rangpur 1	Surendranagar	Harappan Pd. Post Harappan pd.	1. Rice *(Oryza sativa)* 2. Bajra *(Pennisetum typhiodeum)* 1. Bajra, wheat: **Wood remains** *Acacia, Albizzia, Soymida, Fabri-buga, Tanarix, Petrocarpus-Sontalinus*	S.R. Rao: 1963: 161 S.S.Ghosh, 1961: 295 Possehl, *Ibid.*
Surkotada	Kutch	Harappan pd.	1. Finger millet *(ragi)* *(Eleusine coracana)* 2. Italian millet *(Sataria italica)*	*IAR* 1974-75: 78
Nevasa	Ahmednagar	NBPW pd.	1. Wheat 2. Rice 3. Bajra 4. Grams	Sankalia & Mate 1959: 2; Sankalia Deo & Ansari 1960: 529

Chart 5. Faunal Remains of Gujarat *(Selected Sites)*

Site	*Location*	*Domestic*	*Wild*	*References*
Lothal	Ahmedabad	1. Goat 2. Charred animals (not identified)	1. Elephant 2. Shell *Potamilidae* 3 Rhinoceros	*IAR* 1959-60: 80 *IAR* 1961-62: 10
Rangpur	Surendranagar	1. Ox *Bos indicus* 2. Buffalo *Bos bubalus-bubalis* 3. Sheep *Ovis vignei* 4. Goat (*Capra hircus-aegegrus*) 5. Pig (*Sus scrofa Cristatus*) 6. Ass 7. Dog	1. *Chitra Indica gray* 2. *Cervus* unicolour Kerr *Sambhar* deer 3. *Xancus pyrum* Linn. 4. *Shankha* (shell)	Bholanath: 1963: 154-9
Malvan	Surat	1. Ox 2. Buffalo 3. Horse 4. Goat 5. Sheep 6. Dog	1. Wild boar 2. *Barasingha* 3. Spotted deer	*IAR* 1969-70: 3
Jokha	Surat	1. Humped Ox 2. Buffalo 3. Pig 4. Goat 5. Sheep 6. Dog	1. Hyena 2. Rat 3. *Barasingha* 4. Spotted deer	Mehta, Choudhury *et.al.* 1971: 70

Chart 5 (Contd.)

Kanewal	Khera	1. Ox 2. Buffalo 3. Horse 4. Pig 5. Camel	1. Birds 2. *Cheetal* 3. *Neelgai* 4. *Barasingha* 5. Rhinoceros 6. Monitor lizard	Mehta, Momin & Shah 1980: 74-5
Dhatva	**Surat**	1. Humped Ox 2. Buffalo 3. Pig 4. Goat 5. Dog	1. Freshwater Bivalve 2. Monitor lizard 3. Crocodile 4. River turtle 5. Rock pigeon 6. Cattle egret 7. *Barasingha* 8. Spotted deer 9. Hog deer 10. *Nilgai* 11. Mole rat 12. Common rat 13. Rabbit	Mehta *et.al.* and Chowdhary 1975 : 57
Oriyo Timbo	Bhavnagar	1. Ox 2. Pig 3. Goat 4. Sheep		Rissman & Chitalwala 1990: 110-126

Chart 6. Survival/Longevity of the Sites/Settlements

Region/Site	*Layers*	*Timespan*	*Survival*
Mundigak mound A S. Afghanistan	7 occupational periods	1-5 layers are from Ceramic Neolithic to Harappan culture. Last 2 layers belong to late periods	Nearly 3 million years
Deh-Murasi-Ghundai S.W. Afghanistan	4 occupational periods	1-3 periods are contemporary to 1-4 periods of Mundigak. The fourth layer belongs of Islamic period	
Mehrgarh (Kacchi Plains) Baluchistan	1-7 occupational periods	6000-2500 B.C.	More than 3 million years
Gumla (Gomal Plains)	1-6 occupational periods	1-3 belong to pre-Ceramic to Harappan culture. The fifth & sixth layers are of late occupation	nearly 3 million years
Anjira (Kalat region) Baluchistan	1-5 occupational periods	4500-2500 B.C.	2000 years
Kili Gul Mohammad Quetta Valley Baluchistan	1-4 occupational periods	5000-3500 B.C.	1500 years
Amri	1-4 occupational periods	3500-2000 B.C.	1500 years

Chart 6 (Contd.)

Rahman dheri (Gomal plains)	1-3 occupational periods	3500-2000 B.C.	1000 years
Sur Jungal, Baluchistan	1-3 occupational periods		1000 years
Quetta Valley, Baluchistan	1-3 occupational periods	4000-3000 B.C.	1000 years
Rahman dheri	1-3 occupational periods	3500-2500 B.C.	1000 years
Mohenjodaro	1-3 occupational periods	2700-1500 B.C.	Slightly more than 1000 years
Harappa, Punjab	1-3 occupational periods	2700-1500 B.C.	More than 1000 years
Lothal, Gujarat	1-2 occupational periods	2500-1500 B.C.	1000 years
Prabhas Patan, Gujarat	1-3 occupational periods	1800-1000 B.C.	800 years
Rojdi. Gujarat	1-2 occupational periods	2300-1800 B.C.	500 years

Chart 7. Chalcolithic Sites on the River Valleys

Region	*River Valley*	*Cultural types*	*No. of Sites*	*References*
Baluchistan	Gaj, Hingol, Porali, Hab, Nara, Lake Mancchar	Kulli Nal Amri	90 37 7	Possehl, 1986/App B. N.G. Majumdar, 1934: 65 Fairservis, 1971: 158-216
Sindhi-Kohistan	Near perennial or ephemeral streams	Harappan sites	30	Louis Flam 1984: 77-82
Kirthar Mount, Kirthar Piedmont	Ephemeral streams	Harappan sites	10	Louis Flam 1984: 77-82
Lower Indus region	On the ephemeral rivers with seasonal floodings	Harappan sites	21	Louis Flam 1984: 77-82
Cholistan region	Hakra	Hakra ware Early Harappan (Kotijian) Mat Har. Pd. Late Har. Pd. PGW	99 40 174 50 14	Mughal 1982: 85-95 " " " " " " " " " " " "
North Rajasthan (Hanumangarh Tehsil)	Saraswati Drsadwati	Pre. Har Mat Har. Pd. Late Har. Pd. PGW	8 30 10 1	Dikshit, 1979 a 123-133 A. Ghosh 1989

Chart 7 (Contd.)

South Rajasthan	Berach, Wagan Gambhir, Kadmali	Paleolithic & Chalcolithic		V.N. Misra, 1967 : 200-209
Haryana	Saraswati	Mat. Har. Late Har. PGW	3 43 100	Suraj Bhan 1976, 1977
Haryana	Drisadwati Gambhir, Kadmali	Mat. Har. Late Har. PGW	22 51 71	Suraj Bhan *Ibid.*
Haryana	Yamuna	Mat. Har. Late Har. PGW	8 32 87	Suraj Bhan *Ibid*
Western U.P. Saharanpur Distt.	Yamuna, Ganga *Doab* & tributaries to Yamuna	Mat. Har. Mat. Har. OCP GW/PGW NBPW	25 13 75 9 4	Dikshit, 1984 : 253-270
Kanpur Distt.	Ganga Rind *Doab*, Yamuna Rind *Doab*	BRW PGW NBPW EH	9 46 99 141	Makhan Lal 1984. 6 : 170-178
Saurashtra Bhavnagar Distt.	Ghelo, Kalubhar	Mat. Har. (Rangpur II B.C.) Late Har. (Rangpur III)	28 12	Possehl 1980: 44, 50, 89-119

Chart 8. Chalcolithic Sites on the River Valleys of Baluchistan

Periods	*Zhob*	*Lorlai*	*Quetta*	*Sibi*	*Sarawan*	*Jhalwan*	*Kharan*	*Lasbela*	*Makran*
4500-3500	X	1	3	X	X	2	X	X	X
3500-3000	1	8	2	X	7	3	X	X	X
3000-2500	X	1	18	X	13	16	1	1	7
2500-1400	7	8	30	3	16	7	6	9	28
1400-800	X	4	9	5	6	51	4	17	4

This chart is made on the basis of Fairselvis 1971: 398-408. App. : F.

Chart 9. Size of Baluchi Sites of Pre- & Mat. Harappan Periods (Selected sites)

Site	Location	Period	Size (Hectare)	References
Anjira	Kirthar/Sulaiman Kalat distt.	Pre-Harappan	2.5	Shashi Asthana: 1985: 124 De Cardi 1965: 86-103
Damb-Sadat	Quetta Valley	Pre-Harappan	1.47	Shashi Asthana: 1985: 120 Fairservis: 1956: 206; 1971: 443
Edithshahr	Porali river, Las Bella region	Pre-Harappan	0.17	Fairservis: 1971: 195 Possehl: 1986: 56
Gumla	Gomal plains	Pre-Harappan	0.37	Shashi Asthana: 1985: 98
Kaudani	Zhob river bank	Pre-Harappan	3.6	Stein: 1929: 41-43
Kechi Beg	Quetta valley	Pre-Harappan	0.23	Fairservis: 1971: 443
Kulli	Las Bella	Pre-Harappan	10.8	Possehl: 1986: 11 Shashi Asthana: 1985: 129
Mehrgarh	Kacchi plains on the Bolan river	Pre-Harappan III period of habitation	11.14	Nautiyal: 1989: 3-8
Mehi		Pre-Harappan	9.9	Stein: 1931: 154 Fairservis: 1971: 201
Moghul Ghundai	On the river Zhob	Pre-Harappan	0.48 0.18	Stein: 1929: 43-49 Shashi Asthana: 1985: 105

Chart 9 (Contd.)

Nal		Pre-Harappan	6 5.63	Fairservis: 1975: 158 Fairservis: 1971: 158
Niai-Buthi	On the river Poralli, Lasbella region	Pre-Harappan	1.5	Possehl: 1986: 57
Nindowari	Ornach valley Kolawa Distt.	Pre-Harappan	6	Jarrige: 1983 a: 47-50
Nimkai	On the river Anambar	Pre-Harappan	0.83	Stein: 1929: 71
Periano-Ghundai	On the river Zhob	Pre-Harappan	14.6	Shashi Asthana: 1985: 106
Rahman Dheri	Derajat	Pre-Harappan	18.9 21.76	Durrani: 1981: 133-37 Shashi Asthana: 1985: 95
Rana Ghundai	Kirthar Sulaiman	Pre-Harappan	14.4	Stein: 1929: 52
Sandiyar	Zhob river valley	Pre-Harappan	3.14	Stein: 1929: 49
Sunery Damb	Maskai valley	Pre-Harappan (Nal type ware)	3.07	Stein: 1931: 164
Sur Jungal	Quetta Valley	Pre-Harappan	0.49	Stein: 1929: 73
Tando Rahim	Kirthar Piedmont	Pre-Harappan	0.37	Shashi Asthana: 1985: 126
Balakot	East of Sonmiani Bay Makran coast	Mat. Harappan	2.6	Dales: 1974: 1-22; 1977: 241-273

Chart 9 (Contd.)

Dabarkot	Lorlai Valley	Mat. Harappan	18.78	Stein: 1929: 56
Siah-Damb	Makran coast Nundera valley	Mat. Harappan	3.2	Stein: 1931: 138 Shashi Asthana: 1985: 108
Suktagendor	Makran coast	Mat. Harappan	1.78 (or 2)	Wheeler: 1968: 60; Stein: 1929
Rahman Dheri		Mat. Harappan	18.9	Dani: 1970-71: 28

Chart 10. Settlement Pattern in Sindh Multiplicity of the Sites

Region	*Ware*	*No. of Site*
Kirthar-Kohistan	Amri-Kotdijian	30
Kirthar-Kohistan	Mat. Harappan	19
Lower Indus Valley	Amri-Kotdijian	3
	Mat. Harappan	20

Chart 11. Sizes of the Prehistoric Sites of Sindh (Selected sites)

Sites	*Region*	*Ware types*	*Size of (Hectares)*	*References*
Bibi Ji Bhit	Sindh Kohistan	Amrian	0.35	L. Flam: 1981: 221; Table 1
Taung Buthi	Sindh Kohistan	Amrian	0.5	*Ibid.*
Gorandi (a)	Sindh Kohistan	Amrian	0.5	*Ibid.*
Tando Rahimkhan	Kirtmar Piedmont	Amrian	0.75	*Ibid.*
Pokhran	Sindh Kohistan	Amrian	0.8	*Ibid.*
Khajaur	Sindh Kohistan	Amrian	1.16	*Ibid.*
Pandiwahi	Sindh Kohistan	Amrian	1.27	*Ibid.*
Kai Buthi	Sindh Kohistan	Amrian	1.32	*Ibid.*
Chauro	Sindh Kohistan	Amrian	1.38	*Ibid.*
Othmanjo Buthi	Sindh Kohistan	Amrian	7.4	*Ibid.*
Bandhni	Sindh Kohistan	Amrian	7.7	*Ibid.*
Amri	Sindh Kohistan	Kot-Dijian	8	Fairservis: 1967: 32
Phang	Sindh Kohistan	Kot-Dijian	0.39	Majumdar: 1934: 24-28
Kohtrash	Sindh Kohistan	Kot-Dijian	3.5	Majumdar: 1934: 132-34

Chart 11 (Contd.)

Ali Murad	Kirthar-Piedmont	Harappan	10.185	Majumdar: 1934: 89
Allahlino	Sindh Kohistan	Harappan	1	Fairservis: 1975: 429
Amilano	Sindh Kohistan	Harappan	1	Piggott: 1950: 175
Badah	Lower Indus	Harappan	3.2	Deva: 1949: 25
Chanhu-Daro	Lower Indus	Harappan	6.5 4.6	Piggott: 1950: 171 Majumdar: 1934: 35
Dhal Buthi	Sindh Kohistan	Harappan	1.5	L. Flam *op. cit.*
Judieirjodaro	Kacchi	Harappan	25	*Pakistan Archaeology:* 1964: 11-12
Karchat		Harappan	5	Majumdar: 1934: 48
Katasur		Harappan	9	Vats: 1940: 37
Lohumjo-daro	Lower Indus	Harappan	5	Majumdar: 1934: 48
Mohenjodaro	Lower Indus	Harappan	85	Mackay: 1935: 8
Nuru-waro-Dharo	Lower Indus	Harappan	35	*Pakistan Archaeology:* 1964: 43
Pandiwahi		Harappan	1.5	Majumdar: 1934: 91
Rajo	Kirthar Piedmont	Harappan	3.2	Deva: 1949: 25
Thano-Bulakhan	Harappan	Harappan	1.5	Majumdar: 1934: 142

Chart 12. Sizes of Selected Harappan Sites of Punjab

Sites	*Size in Hectares*	*References*
Bara	1.6	*IA*: 1953-54: 38
Chakpurbane	2.02	Vats: 1940: 475
Harappa	45	Vats: 1940: 3
Harappa Md. F	7	Vats: 1940: 17
Jalilpur	15	Dales: 1973: 121
Kotla Nihang Khan	4.86	Vats: 1940: 477
Rahman Dheri	21.7	Durrani: 1981: 133-37
Rupar	35	*IA*: 1954-55: 9-11

Chart 13. Settlement Pattern of Bahawalpur state (Cholistan)

Period	*Ware type*	*No. of Sites*	*References*
Fourthern millenium B.C.	Hakra wares	99	Mughal: 1982: 85-97
Early third millenium B.C.	Kot Dijian wares	40	*Ibid.*
Mid & late third millenium B.C.	Mature Harappan ware	174	*Ibid.*
Early 2000 B.C.	Late Harappan ware	50	*Ibid.*
End of second & early first millenium B.C.	Post Harappan (PGW)	14	*Ibid.*

Chart 14. Size of the Harappan sites in Hakra/ Ghaggar valley (Selected Sites)

Sites	*Size in Hectares*	*References*
Ahmadwala	7.29	Stein: 1934: 114
Ahmad-Khan Dheri	2.07	Stein: 1934: 197 Mughal: 1970: 158
Dewaliana-Ther	22.2 20.5	Mughal: 1970: 158 Stein: 1943: 168
Gumanwala	27.3	Mughal: 1982: 85-95
Ganwariwal	81.5	Mughal: 1982: 85-95
Jalwali	22.5	Mughal: 1982: 85-95
Kalapur	17.5	Stein: 1943: 74
Kalibangan	15 22	Lal and Thapar: 1967: 79 Mughal: 1982: 85-95
Lurewala ther	82	Mughal: 1970: 159
Qadarwali Ther	5.5	Mughal: 1970: 159
Sandhanwala Ther	5.5	Mughal: 1982: 85-95
Satwali	13.7	Mughal: 1982: 85-95
Trekoe	42	Mughal: 1970: 160

Chart 15. Settlement pattern of pre Harappan and Mature Harappan Rajasthan (North Western)

	Pre-Harappan	*Mature Harappan*	*Late Harappan*	*PGW*
Ganganägar district (Hanumangarh tehsil) (Sothi ware)	8	30	10	1
Sikar district (Ganeswar culture)	46	X	141 (Ocp sites)	—

Chart 16. Settlement pattern in East/South Rajasthan

District	*Ahar/BRW*	*OCP*	*BRW/PGW*
Alwar	X	4	1
Ajmer	X	X	2
Bharatpur	X	7	20
Bhilwara	X	X	12
Chittorgarh	19	X	X
Dholpur	1	X	X
Dungarpur	6	X	X
Jaipur	7	19	5
Jhunjhunu	2	7	X
Sawai Madhopur	X	1	X
Tonk	1	X	X
Udaipur	15	X	X

Chart 17. Size of the Selected Gujarati sites of Harappan times

Site	*Location*	*Period*	*Size in (Hectare)*	*References*
Desalpur	Kutch	(IIa) Early Harappan	1.3	Possehl: 1980: 95
Kerasi	Kutch	(IIa) Early Harappan	0.003	Joshi: 1972: 6: 27
Kotadaadli II	Kutch	(IIa) Early Harappan	0.0008	Joshi: *Ibid.*
Kotadi (Md. I)	Kutch	(IIa) Early Harappan	1.5	Possehl: 1980: 106
Lothal	Ahmedabad	(IIa, b, c) Early + Mat. Harappan	7.1 4.75	Possehl: 1980: 108 D.K. Chakrabarti: 1979: a 205-15
Surkotada	Kutch	(IIa, b, c) Early + Mat. Harappan	2.6	Joshi: 1972: a: 98-144 Possehl: 1980: 116
Akru	Ahmedabad	(IIb, c) Mature Harappan	4	Rao: 1963: 186
Adatala	Bhavnagar	(IIb, c) Mature Harappan	7	*IAR*: 1960-61: 7
Bhimpatal	Ahmedabad	(IIb, c) Mature Harappan	1.1	Rao: 1963: 184
Bhojvadar	Bhavnagar	(IIb, c) Mature Harappan	3.3	Possehl: 1980: 92
Bhokil Dhar	Bhavnagar	(IIb, c) III, Mature Harappan & Late Harappan	5.6	Possehl: 1980: 92

Chart 17 (Contd.)

Budhel	Bhavnagar	(II b, c) Mature Harappan	23	Possehl: 1980: 93
Budhel	Bhavnagar	(II b, c) Mature Harappan	23	Possehl: 1980: 93
Charnio	Bhavnagar	(II b, c) Mature Harappan	7.5	Possehl: 1980: 93
Devaliyo	Amreli	(II b, c) Mature Harappan	32	Rao: 1963: 184; Chakrabarti: 1979: a: 212
Ghelo Bund	Bhavnagar	(II b, c) Harappan	4.2	Possehl: 1980: 98
Hanuman-no-timbo	Bhavnagar	(II b, c) Mature Harappan	11.9	Possehl: 1980: 99
Kaj	Amreli	(II b, c) Mature Harappan	11.7	*IAR*: 1957-58: 19
Kunjetar	Amreli	(II b, c) Mature Harappan	2	Rao: 1963: 181
Kindrkhera	Junagarh	(II b, c) Mature Harappan	1	Rao: 1963: 183
Kotadi (Md. 2)	Kutch	(II b, c) Mature Harappan	14	Joshi: 1972: 108
Malva	Surat	(II b, c) Mature Harappan	2	*IAR*: 1967-68: 10
Malgam	Rajkot	(II b, c) Mature Harappan	10.26	Possehl: 1980: 109
Mahadevio		(II b, c) Mature Harappan	1.32	Possehl: 1980: 109
Wasai	Jamnagar	(II b, c) Mature Harappan	0.08	Rao: 1963: 207

Chart 18. District-wise Distribution Pre-historic Sites of Punjab (India)

District	*Pre/Early Harappan*	*Mature Harappan*	*Late Harappan*	*BRW/PGW*
Amritsar	X	2	4	7
Bhatinda	11	13	10	X
Chandigarh	X	1	4	2
Faridkot	2	2	1	1
Firozpur	1	1	X	X
Gurdaspur	X	X	10	11
Hoshiarpur	X	X	2	1
Jullundur	X	4	15	17
Kapurthala	2	2	2	X
Ludhiana	2	7	39	6
Patiala	X	4	36	30
Ropar	2	10	18	11
Sangrur	6	6	10	5
TOTAL	26	52	151	91

Chart 19. District-wise Distribution of Pre-historic Sites of Haryana

District	*Pre/Early Harappan*	*Mature Harappan*	*Late Harappan*	*PGW/GW*
Ambala	X	2	23	54
Bhiwani	2	2	3	2
Gurgaon	8	X	16	42
Hissar	37	25	33	31
Jind	44	12	110	33
Karnal	8	8	69	42
Kurukshetra	3	2	60	98
Mahendragarh	2	X	9	X
Rohtak	5	2	10	17
Sirsa	X	X	1	12
Sonipat	4	X	11	23
TOTAL	113	55	345	354

Chart 20. Remains of grass grazing animals a selected (North western regions)

Site	*Location*	*Ox*	*Sheep/ Goat*	*Buffalo*	*Gazelle*	*Others*	*References*
Mehrgarh	Kacchi plains	38% to 65%	85% in pd. I 4,62% in pd. I, 1	Two specimens	36% in early period	X	Meadow: 1979: 334 1981: a : 143
Mundigak	Afghanistan	*Bos* indicus *Bos* taurus 70 frag-ments	436 pieces of goat bones, 144 pieces of sheep bones	X	23 frag-ments of bones of gazelles	95 pieces of *Equus hydrontinus* and 33 pieces of *Equus caballus*	Poullain: 1966: 119; Shaffer: 1978: 111; Jarrige, Tosi: 1979: 115
Tarakaiqila & Lewan	Bannu Basin	*Bos* indicus Predomi-nates	*Ovis/Capra* bones traced	Babalus-Babulis bones found	X.	X	Allchin, Knox: 1979: 241-45 Thomas: 1979: 227; 1983: 127-144
Loebanr III & Aligrama	Swat valley	Total 2069 pieces i.e. 67% of total bones	Total 610 pieces i.e. 19% of total bones	X	11 pieces i.e. 0.4 % total bones	2.5 pig bones only in Loebanr	Compagnoni: 1979: 697-702

Chart 20 (Contd.)

Shahr-i-sokhta Seistan		3678 fragments of Ox, *zebu* and *Bos indicus bones*	X	Wild species	X	X	Caloi & Compagnoni: 1979: 187
Balakot	S.E. of Las Bella Valley	74% of total bones	37% sheep, 50% goats	1 piece of water buffalo bone	13% of total bones	17 pieces of Nilgai bones	Meadow: 1977: 275

Chart 21. Remains of grass grazing animals of Sindh and Punjab

Site	*Location*	*Ox*	*Sheep/ Goat*	*Buffalo*	*Gazelle*	*Others*	*References*
Chanhu-daro	Sindh	Fragments of *Bos* sp., ox bones	2 lower molars of goats	X	A number of deer bones	X	Mackay: 1943 : 246
Mohenjo-daro	Sindh	23 *Bos indicus* fragment bones listed	5 fragments of bones of Ovis	6 speci-mens of *Bos Bubalus-Bubalis*	2 fragments of stag. 18 of rusa deer, 6 of Hog deer	46 frag-ments of *Sus cristatus*	Sewell & Guha: 1931: 2: 649
Harappa	Punjab	Zebu (*Bos indicus*) 103 pieces	38 sheep & 25 goat bone fragments listed	20 frag-ments of *Bos Bubalus*-bubalis	12 frag-ments of *Barasingha*	6 bones of domestic-ated ass, 1 piece of humped camel bone	Prasad: 1936: 31-51

Chart 22. Remains of grass grazing animals of Gujarat (As studied by Possehl: 1989: 174)

Site	*Ox*	*Sheep/ Goat*	*Buffalo*	*Deer, etc.*	*Others*	*Total Assemb-lage*	*References*
Oriyo	84%	13.9	X	X	X	1,190	Possehl and Raval : 1989 : 174
Dhatva	76.4 %	0.2 %	3.0 %	12.8 %	4.9 %	657	Shah: 1975: 57-60
Kanewal	50 %	X	X	X	X	X	Shah: 1980: 74-76
Khanpur	62 %	X	X	X	X	X	Thomas: 1984: 355-362
Nageswar (urban phase)	48.3 %	19.8 %	11 %	13.4 %	X	611	Hegde, Bhan, Sonawane: 1984-85: 1-9
Nageswar (post urban)	41.8 %	33.1 %	3.1 %	10.7 %	9.1 %	total bone count for both pds.	
Prabhaspa-tan	55 %	X	X	X	X	X	Thomas: 1984: 355-362
Rangpur (all pds.)	78 %	11 %	2 %	X	X	1,847	Bholanath: 1963: 154-159

Chart 22 (Contd.)

Rojdi (all pds.)	74.5 %	15.9 %	X	X	X	804	Possehl: *etal* : 1985: 80-100
Lothal	56.3 %	20.4 %	4.5 %	0.3 %	0.3 %	4,602	Bholanath: 1985: 636-50 Possehl & Raval: 1989: 174

Chart 23. Forests as Mentioned in the Literacy Sources

Name of Forest	*Location*	*References*
Puragavana	Pataliputra	Aṣṭadhyāī VIII. 4.4.5
Misrakavana	Sitapur district	*Ibid.*
Sidhrakavana	Not specified	*Ibid.*
Kotaravana	Not specified	*Ibid.*
Agrevana	Not specified	*Ibid.*
Saravana	Sravasti	*Ibid.* (see V.S. Agarwal, 1953: 41)
Iksuvana	Not specified	*Ibid.*
Plakshavana	Not specified	*Ibid.*
Amravana	Rajgriha, Kampilya, and, Mallaratha	*Ibid.*; *D.N.* I. 47, 47 *S.N.* IV. 121
Khadirvana	Not specified	*Ibid.*
Anjanavana	Saket	*S.N.* I. 54; V. 219
Kantakivana	Saket	*Ibid.*
Andhavana	Savatthi	*S.N.* V. 302
Dandakaranya	Vindhya mountains	*MBH.* III, 8183 & *Milindapañho* p. 130
Icchanangala	Kosala	*A.N.* III. 30, 341; IV. 340
Jetavana	Sravasti	*D.N.* I. 178
Jatiyavana	Bhaddiya country	*A.N.* III. 36
Ketakavana	Kosala	*Nalapana Jātaka* (No. 20 para 170)
Latthivana	Rajgriha	*Jāt* No. 544 para 220; *Jāt* No. 485 and 282
Lumbinivana	Kapilavastu	*S.N.* I.P. 26; *S.N.* I. 29-30
Amalakivana	Kapilavastu	*Ibid.*
Makkarattha	Avanti	*S.N.* IV. p. 116

Chart 23 (Contd.)

Mahavana	Kapilavastu, Vaisali	*S.N.* I. p. 26; *S.N.* I. 29-30; *Jāt.* No. 108; No. 149; No. 152
Nagavana	Vajji country	*A.N.* IV p. 213
Bhaskalavana	Sumsumaragiri	*A.N.* II. 61; III. 296; *Majjhima* I. 95; II 91
Simsapavana	Kosala	*D.N.* II. 316
Simsapavana	Kosambi	*S.N.* V. 437
Simsapavana	Alavi (Unnao dt.)	*A.N.* I. 136
Sitavana	Rajgriha	*S.N.* I. 210-12
Veluvana	Rajgriha, Kampila, Kajangala	*S.N.* I. 52
Velukantaka	Dakshingiri	*A.N.* IV. 64
Vinjhatavi	Vindhya forest	*Dīpavaṃśa* 75-87
Salavana	Kushinara	*D.N.* II. 146
Parileyyakavana	Cheti kingdom	see-B.S. Upaddhyaya p. 145
Ambatakavana	Kasi	*Ibid.*
Pippalivana	Moriya kingdom	*Ibid.*
Saugandhikavana	Gandhamadana mountain	*MBH. Āraṇyakaparva*, ch. 155
Kahdirvana	Himalayas	*Jāt.* No. 210 para 163
Salavana	Himalayas	*Jāt.* No. 210, para 163
Chitraratha vana	North Kuruksetra	*MBH, Udyogaparva 109. 1;* 111.1; 111.10-11
Anjanavana	Near Saket (Ayodhya)	*Jāt.* No. 68 para 309
Dvaitavana	North of Sravasti	*MBH Āraṇyakaparva* III. 453
Kamyakavana	On Marudesa on Saraswati (identified with the region from Kalka to Thaneshwar)	*MBH Āraṇyakaparva* III. 218
Nishadabhumi	Gwalior, Narwar, Guna regions of M.P.	*MBH Āraṇyakaparva* III. 61

Chart 24. Identification of Trees mentioned in Literacy Sources

Name of Forest	*Locations*	*Modern Name of the Plant*
Sala tree	Himalayan region and Kushinara	*Shorea robusta*
Amba or *Amra*	Rajgriha, Kushinara, Kamanda	Mango tree
Anjana tree	Saket	A type of medicinal plant
Amalaki tree	Lumbini, Kapilavastu	*Phyllanthus emblica* vin
Ketaki tree	Kosala	A type of flower
Pippali	Moriya land	Pepper vin
Simsapa tree	Kosambi, Kosala, Alavi	*Dalbagga sissoo*
Sita tree	Rajgriha	Camphor (or *Durva* grass)
Venu or *Velu*	Rajgriha, Dakhinagiri,	Bamboo
Ambataka tree	Kashi	Hogplum or *Spondias mangifera* vin
Khadir	Not mentioned	*Khair Acacia*
Plaksa	Not mentioned	Fig tree
Sara	Not mentioned	Reed
Iksu	Not mentioned	Sugarcane

Chart 25. Floral Remains from Mehrgarh

Period	*Specimens*	*References*
I Aceramic	1. Two-row hulled barley 2.5 % *Hordeum distichum* 2. Six-row barley 91 % *Hordeum vulgare* and *Hordeum vulgare* var. *nudum* 3. Einkorn wheat 4 % *Triticum Monococcum* 4. Emmer *Triticum dicoccum* and bread wheat 0.7 % *Triticum aestivum* 5. Jujube plants *Zizyphus jujuba* 6. Date palm *Phoenix dactylifera*	Constantini 1984: 22-23 Jarrige and Meadow, 1980: 122
II Ceramic Neolithic	1. Wheat 2. Barley 3. Some cottonseed (*Gossypium* sp.)	Jarrige and Meadow: 1980: 128: Constantini, 1984: 30-31
III	In addition to the earlier crop types, new cereals were introduced. 1. Two new types of bread wheat a. *Triticum aestivum compactum* b. *T. aestivum sphaerococcum* 2. A new cereal oats (*avena*)	
IV	In addition to earlier ones, a new cultivar, wine grapes was introduced.	

Chart 26. Earliest Iron Finds

Site	*Region*	*Cultural Phase*	*Appx. Date*	*Iron*
Ahar	Udaipur	Pd. I Chalcolithic	1500-2000 B.C.	Iron slags.
Hallur	Dharvar	Megalithic	1000 B.C.	Arrowheads spearheads
Nagda	Malwa	Post-Chalcolithic	1000 B.C.	Dagger, socket of axe, spoon, knife, sickle
Eran	Malwa	BRW-Pre-NBPW	700-200 B.C.	Iron objects
Jodhpur	Rajasthan	BRW along with NBPW	700-100 B.C.	Iron objects
Mahisadal	W. Bengal	Post-Chalcolithic	750 B.C.	Arrowheads, spearheads, chisel, nails
Pandu Rajar Dhibi	W. Bengal	Post-Chalcolithic		Iron objects
Bahal	Tapti valley	PRW-pre-NBPW	600-300 B.C.	Arrowheads spearheads, knife, dagger, sickle
Besnagar	Vidisa	BRW		Negligible quantity of iron
Chirand	Saran	BRW		Iron objects

Chart 27. Major Iron Bearing PGW Sites

Sites	*Iron Objects*
Ahicchatra	Spears, arrows, points, axes
Alamgirpur	Hoe
Allahpur	Sickle
Atranjikhera	Knives, blades, rods, tongs, sickle
Jakhera	Hoe, ploughshare, sickle
Hastinapur	Nails, pins, iron slags

Chart 28. Storage Capability

Site	*District*	*Period*	*Store Jars*	*Storing Pits*	*Store House*
Ahar	Bulandshahar	Pd. I Chalcolithic	Yes	Yes	No
Ambkheri	Saharanpur	OCW Period	Yes	No	No
Apegaon	Aurangabad	Pd. I (1600-1300 B.C.) Malwa ware + Jorwe ware	Yes	No	No
Bahal	Jalgaon	Pd. I. Chalcolithic	Yes	No	No
Banwali	Hissar	Pd. II (2300-1700 B.C.) Pre Har. and Har. pd.	Yes	No	No
Bara	Rupnagar	Bara ware cultural stage (2000-1600 B.C.)	Yes	No	No
Chandoli	Pune	Malwa and Jorwe cultural site	Yes	Yes	No
Daulatpur	Kurukshetra	Contemporary to Bara ware cultural stage. Pre Harappan and Harappan	Yes	No	No
Dwarka	Jamnagar	Pd. III 7th 8th century B.C.	Yes	No	No
Eran	Sagar	Pd. J. 2100-700 B.C. Chalcolithic RW/BRW-Periods	Yes	No	No
Gilund	Udaipur	Pd. I. middle 2nd mill BC Chalcolithic BRW site	No	Yes	No

Chart 28 (Contd.)

Harappa	Montgomery	Mature Harappan period	No	No	Yes
Hastinapur	Meerut	Pd. III NBPW period. 8th to 6th century B.C.	Yes	No	No
Kakoria	Varanasi	Megalithic grave site, 1st half of the second mill. B.C.-700 B.C.	Yes	No	No
Kayatha	Ujjain	Pd. I. 2000-1800 B.C.	Yes	No	No
Kotla Nihang Khan	Rupnagar	Pd. I. Harappan	Yes	No	No
Lal Qila	Bulandshahr	OCW Period	Yes	No	No
Maheswar-Navdatoli	Nimar	Pd. III. 1500-1200 B.C. Chalcolithic	Yes	No	No
Mehrgarh	Kacchi plains	Pre-Harappan *c* 5000 B.C.	No	No	Yes
Mirzapur	Kurukshetra	Pd. I. Late Harappan	Yes	No	No
Mitathal	Bhiwani	Pd. II. Harappan and Late Siswal tradition	Yes	No	No
Mohenjodaro	Larkana	Mature Harappan period	No	No	Yes
Nevasa	Ahmadnagar	Pd. III Chalcolithic1500-1000 B.C. and Pd. IV. NBPW period	Yes	Yes	No

Chart 28 (Contd.)

Rajgir	Nalanda	2nd-1st B.C.	No	No	Yes
Rakhigarhi	Hissar	Harappan period. Late Harappan period	Yes	No	No
Rangpur	Surendranagar	Pd. II. Harappan	Yes	No	No
Rojdi	Rajkot	Pd. I. Harappan	Yes	No	No
Ropar	Rupnagar (formally Dt. Ambala)	Pd. I. Harappan, Pd. II PGW period	Yes	No	No
Sarnath	Varanasi	NBPW period	Yes	No	No
Sirpa Baram	Varanasi	NBPW period site	No	No	Yes
Sonpur	Gaya	Pd. I. B. Chalcolithic BRW	Yes	No	No

BIBLIOGRAPHY

Agarwal, D. P. and Sood, R. R., 1982. 'Ecological factors and Harappan civilization'. In *Harappan Civilization*, Possehl, G.L. (ed.) Oxford and IBH, Delhi. pp. 223-233.

Agarwal, V. S., 1953. *India as known to Panini*, Lucknow University, Lucknow.

Agashe, R. R. (ed.), 1977; 1979. *Aitareya Brahmana* (Part I and II, 3rd edn.; Part I 3rd edn.), Anandashram, Poona.

Ahmad, K. S. 1963. 'Land use in the semi-arid zone of West Pakistan', *Pakistan Geographical Review*, Vol. XVIII, pp. 1-18.

Aiareya Brahmaṇa, See Agashe, R. R., 1977, 1979; Keith, A. B., 1920.

Ali, S. M., 1966. *History of the Puranas*, PPH, New Delhi.

Allchin, B. and F. Raymond, 1983. *The rise of civilization in India and Pakistan*, Select Book Syndicate, New Delhi.

Allchin, F. R., 1979. 'Early domestic animals in India and Pakistan'. In Allchin, F. R. and Chakrabarti, D. K., (eds.), *A source book of Indian archaeology*, p. 324-327, New Delhi. Munshiram and Manoharlal; 1979. 'Early cultivation plants in India and Pakistan'. In Allchin, F. R., and Chakrabati, D.K., (eds.), *A source book of Indian archaeology*, Vol. I, p. 275, New Delhi. Munshiram and Manoharlal; and Knox, J. R., 1979. 'Preliminary report on the excavation at Tarakai Qila' (1978-79), In M. Taddic (ed.) Naples. *SAA*. pp. 241-250.

Altekar, A. S. and Misra, V., 1959. *Kumrahar Excavation, 1951-55*, K.P. Jayaswal Research Institute (Historical Research Series, Vol. 3), Patna.

Amarakoṣa, Amara Simha, 1941. *Nāma-ling-ānuśāsana or Amarkoṣa*, (tr.) Hargovind Sastri, Banaras. Chowkhmba Sanskrit Series.

Anderson, E., 1960, 'The evolution in domestication'. In Tax, Sol (ed.), *Evolution after Darwin: The Evolution of Man: Man, Culture and Society*, Vol. II: University of Chicago Press, Chicago.

Anguttara Nikāya, 1960. Bhikkhu J. Kashyap (ed.), 4v: Pali Publishing Boards.

Arrian, *see* McCrindle, J.W., 1877 and Majumdar, R.C. 1960.

Arthaśāstra of Kautalya, *see* Kangle, R.P. 1960-63-65; Shamshastry, R. 1967.

Aṣṭadhyāyī of Pāṇinī, 1891-98. Vasu, S. C. (ed. and tr.), 2 vols. Allahabad, Indian Press.

Asthana, Shashi, 1985. *Pre-Harappan Cultures of India and Borderlands*, Delhi.

Atharva Veda, 1905. Whitney, W. D. and Lanman, C. R. (tr) 2 vols. Harvard University, Cambridge, Mass.

Aṭṭhakathā see *Dhammapada Atthakathā*.

Aurora, D. and Mehra, D. S., 1974. *Agricultural Studies in India*. Directorate of Economics and Statistics, Ministry of Agriculture, Government of India, Vol. XXIX, No. 5, Delhi.

Avadanāśataka, 1902. Speyer, J. S., (ed.) Imperial Academy of Sciences, Petrograd.

Āvaśyak Niruktī, Curnī. Jinadasagani (ed.). Ratlam, 1928.

Banerji, N. R., 1965. *The Iron Age in India*. Munshiram, Manoharlal, Delhi.

Basu, J., 1969. *India of the Age of the Brahmanas*. Sanskrit Pustak Bhandar, Calcutta.

Beal, S., 1883. (tr.) *Si-Yu-Ki. Buddhist Records of the Western World*. 2 vols. Trubner and Co. Ludgate Hill. London.

Bhagavata Purāṇa, 1840-98. Burnouf, E. and others (tr.) 5 vols. Paris. Imprimeric Royal.

Bhan, Suraj, 1972. Changes in the course of Yamuna and their bearing on the proto-historic cultures of Haryana. *Archaeological Congress and Seminar Papers*. Deo, S. B., (ed.), pp. 125-28, Nagpur.

Bhan, Suraj, 1976. Early settlements in Haryana: A study in the urbanization. *JIH*. Vol. 8, No. 1.

Bhan, Suraj, 1977. Settlement patterns of proto-historic cultures of Haryana. Seminar Papers—*Indus Civilization: Problems and Issues*. Simla.

Bhan, Suraj and Shaffer, J. G. 1978. New discoveries in northern Haryana. *Man and Environment*. Vol. 2 pp. 59-68.

Bhandarkar, D. R., 1914-15. (Reprint 1990) *Excavations at Besnagar*. Archaeological Survey of India. Annual Report, Swati Publications, Delhi.

Bhargava, P. L., 1956. *India in the Vedic Age*, Lucknow, Upper India Publishing Co.

Bhargava, M. L., 1965. *Geography of Rig Vedic India (a physical geography of Sapta Saindhava)*, Lucknow. Upper India Publishing Co.

Bhatia, B. M., 1967. *Famines in India (1860-1965)*, 2nd edn., Asia Publishing House, Delhi.

Bhattacharya, N. N., 1975. *Ancient Indian Rituals and their Social Context*, Manohar Book Service, Delhi.

Bholanath, 1963. Animal remains from Rangpur. *Ancient India*. Vols. 18-19, pp. 153-160.

Bholanath, 1979. Animal remains from Harappa. In *A Source Book of Indian Archaeology*. Allchin, F. R. and Chakravarty, D. K. (eds.) Vol. I, pp. 319-24, Munshiram Manoharlal, Delhi.

Bholanath, 1985. Animal remains from Lothal excavations. *Lothal : A Harappan port town*. Rao, S. R. *Memoirs of Archeological Survey of India*, No. 78, Vol. II, pp. 636-50.

Biscione, R., Salvatoris, S., Tosi, M., 1977. Shahr-i-Sokhta, L'abitate prehistorico e la sequenza cronologica. *La Citta Bruciata del Deserte Salate*, Venice, pp. 77-112.

Bisht, R. S., 1976. *Banawali*. Booklet published by Department of Archaeology, Haryana.

Bisht, R.S. 1978. Banawali: A new Harappan site in Haryana. *Man and Environment*. No. 2, pp. 86-88.

Bloomfield, M. 1908. *The Religion of the Veda*. Indological Book House, Delhi.

Boserup, E., 1965. *The Condition of Agricultural Growth: The Economics of Agrarian Change under Population Pressure*. Allen, London.

Brahamāṇḍa Purāṇa, 1983. Shastri, J. L. (ed.), Motilal Banarasidas, Delhi.

Braidwood, R. J., 1960 (ed.). Levels in pre-history: A model for consideration of the evidence. In Tax, Sol. (ed.), *Evolution after Darwin: The evolution of man: man, culture and society*. University of Chicago Press, Chicago.

Datta, Breham, 1980. *Settlement of PGW in Haryana*. Unpublished Ph.D. Thesis, Kurukshetra University, Kurukshetra.

Brhad-āraṇyaka Upanīṣad, 1950. Gita Press, Gorakhpur. 1972; 1933. Vasu, S.C., (ed. and tr.) Allahabad.

Brhaspati Smṛti, 1941. Aiyangar, K. V. R. (ed.) *GOS*, Vol. LXXXV, Baroda; 1889. Jolly, J. (tr.) *SEB*. Vol. XXXIII Oxford.

Brhatkalpa Bhāṣya. 1933-38. Sanghadasagani Ksamasarmana (com.) Malayagiri and Ksemakirti, Atmananda Jain Sabha, Bhavnagar.

Brhatkalpa Sūtraṃ, 1905. Schubring, W. S. (ed.) Leipzig.

Brhatkathā Koṣa of Harisena, 1943. Upadhye, A. N. (ed.), Bhartiya Vidya Bhavan, Bombay.

Brhat Saṃhitā of Varāhamihira, 1947. Sastri, V. S. and Bhat, R., 2 Vols., Bangalore. (Reprint) Delhi. 1981 Motilal Banarasidas.

Buddhacarita of Aśvaghoṣa, 1977. Cowell, E. B. and Neil, A. (First Published as SBE & Vol. 49) Cambridge, 1894, (Reprint). Cosmo.

Bühler, G. 1967. (tr.). *The Laws of Manu*, Delhi, Motilal, Banarasidas, *(SBE*. Vol. XXV), (Ist Pubs. 1886).

Bühler, G. 1969 (tr.). *The Sacred Laws of the Aryas*, 2 Vols. Delhi: Motilal Banarasidas. *(SBE*. 2.14), (Ist Pubs. 1879-82; Apastamba Gautam, Vasistha, Bundhayana Dharmasutras in trans.).

Burgess, J., 1971. *Report on the Antiquities of Kathiawar and Kaccha*, (Archaeological Survey of Western India 1874-75), (Reprint) Indological Book House, Varanasi.

Caloi, L. and Compagnoni, B., 1979. Preliminary remarks on the bovine remains at the archaeological site of Shahr-i-Sokhta (Iranian Seistan) 3200-1800 B.C. In H. Hartel (ed.) 1981. Ber lin. *SAA*., pp. 181-190.

Carney, T. F., 1973. *The Economics of Antiquity*, Lawrence, Kansas.

Casal, J. M., 1961. *Fouilles de Mundigak*, (Memories de la Delegation Archaeologique Francaise en Afghanistan, Vol. XVII), Paris; 1964, *Fouilles D'Amri*, Vols. I and II, (Publication de la Commission des Fouilles Archaeologiques, Fouilles du Pakistan), Paris; L. braric C. Klincksieck; 1973. Excavation at Pirak, West Pakistan, *SAA*, pp. 171-79.

Chakrabarti, D. K., 1976. The beginning of iron in India, *Antiquity*, Vol. L, pp. 114-24; 1979a. Size of the Harappan settlement. *Essays in Indian Proto-History*, Chakrabarti, D. K. and Agarwal, D. P. (eds.) pp. 205-15, D.R. Publishing Co., Delhi; 1979b. Domestication of plants and animals. *A Source Book of Indian Archaeology*, Allchin, F. R. Chakrabarti D.K. (ed.) pp. 271-352. New Delhi; Munshiram Monoharlal 1980. Early agriculture and development of towns in India. *Cambridge Encyclopaedia of Archaeology*. Sharratt, A. (ed.) pp. 162-67, Cambridge. Cambridge University Press.

Chakravarti, U., 1987. *The Social Dimensions of Early Buddhism*, Oxford University Press, Delhi.

Chakrawarti, H. P., 1986. *Socio-Economic Life of India in the Vedic Period*, Sanskrit Pustak Bhandar, Calcutta.

Chamber's Encyclopaedia, 15 Vols., London, 1961.

Chang, T. T., The rice culture in the early history of agriculture. *Phil. Trans. R. Soc. London*, Ser. B., Vol. 275: pp. 143-55.

Chhāndogya Upaniṣad, 1983. Swami, Gambhirananda (ed. and tr.), Advaita Asram, Calcutta.

Childe, V. G., 1953. Old world pre-history: Neolithic. *Anthropology Today.*

Childe, V.G., 1956. *Piecing Together the Past*, the Interpretation of Archaeological Data. London: Routledge and Paul.

Childe, V.G., 1979. The urban revolution. *Ancient Cities of the Indus*, G. L. Possehl, Durham: Carolina Academic Press, pp. 12-17.

Chitalwala, Y. M., 1979. Harappan and post-Harappan settlement pattern in Rajkot district of Saurashtra. In *Essays in Indian Protohistory*. Agarwal, D. P. and Chakrabarti, D. K. (ed.), pp. 113-121, B.R. Publishing Corporation, Delhi.

Chowdhury, K. A., Saraswat, K. S. and Ruth, G. M., 1977-78. *Ancient Agriculture and Forestry in North India*, Asia Publishing House, Bombay.

Cleuzion, S. and Constantini, L., 1979. *An Early Evidence of Sorghum from Proto Historic South East Arabia*, Paris.

Compagnoni, B., 1977. Preliminary report on the faunal remains from protohistoric settlements of Swat. *SAA*, 1979, Vol. 2, pp. 697-702. Taddei, M. (ed.), Naples.

Constantini, L., 1977a. Wood remains from Shahr-i-Sokhta—A source of information for the ancient environment and technology of proto-historic Seistan. In M. Taddei (ed.) 1979 *SAA*., pp. 87-121;

1979a. Paleo-ethnobotany at Pirak: a contribution to 2nd millennium B.C. agriculture of the Sibi-Kachi plain, Pakistan. In H. Hartel (ed.) 1981. *SAA*, pp. 271-78; 1979, b. The table of identified plant species from Shahr-i-Sokhta as compiled by Constantini, L., for the article of C. Jarrige and M. Tosi, *The natural resources of Mundigak*. In H. Hartel (ed.) 1981. *SAA*, pp. 115-142; 1979c. Plant remains at Pirak. *Foullies de Pirak*, Jarrige. J. F., Enault, J. F. and Santoni, (ed.) pp. 326-333; Paris, Diffusion de Boccasd; 1984. The beginning of agriculture in the Kacchi plains: The evidence of Mehrgarh. In B. Allchin (ed.) *SAA*. 1981, Cambridge. Cambridge Press, pp. 20-23.

Constantini, L., 1977. Notes on Palacoethnobotany of Protohistorical Swat. *SAA*. pp. 703-708.

Constantini, L., and Biasini, L. C., 1985. Agriculture in Baluchistan between the seventh and third millennium B.C. *Baluchistan Studies*, Vol. I, p. 160, plates 1-7.

Constantini, L. and Biasini, L.C., 1986. Catalogue of the material from the excavations carried by the Italian archaeological mission of ISMEO in Pakistan: Laboratory of bio-archaeology. *East and West*, Vol. 36, No. 4, pp. 354.

McGindle J. W. 1877. *Ancient India as Described by Megasthenes and Arrian, Calcutta*, (reprint) 1960, Calcutta. Chuckervertty, Chartterjee and Co. Ltd.; 1885. *Ancient India as described by Ptolemy being a Translation of the Geography*. Calcutta; R.C. Jain, New Delhi Today and Tomarrow's; 1893. *Invasion of India by Alexander the Great as described by Arrian, Q. Curtius, Diodorus, Plutarch and Justin*. Westminister: Archibald Constable and Co.; 1901. *Ancient India as Described in Classical Literature*, Westminister: Archibald Constable and Co.

Cullavagga, 1956. Kashyap J. Bhikkhu (ed.), Bihar Pali Publication Board.

Cunningham, A. 1963. *The Ancient Geography of India*, Calcutta: Majumdar Sastri, S. N. 1924. (Reprint) Indological Book House, Varanasi.

Curtius, *see* McCrindle, 1893.

Dales, G. F., 1973. Recent pre- and proto-historic research in Pakistan and Afghanistan. *Radiocarbon and Indian Archaeology*, pp. 118-130; Tata Institute of Fundamental Research, Bombay.

Dales, G.F., 1974. Excavation at Balakot, Pakistan. *Journal of Field Archaeology*, Vol. I. (1-2).

Dales, G.F., 1977. The Balakot project: Summary of four years' excavation in Pakistan. *SAA*. pp. 241-73.

Dani, A. H., 1970. Excavation in the Gomal valley. *Ancient Pakistan*, Vol. 5, (Special number) pp. 1-177.

Daśakumāracharita of Daṇḍin, Ryder, A.W. (tr.) Chicago. University of Chicago, 1960.

Dayal, P., 1947. *The Agricultural Geography of Bihar*. Ph.D. thesis, London University, London.

De Cardi, B., 1965. Excavations and reconnaisance in Kalat, West Pakistan. *Pakistan Archaeology*, Vol. 2, pp. 86-182.

Deva, K. and McCown, D. E., 1949. Further explorations in Sindh, 1938. *Ancient India*, Vol. 5, pp. 12-30.

Deva, Krishna, 1969. Problems of Ochre Colour Pottery, *Potteries in Ancient India*. Sinha, B. P. (ed.) pp. 75-82, Patna University.

Dhammapada, MaxMuller, F. (tr.) Motilal, 1968, Oxford, 1881.

Dhammapada Aṭṭhakathā, 1969. Burlingame, E. W., (tr.) *Buddhist Legends*: from the original Pali text of the Dhammapada Commentary, 3 Vols.

Dhavlikar, M. K. Sankalia, H. D. and Ansari, Z. D., 1988. *Excavations at Inamgaon*, Deccan College, Pune.

Digby, W., 1901, *Prosperous British India*, London. Fisher Unwin.

Dīgha Nikāya, Rhys Davids, T. W. and Carpenter, J. E., (tr.), 1899, 1900, 1921. *Dialogue of the Buddha*, 3 Vols. *SBE*, London.

Dikshit, K. N., 1968. The copper hoards in the light of recent discoveries. *Bulletin of Ancient Indian History and Archaeology*, Sagar, Vol. II, pp. 43-50; 1977, Distribution and relationship of proto-historic sites along old river channels of the Ghaggar system. *Ecology and Archaeology in Western India*, Agarwal, D. P. and Pandey, B. M. (eds.), pp. 61-66, Concept Publishing Company, Delhi; 1979a. The late Harappan cultures in India, *Essays in Proto History*, Agarwal, D.P. and Chakrabarti, D.K. (eds.), pp. 123-133. B.R. Publishing Corporation, Delhi; 1979b. Hulas and the late Harappan complex in western *U.P. Papers on Harappan Civilization, Srinagar Seminar*, pp. 213, Srinagar; 1981. The excavations at Hulas and further exploration of the upper Ganga-Yamuna *doab*. *Man and Environment*, Vol. 5, pp. 70-75.

Dikshit, K.N., 1984. Late Harappan period in northern India. *Frontiers of the Indus Civilization*, Lal, B. B. and Gupta, S. P. (eds.), (Wheeler Commemorative Volume), N. Delhi, pp. 253-270. Books and Books.

Diodorus, *see* McCrindle, 1893.

Dīpavaṃśa, Oldenberg, H. (ed), New Delhi. Asian Education Services, 1982.

Divyāvadāna, 1886. Cowell, E. B. and Neil, R. A. (eds.), Cambridge University Press, Cambridge.

Dow, A., 1973. *A History of Hindustan*, 3 vols., 2nd, edn. 1770, (Reprint), Today and Tomorrow Printers London.

Durrani, F. A., 1977. Excavations at Rahman Dheri, Paper read at Fourth International Conference of the South Asian Archaeology, Naples (cyclostyled copy);

Durrani, F.A., 1981. Indus civilization: Evidence west of Indus. *Indus Civilization—New Perspective*. Dani, A. H. (ed.), pp. 133-37, Islamabad. Quaid-i-Azam University.

Elliot, H. M. and Dowson, S., *History of India as told by its own Historians: The Muhammadan Period*, 8 vols. London 1867-77 (dates of the referred vols.). Vol. II, London, 1869, Allahabad 1952; Vol. III, London, 1871, Allahabad, not dated; Vol. VI, London 1875, Allahabad, 1964; Vol. VII, London, not dated, Allahabad, 1964. Kitab Mahal.

Encyclopaedia of Social Sciences, 1957. Seligman, E. R. A. (ed.) 15 Vols., 12th ed. New York.

Fairservis, W. A., 1956. Excavations at the Quetta Valley in Pakistan. *Anthropological Papers of the American Museum of Natural History*, Vol. 45, pp. 169-402.

Fairservis, W. A., 1959. Archaeological surveys in the Zhob and Lorlai districts in west Pakistan. *Anthropological papers of the American Museum of Natural History*, Vol. 47, pp. 273-448.

Fairservis, W.A., 1967. The origin, character and decline of an early civilization. New York : American Museum of Natural History. *Novitates*, No. 2302, pp. 1-48.

Fairservis, W.A., 1971. *The Roots of Ancient India*, New York: Macmillan.

——— 1975, 2nd (ed.), Chicago. University of Chicago Press.

Famine Commission Report, 1880, Strachey, R., 3 Pts., H.M.S.O., London.

Fentress, M. A., 1976. Resource access, exchange systems and regional intercourses in the Indus valley: an investigation of archaeological viability at Harappa and Mohenjodaro. Ph.D. Dissertation, University of Pennsylvania.

Fentress, M.A., 1982. From Jhelum to Yamuna: city and settlements in the 2nd and 3rd millennium, B.C., *Harappan Civilization—A Contemporary Perspective*, Possehl, G. L. (ed.) pp. 245-260; Oxford, IBH, New Delhi.

Fentress, M.A., 1984. The Indus granaries: Illusion, imagination and archaeological reconstruction,

Studies in the Archaeology and Paleonthropology of South Asia. Kennedy, K. A. R., and Possehl, G. L. (eds.), pp. 89-98, New Delhi.

Flam, L., 1981. The palaeography and prehistoric settlement pattern in Sind, Pakistan (c. 4000-2000 B.C.). Ph.d. dissertation. University of Pennsylvania, Philadelphya.

Flam, L., 1984. The palaeogeography and prehistoric settlement pattern of the lower Indus valley, Sind, Pakistan. *Studies in the Archaeology and Palaeoanthropology of South Asia.* Kennedy, K. A. R., and Possehl, G.L. (eds.), pp. 77-82, New Delhi. Oxford and IBH.

Flam, L., 1986. Recent explorations in Sind: Palaeogeography, regional ecology and prehistoric settlement pattern: (c. 4000-2000 B.C.). *Studies in the Archaeology of India and Pakistan,* (ed.) Jacobson, J., pp. 65-90. New Delhi.

Fleet, J. F., 1916. *Inscriptions of the Early Gupta Kings and their Successors,* Indological Book House, Varanasi, 1963.

Forbes, R. J., 1955. *Studies in Ancient Technology, Vol. II, Irrigation and Drainage,* Leiden. Brill.

Foster, W., 1906-27. *English Factories in India:* A calendar of documents in the India Office, British Museum, Oxford.

Gadre, A. S., 1943. *Important Inscriptions from Baroda State,* Pratap Simha Maharaj Rajyabhisheka Granthamala, Memoir No. II, Baroda.

Gambhirananda, Swami (ed. and tr.) 1983. *Chāndogya Upanīṣad,* Advaita Asram, Calcutta.

Gaur, R. C. and Nurul Hasan, S., 1967. Excavation at Atranjikhera. A cyclostyled preliminary report, informally circulated, Aligarh.

Gaur, R. C., 1982. Authors of OCP, *Indian Archaeology : New Perspective,* Sharma, R. K., (ed.) pp. 131-135, Agam Kala Prakashan, Delhi.

Gaur, R. C., 1983. *Excavations at Atranjikhera*, Delhi: Motilal Banarasidas.

Geddes, A., 1960. The alluvial morphology of the Indo-Gangetic plain, *Transactions and Papers, Institute of British Geographers*, London, p. 262.

Ghosh, A., 1952. The Rajputana desert: its archaeological aspects. *Proceedings of the Symposium on the Rajputana Desert*, Bulletin of the National Institute of Sciences of India, Vol. I, pp. 37-42, Calcutta.

Ghosh, A., 1953. Explorations in Bikaner. *East and West*, Vol. 4(1) pp. 31-34.

Ghosh, A., 1989, *Encyclopaedia of India Archaeology*, Munshiram Manoharlal. New Delhi.

Ghosh, R.N., 1977. Photogeological studies on ancient water regimes of Rajasthan rivers. *Ecology and Archaeology of Western India*, Agarwal, D. P. and Pande, B. M. (eds), pp. 157-166, Delhi: Concept Publishing Company.

Ghosh, S.S., 1961. Further records of rice from ancient India. *Indian Forester*, Vol. 87, No. 5, pp. 295-301.

Ghosh, S.S. and Krishna Lal, 1963. Plant remains from Rangpur. *Ancient India*, No. 18-19, pp. 161-171.

Ghurye, G. S., 1979. *Vedic India*. Popular Prakashan, Bombay.

Gluckman, Max., 1965. *Politics, Law and Rituals in Tribal Society*, Oxford. Basil Black will.

Goudie, A. S., Allchin, B. and Hegde, K. T. M., 1973. The former extension of the Great Indian Desert. *Geographical Journal*, pp. 243-57.

Grhya Sutras, Oldenberg, H.,(tr.) Pt. 1, 1886; Pt. 2, 1982, (Reprint) 1964, Motilal Banarasidas, New Delhi.

Gupta, S. P., Asthana, Shashi and Amarendra Nath, 1977. PGW sites in relation to old river beds in Rajasthan. *Ecology and Archaeology of Western India*, Agarwal, D. P. and Pande (eds.) pp. 79-92, Delhi. Concept Publishers.

Hargreaves, H., 1929. Excavations at Baluchistan in 1925. *Memoirs of Archaeological Survey of India*, No. 35. Calcutta.

Harivaṃśa Purāṇa, Jinasena Suri, 1930. Manikchand Digambara Jain Granthamala, Bombay.

Hegde, K.T.M., Bhan, K.K. and Sonawane, 1984, Excavations at Nageswar. *Journal of the M. S. University*, Baroda, Vols. 33-34(1), 1985, pp. 1-9.

Herre, W. and Rohrs, M., 1976. The evolution of domestic animals. *Encylopaedia of Evolution*, Grzimek, B. (ed.), New York. Van Nostrand Reinhold Co.

Huen-tsang, *see* Watters, T., 1904-5 and Beal, S., 1883.

Hume, R. A., (tr.) 1921. *Thirteen Principal Upanisads*, London. Oxford University Press.

Imperial Gazetteer of India, Vol. XXIII. Singhbhum to Trashi-chod-zong. Published His Majesty's Secretary of State for India in Council. Oxford. 1908. Clasendon Press.

Jacobi, H., 1964. *Jain Sutras*, (tr.) Pt. I., *The Acaranga Sutra, The Kalpa Sutra*, Pt. II., *The Uttaradhyayana Sutra*, Motilal Banarasidasa, Delhi. (*SBE 22.45*) (Rpt. 1884-95 ed.).

Jaiminīya Brāhmaṇa, see Macdonald, K.S. 1979.

Jain, J.C. 1947. *Life in Ancient India as Depicted in the Jain Canons and Commentaries*, Bombay. 2nd edn. 1989, Munshiram Manoharlal, Delhi.

Jansen, M., 1979. Settlement pattern in the Harappan culture. *SAA*. pp. 251-259.

Jarrige, J.F., 1979. Economy and society in early Chalcolithic/Bronze Age of Baluchistan: New perspectives from recent excavations at Mehrgarh. *SAA*, pp. 93-114.

Jarrige, J.F., 1980. The antecedents of civilization in the Indus valley. *Scientific American*, Vol. 243: 2, pp. 122-33.

Jarrige, J. F., and Meadow, R.H., 1980. The antecedents of civilization in the Indus Valley. *Scientific American* Vol. 243: 2. pp. 122-133.

Jarriage, J.F., 1982. Excavations at Mehrgarh: Their significance for understanding the background of the Harappan civilization. In *Harappan Civilization a contemporary perspective*, Possehl, G. L. (ed.), New Delhi. Oxford. IBH. pp. 79-85.

Jarrige, J.F., 1983a. Nindowari, a 3rd millennium site in South Baluchistan. *Newsletters of Baluchistan Studies, Vol.* I. pp. 47-50. Seminario de Studi Asiatici, Instituto Universitatio Orientale, Naples.

Jarrige, J.F., 1983b. Continuity and change in the north Kachi plain (Baluchistan, Pakistan) at the beginning of the second millennium B.C. *SAA*, pp. 37-68.

Jarrige, J.F., 1986. Excavations at Mehrgarh, Nausharo. *Pakistan Archaeology*, Vol. X. 22, pp. 63-123.

Jarrige, J. F. and Tosi, M., 1979. The natural resources of Mundigak. *SAA*, pp. 115-42.

Jatakas, Cowell, E. B. and others (tr.) 1895-1907. 7 Vols., London: Luzac 1969.

————, Fausball, V. (ed.), Rhys, Davids, T. W., 1880 (tr.). Trubner and Co, London.

Jayaswal, K. P., 1943. *Hindu Polity*, Bangalore. Bangalore Printing and Publishing Co.

Jolly, J., 1880. *The Institute of Viṣṇū, SBE*, Vol. VII, Oxford.

Joshi, J. P., 1972a. Exploration in Kutch and excavation at Surkotada and new light on Harappan migration. *Journal of the Oriental Institute*, M.S. University, Baroda, Vol. XXII (1-2), pp. 98-144.

Joshi, J. P., 1972b. Fresh light on the archaeology of Kutch. In *Proceedings of the Faith Indian. Archaeological Congress and Seminar Papers*, Deo, S.B. (ed.), pp. 21-35, Nagpur University, Nagpur.

Joshi, J. P., 1978. Interlocking of late Harappan culture in PGW culture in the light of recent excavations. *Man and Environment*, Vol. 2, pp. 98-101.

Joshi, J. P., 1979. The nature of settlement at Surkotada. *Essays in Proto-History*, Agarwal, D. P. and

Chakrabarti, D. K. (eds.), pp. 59-64, Delhi. B.R. Publishing Co.

Joshi, J. P., and Madhubala, 1982. Manda: A Harappan site in Jammu and Kashmir. *Harappan Civilization A New Perspective, Possehl,* G. L. (ed.), New Delhi, Oxford and IBH pp. 185-197.

Kādambarī, of Bana, Kale, M.R., 1924. (tr.). Bombay. V. Yashvant.

Kalpasūtra and Navajatva, (tr). J. Stevenson : Varanasi Bharat Bharati 1972 (Ist Pub. 1848).

Kane, P. V., 1930-58. *History of Dharma Sastras, Ancient and Medieval, Religious and Civil Laws,* 6 Vols, Pune. BORI.

Kangle, R. P. (ed. & tr.) *Arthaśāstra of Kautalya,* 3 Vols. Pt. 1 text, 1960; Pt. 2, translation, 1963; Pt. 3, critical study, 1965. Bombay: 4 of Bombay.

Kathāsaritsāgar of Somadeva, 1925-28. *The Ocean of Story,* Tawney, C. H. (tr.), Penzer, N. (ed.), 10 Vols. London. Delhi : Motilal Banarasidas, 1968.

Katha Saṃhitā, (ed.) S.D. Satvalekar Aundhanagar Svadhyaya, Mundala, 1943.

Kātyāyana Śrauta Sūtra, (ed.), 1904. Nityananda. Benaras Chaukhamba, 1928, 39.

Kausitakī Brāhmaṇa, (tr.) Keith, A. B., 1920. *Rig Veda Brahmanas,* Cambrige Harvard University Press.

Keith, A. B., 1920. *Rig Veda Brāhmaṇas,* Mass. Harvard University Press, Cambridge.

Khan, F. A., 1959. *Preliminary report on Kot Diji Excavation 1957-58,* Department of Archaeology, Pakistan.

Konow, Sten, 1929. *Kharosti Inscriptions with the exception of those of Asoka,* C.I.I., Vol. II, Calcutta.

Krishna, A., 1970. Some aspects of water management for crop production in arid and semi-arid zones of India. *Annals of Arid Zone,* No. 8, pp. 1-17, Jodhpur.

Lal, B. B., 1954-55. Excavation at Hastinapur and other explorations in the upper Ganga and Sutlej basin—1950-52. *Ancient India,* Nos. X-XI, pp. 5-151.

Lal, B. B., 1955. Excavations at Hastinapur. *Ancient India,* Vols. X, XI, pp. 31-32.

Lal, B. B. and Thapar, B. K., 1967, Excavation at Kalibangan—new lights on the Indus civilization. *Cultural Forum,* Vol. 9, No. 4, pp. 78-88.

Lal, B.B., 1968. A deluge? Which deluge? Yet another facet of the problem of the Copper Hoard Culture. *American Anthropologist,* Vol. LXX, pp. 857-63.

Lal, B.B., 1969. The ochre colour pottery. *Potteries in Ancient India,* Sinha, B. P. (ed.), pp. 83-94, Patna Unversity.

Lal, B.B., 1971-72. OCP—a geochronological study, *Puratattva,* Vol. 5, p. 49.

Lal, B.B., 1979. Kalibangan and Indus civilizations. In *Essays in Indian Proto-History.* Agarwal, D. P. and Chakrabarti, D. K. (eds.), pp. 65-97, Delhi: B.R. Publishing Corp.

Lal, Makhan, 1978. The settlement pattern of PGW culture in the Ganga valley. Paper presented at the symposium on the 'Recent Advances in Indo-Pacific Prehistory', Pune.

Lal, Makhan, 1981. Settlement history of the Ganga valley from 1500 B.C. to 150 A.D. Paper presented in VIII Indian Society of Prehistory.

Lal, Makhan, 1984. Summary of four seasons of explorations in Kanpur district, U.P. *Man and Environment,* Vol. VIII, pp. 61-88.

Lal, Makhan, 1984. *Settlement History and Rise of Civilization in Ganga Yamuna Doab,* B.R. Publishing Corporation, Delhi.

Lal, Makhan, 1986. Chronology of the proto-historic and historic cultures of the upper Ganga plains. *East and West,* Vol. 36, Nos. 1-3, pp. 83-100.

Lamb, H. H., Lewis, R. P. W., Woodroff, A., 1966. World climate from 8000 B.C. to 0 B.C. *Proceedings of the International Meterological Symposium.* The Royal Meterological Services, Oxford.

Lambrick, H. T., 1964. *Sindh—a General Introduction,* (History of Sindh Series, Vol. I), Hyderabad. Paksitan: Sindhi Abadi Board.

Lambrick, H. T., 1967. The Indus flood plain and the Indus civilization. *The Geographical Journal,* Vol. 133 (4), pp. 483-495.

Lambrick, H.T., 1967. The Indus flood, *Antiquity,* Vol. 41, pp. 313-32.

Laṭyayana Śrauta Sūtras, Vedantavagisa, A.C. (ed.), 1872. (Reprint), 1982, Munshiram Manoharlal, Delhi.

Law, B. C. 1941. *India as Described in Early Texts of Buddhism and Jainism,* Luzac, London.

Lechavallier, M., Quivron, G., 1979. The neolithic in Baluchistan: New evidence from Mehrgarh. In M. Taddi, (ed.), Naples. *SAA,* pp. 71-72.

Leshnik, L. S., 1973. Land use and ecological factors in prehistoric N.W. India. *SAA,* pp. 67-84.

Loveday, A., 1914. *History and Economics of Indian Famines. Appx. A.,* London. G. Bellanl Sons Ltd.

Luder, H., 1961. *Mathura Inscriptions,* Gottingen. Vandenhoeck and Ruprecht.

Macdonald, A. A., Keith, A. B., 1958. *Vedic Index of Names and Subjects,* 2 Vols. (1912), (Reprint) Motilal Banarasidas, New Delhi.

Macdonald, K. S., 1979. *The Brāhmaṇas of the Vedas,* Bharatiya Book Corporation, Delhi.

Mackay, E. J. H., 1935. *Early Indus Civilization,* London; Clay and Sons Ltd.

Mackay, E. J. H., 1943. *Chanhudaro Excavations 1935-36.* American Oriental Society, Vol. XX, New Haven: American Oriental Society.

Mahābhārata, (tr.), Dutt, M. N., 1988. Vols. 7, (Reprint), Parimal Publication, Delhi.

Mahābhāṣya of Patanjali, *see Vyākaraṇa Mahābhāṣya.*

Mahāparinibbāna Suttanta, 1965. Rhys Davids, T. W. (tr.), *Buddhist Suttas* translations from Pali, *SBE,* vol.

XI, Oxford, 1881, (reprint), Motilal Banarasidas, Delhi.

Mahāvagga, 1956. Bhikku J. Kashyap, (ed.) Nalanda Devanagari Pali Series. Bihar Government, Patna.

Mahavaṃśa, 1912. Geiger. W., (tr.) Pali Text Society, London.

Mahāvastu, (tr.) J.J. Jones. London: Luzac and Co. 1949-52.

Mahāvastu Avādana 1963. Basak, R. G. (ed. Bengali tr.) Calcutta, Sanskrit College.

Maity, S. K., 1957. *Economic Life of Northern India in the Gupta period*, Calcutta. (rev. 2nd ed. Delhi. Motilal, 1970).

Majjhima Nikāya, Lord Chalmers, (tr.). *Further Dialogues of the Buddha*, Vols. 2, *SBB.*, London, 1926-27.

Majjhima Nikāya, Rahul Sankrityayana and Bapat, P. V., (ed. tr.) Vols. 3, Nalanda Devanagari Pali Series, Bihar Government, 1958.

Majjhima Nikāya, Horner, I. B., (tr.) *The Middle Length Sayings*, Vols. 3, *PTS*, London, 1976.

Mahaparinibbāna Sutta Arhat Tathagater Antim Avadana (Bengali tr.) Dharmaratna Mahasthavir, Chittagong, 1941.

Maitrayanī Saṃhitā, 1923. Leopold von Schrodor, (ed.) F. A. Brock haus, O. Harrassowitz: Leipzig.

Majumdar, G. P., 1935. *Translation of Ūpavanavinoda.* Indian Research Institute, Calcutta.

Majumdar, N. G., 1934. *Explorations in Sind.* Memories of Archaeological Survey of India, No. 48, Delhi. Govt. of India.

Majumdar, R. C., 1960. (ed.) *The Classical Accounts of India.* Calcutta. K. L. Mukhopadhyaya.

Mālavikāgnimitram of Kālidasa, Text with Hindi translation, Mishra, R., CSS, Varanasi.

Mankal, D. R., 1951. *Puranic Chronology* Ciangajuli Prakashan, Anand.

Manusmriti, 1964. Buhler, G. (tr.) Laws of Manu, *SBE*, Vol. 25, (Reprint), Motilal Banarasidas, Delhi.

Manusmriti, with *Manubhāṣya* of Medatithi, 1932. M. Ganganath Jha, (ed.) Vols. 3, Asiatic Society of Bengal, Calcutta.

Marshall, J., 1931. *Mohenjodaro and the Indus Civilization*, Vols. 3, London, Arthur Probsthain.

Mate, M. S., 1969-70. Early historical fortification in the Ganga Valley. *Puratattva*, No. 3, p. 58.

Matsya Purāṇa, Akhtar, J.D. (ed.). Delhi: Oriental Pub., 1972 (Sacred Books of the Aryans., 1).

Meadow, R. H. 1977. Prehistoric subsistence at Balakot-initial consideration of the faunal remains. M. Tadei, (ed.). 1979. *SAA*, Naples, pp. 275-316.

Meadow, R. H., 1979. A preliminary note on the faunal remains from Pirak. *Fouilles de Pirak*, Jarrige, J.F., Enault, J. F., Santani, M., (eds.), Paris, pp. 334.

Meadow, R.H., 1981a. Early animal domestication in South Asia. A first report on the faunal remains from Mehrgarh. (ed.) Hartel, H., *SAA*, Berlin, pp. 143-180.

Meadow, R.H., 1981. Faunal exploration pattern in eastern Iran and Baluchistan: A review of recent investigations. *G. Tucci Commemorative Volume, ISMEO*, Rome.

Meadow, R.H., 1986. Faunal exploration in the Greater Indus valley. A review of recent works up to 1980. *Studies in the Archaeology of India and Pakistan*. Jacobson, J., (ed.) American Institute of Indian Studies, New Delhi, pp. 43-61.

Meadow, R.H., 1981. Notes on the faunal remains from Mehrgarh, with a focus on cattle *(Bos)*, *SAA*, Allchin, B., (ed.) Cambridge, pp. 34-40.

Meadow, R.H., 1985. A note on the distribution of faunal remains during the later periods at Mehrgarh, Baluchistan, Pakistan. *SAA*, pp. 167-176.

Megasthenes, *see* McCriadle J. W., 1877.

Mehta, Ratilal, 1939, *Pre-Buddhist India*, Examiner Press, Bombay.

Mehta, R.N., 1982. Some rural Harappan settlements in Gujarat. *Harappan Civilization : A Contemporary Persepective*. Possehl, G. L., (ed.) pp. 167-75. New Delhi. Oxford and IBH.

Mehta, R. N., Chaudhary, S. N., 1975. *Excavation at Dhatwa*, Baroda. M. S. University of Baroda.

Mehta, R. N., Chaudhary, S. N., *et al.*, 1971. *Excavation at Jokha, 1966-67*. Baroda. M. S. University of Baroda.

Mehta, R. N., Momin, K.N., *et al.*, 1980. *Excavation of Kanewal*, Baroda. M.S. University of Baroda.

Mehta, R. N., Shah, D. R., 1968. *Excavation at Nagara*. Baroda. M. S. University of Baroda.

Milindapañho, 1980. Rhys Davids, T. W., (tr.) *The Questions of King Milinda. SBE.*, Vol. 35, Clarendon Press, Oxford. Delhi: Motilal 1965.

Misra, G. S. P., 1972. *The Age of the Vinayas*, New Delhi. Munshiram Manoharlal.

Misra, V. N., 1967. *Pre- and Proto-history of the Berach Basin, South Rajasthan*, Poona. Deccan College Poona.

Misra, V. N., 1984. Climate : A factor in the rise and fall of the Indus civilization, Evidence from Rajasthan and beyond. *Frontiers of Indus Civilization*, Lal, B. B. and Gupta, S. P., (eds.) pp. 481. New Delhi: Books and Books.

Monier, Williams, M. 1951. *Sanskrit-English Dictionary*, Oxford.

Moreland, W. H., 1929. *The Agrarian System of Moslem India*, Cambridge. Delhi Oriental Books Reprint Corporation 1968.

Moti Chand, 1945. Rationing and other famine relief measures in ancient India. *Journal of U.P. Historical Society*, pp. 18-30.

Mughal, M. R., 1970. *The Early Harappan Period in the Greater Indus Valley and Northern Baluchistan* (c. 3000-2400). Ph.D. dissertation, University of Pennsylvania, Philadelphia.

Mughal, M.R., 1972. A summery of excavations and explorations in Pakistan (1971-72), *Pakistan Archaeology*, Vol. VIII, pp. 114-58.

Mughal, M.R., 1974. New evidence of the early Harappan culture from Jalilpur. Pakistan *Archaeology*, Vol. XXVII, pp. 106-13.

Mughal, M.R., 1982. Recent archaeological research in the Cholistan desert. *Harappan Civilization : A Contemporary Perspective*, Possehl, G. L., (ed.) pp. 85-97. New Delhi : Oxford and IBH.

Max mueller, F., 1879-82. (tr.) *The Upanisads*, Vols. 2, Oxford, (Reprint) 1969, Motilal Banarasidas, New Delhi.

Nārada Smriti, Jolly, J. (ed.) Calcutta, 1885, (tr.) Jolly, J. *SBE*, Vol. 33, Oxford, 1889.

Nautiyal, K. P., 1989. *Protohistoric India*, Agam Kala Prakashan, Delhi.

Nirukta of Yāska, (ed. & tr.) Lakshman Sarup, Text, 1927, University of Punjab, Trans., 1921, Oxford.

Niṣītha Sūtram, Bhāṣya Cūrni, Jinadasgani Mahattara. Upadhyaya Kavi Amar Muni and Muni Kanhaiyalal, (eds.) (2nd ed.) Sunmati Jnana Pith. Agra, 1982.

Niṣītha Cūrni, *see* Sen, Madhu, 1975.

Niyogi, Pushpa, 1962. *Contribution to the Economic History of Northern India from the 10th to 12th century A.D.*, Calcutta. Progressive Publishers.

Pācittīya, 1958. Bhikkhu, J. Kashyap, (ed.) *Nalanda Devanagari Pali Series*, Bihar Government.

Pañcaviṃśa Brāhmaṇa, 1931. (tr.) W., Asiatic Society of Bengal, Calcutta.

Pande, B.M., 1977. Archaeological remains on the ancient Saraswati. Ecology and Archaeology of Western

India, Agarwal, D. P. and Pande, B. M. (eds.) pp. 55-60, Delhi. Concept Publishers.

Pandey, L.P. 1975. Famines in Ancient India. In *JIH*, Vol. 53. 1, pp. 25-32.

Pandey, M. S., 1963. *Historical Geography and Topography of Bihar,* Delhi. Motilal Banarasidas.

Pārājika Samantapasādikā nāma Vinaya Atthakathā of Buddhaghosh Thera, 1964. Sharma, Birbal, (ed.) *Nava Nalanda Mahavihara Granthamala,* Patna.

Paramatthajotikā, see *Sutta Nipāta.*

Pargitar, F. E., 1913, *Purana Text of the Dynasties of Kali Age,* Oxford. (Reprint. Deep Publishers. Delhi, 1975).

Parisiṣṭaparvan of Hemachandra, 1932. Jacobi, H., (ed.) Calcutta.

Piggott, S., 1950. *Prehistoric India,* Baltimore : Penguin Books.

Pliny, *Natural History,* (trs.) Rackham, H., Jones, W. H. S., and Eichholz, D. E., Vols. 11, (*Loeb*) London, 1938-62.

Possehl, G. L., 1977. Pastoral nomadism in the Indus civilization—a hypothesis, M. Jaddei (ed.) *SAA.*, Naples, 1979, pp. 537-51.

Possehl, G. L., 1979. *Ancient Cities of the Indus.* Durham: Casdlina Academic Press.

Possehl, G. L. 1980. *Indus Civilization in Saurastra,* B. R. Publication Corporation, Delhi.

Possehl, G. L. 1982. *Harappan Civilization.* Delhi American Institute of Indian Studies.

Possehl, G. L., 1986. *Kulli: An Exploration of Ancient Civilization in South Asia,* Durham, Academic Press, Carolina.

Possehl, G. L., Chitalwala, Y. M., *etal.*, 1985. Preliminary report in the second season of excavations at Rojdi, 1983-84. *Man and Environment,* Vol. IX, pp. 80-100.

Possehl, G. L. and Raval, M. H., 1989. *Harappan Civilization at Rojdi*, Oxford and I.B.H., New Delhi.

Poulain, T. 1966. Fouilles de Mundigak II. Etude de la faune. *Bulletin d'l' Ecole Francaise d' Estreme Orient*, Vol. LIII (i), pp. 119-135.

Pran Nath, 1980. *A Study in 'the Economic Conditions of Ancient India*, London, 1929, (Reprint), Abinash Prakashan, Allahabad.

Prasad, B., 1936. Animal remains from Harappa. *Memories of the Archaeological Survey of India*, No. 51, Delhi.

Ptolemy, *See* McCrindle, 1885.

Ragozin, E. A., 1984. *History of Vedic India*, Mittal Publication, Delhi.

Raikes, R. L. 1964. The end of the ancient cities of the Indus. *American Anthropologist*, Vol. 66, pp. 284-299.

Rakies, R. L. 1965. The Mohenjodaro floods. *Antiquity*, Vol. 39, pp. 196-203.

Raikes, R. L. 1968a. Kalibangan: Death from natural causes. *Antiquity*, Vol. XLII, pp. 286-291.

Raikes, R. L., 1968b. Archaeological explorations in southern Jhalawan and Las Bela (Pakistan), *Origini*, Vol. II, pp. 103-171.

Raikes, R.L., 1984. Mohenjodaro environment. *Frontiers of the Indus Civilization*, Lal, B. B. and Gupta, S. P. (ed.) New Delhi, pp. 455-460. Books and Books on behalf of Indian Archacological Society.

Rājataraṅgini of Kalhana, 1961. Stein, M. A., (tr.) 1900, (Reprint) Motilal Banarasidas, Delhi.

Ramaswamy, C., 1968. Monsoon over Indus valley during the Harappan period. *Nature*, Vol. 217, No. 5129, pp. 628.

Rāmāyaṇa of Valmiki, 1963. Griffith, R. T. H. (tr.) 3rd ed. Chawkhamba Benaras.

Randhava, M. S. 1980. *A History of Agriculture in India*, Vol. I, Ancient Period, *ICAR*, New Delhi.

Rao, K. R., and Krishan Lal, 1979. Plant remains from *Lothal : A Harappan Port Town, (1955-62), Memories of Archaeological Survey of India*, Rao, S. R. (ed.) No. 78, Vol. 2, pp. 667-78, New Delhi.

Rao, S. R., 1963. Excavations at Rangpura and other explorations in Gujarat. *Ancient India*, Vol. 18-19, pp. 5-207.

Roa, S.R., 1973. *Lothal and the Indus Civilization*. Asia Publishing House, Bombay.

Raverty, H. G., 1880. *Notes on Afghanistan and Part of Baluchistan*. Secrtary of State for India in Council, Eyre and Spottiswoods. London.

Reddy, N. B. K. and Singh, V. R., 1979. Determination of drought-prone areas of India—archaeological approach. *Proceedings of All India Symposium of Drought Prone Areas of India*, Reddy, N. B. K., (ed.) Rayalseema Geographical Society, pp. 40.

Rig Veda 1973. Griffith, R. T. H., (tr.) 2 vols. 2nd Ed. Benaras 1896-97, (new revised edition).

Rissman, P. C. and Chitalwala, Y. M., 1990. *Harappan Civilization and Oriyo Timbo*, IBH and Oxford Publication, New Delhi.

Ross, E. J., 1946. A chalcolithic site in northern Baluchistan, *Journal of the Near Eastern Studies*.

Roth, R., and Otto, Botlingk., 1855-75, *St. Petersberg Dictionary*, 7 vols., St. Petersberg.

Roy, T. N., 1983. *The Ganges Civilization : A critical archaeological study of PGW and NBPW periods of the Ganges plains*, New Delhi. Ramananda Vidya Bhavan.

Roy, T. N., 1986. *A Study of the Northern Black Polish Culture*, New Delhi. Ramananda Vidya Bhavan.

Roy, T. N., and Narain, A. K., 1976, *Excavations at Rajghat*, (1957-58, 1960-65). 3 Vols., Benaras Hindu University, Varanasi.

Rupavatī Avadāna see Divyāvadana.

Śabda-kalpadruma, see *Rothav, St. Petersberg Dictionary*.

Sahai, B. 1983, *The Descriptions of Bihar.* New Delhi, Ramandanda Vidya Bhavan.

Sahi, M. D. N., 1978, New light on the life of *PGW* people as revealed from the excavation at Jakhera (dt. Etah, U.P.). *Man and Environment,* Vol. 2, pp. 101-104.

Sahi, M. D. and Ara Sarvara, 1985. Antiquity of food production: Survey of new evidences. Paper read in Indian History Congress, 46th session, Amritsar.

Sahni, M. R., 1956, Bio-geological evidence bearing on the decline of the Indus valley civilization. *Journal of the Palaeontological Society of India.* Vol. I (1), pp. 101-107.

Sankalia, H. D. and Mate, M. S., 1959. *Antiquities of Nevasa,* State Board for Historical Records and Ancient Monuments, Monograph, No. 1, Bombay. Goverment Press.

Sankalia, H. D., Deo, S. B. and Ansari, Z. A., 1960. *From History to Prehistory at Nevasa,* Poona.

Sankalia, H.D., 1974. The Prehistory and Protohistory of India and Pakistan. 2nd ed. Poona : Deccan College Postgraduate and Research Institute.

Samantapasādikā, 1963. The commentary on Vinaya by Buddhaghosh Thera, Birbal Sharma, (ed.) Nalanda.

Samyutta Nikāya, 1917-29. Leon Feer, M., (ed.) Vol. 4, PTS, London 1884-94, Rhys Davids, C. A. F. (tr.) Vols. 1, 2 and Woodward, F.L., Vols. 3, 4, London.

Sānkhāyana Gṛhya Sūtra, 1960. Sehgal, S. R., (ed.) Munshiram Manoharlal, New Delhi.

Sānkhāyana Śrauta Sūtra, 1980. Caland, W., (tr.) Motilal Banarasidas, Delhi.

Śatapatha Brāhmaṇa 1963. Eggeling, J., (tr.) Vols. 5, *SBE,* 1882-1900, (Reprint) Motilal Banarasidas, New Delhi.

Saundarānanda of Aśvaghoṣa, 1975. Johnston, E.H., (tr.) (Reprint) Motilal Banarasidas, Delhi. (Reprint of 1928-32 ed.)

Sen, Madhu, 1975. *A Cultural Study of the Nisītha Cūrni,* Amritsar : Sohanlal Jaindharma Pracharak Samiti.

Sewell, S., Guha, B.S., 1931. *Human remains.* In *Mohenjodaro and the Indus Civilization* Marshall, Sir J., (ed.) Vol. II, pp. 649-673. London: Arthur Probsthain.

Shaffer, J. G., 1978a. The later prehistoric periods. *The Archaeology of Afghanistan,* Allchin, F. R., and Hammond, H., (eds.) pp. 72-187, Academic Press, London.

Shaffer, J. G., 1978c. *Prehistoric Baluchistan,* B.R. Publishers, Delhi.

Shaffer, J. G., 1982. Harappan culture and recosideration. *Harappan Civilization,* Possehl, G. L., (ed.) New Delhi. American Institute of Indian Studies, pp. 41-51.

Shah, D. R., 1975. Animal remains from Dhatva. *Excavation at Dhatva.* Mehta, R. N., and Choudhary, S. N., (eds.) M. S. University Archaeological Series No. 12, pp. 57-60, Baroda.

Shah, D. R., 1980. Animal remains from Kanewal. *Excavations at Kanewal.* Mehta, R.N., Momin, K.N., Shah, D.R., (eds.) M. S. University Archaeological Series No. 17, pp. 74-76, Baroda.

Shamshastry, R., 1961. (ed., tr.) *Arthaśāstra of Kautalya,* 7th edn., Mysore: Mysore Print and Pub. House.

Sharma, G. R., 1969. *Excavation at Kausambi* (1949-50), Manager of Publications, Delhi.

Sharma, G. R., Mishra, V. D., Mandal, D. and Pal, J. N., 1980. *Beginning of Agriculture.* Allahabad University Publication, Allahabad.

Sharma, R. S., 1965. *Indian Feudalism: c. 300-1200,* Calcutta. (2nd ed. 1980, Memillan).

Sharma, R.S., 1977. Conflict, distribution and differentiation in Rig vedic society. *IHR,* Vol. 4, No. 1 pp. 1-12.

Sharma, R.S., 1983, *Material Culture and Social Formation in Ancient India,* Delhi.

Sharma, Subhara, 1985. *Life in the Upanisads*, Delhi. Abhinav Publications.

Sharma, Y. D. 1955-56. Past pattern of living as unfolded by excavations at Rupar. *Lalit Kala*, Nos. 1-2, pp. 121-129.

Shastri, A. M., 1969. *India as Seen in the Brihat Samhita*, Delhi. Motilal Banarasidas.

Singh, G., 1971. The Indus valley culture. *Archaeology and Physical Anthropology in Oceania*, Vol. 6, No. 2, pp. 177-189.

Singh, G., Joshi, R. D., Chopra, S. and Singh, A. B., 1974. Late quarternary history of vegetation and climate of Rajasthan desert, India, *Phil. Tran. Royal Society*, London, Series, B Vol. 267, No. 889, pp. 467-501.

Singh, R. L., 1971. *India and Regional Geography*, Varanasi. National Geographic Society of India.

Singh, S. and Ghose, B., 1977, Geomorphology of the Luni basin and its paliaeoclimatic inferences. *Ecology and Archaeology of Western India*, Agarwal, D. P. and Pande, B. M., (eds.) pp. 135-145, Delhi. Concept Publishers.

Sircar, D. C., 1963. *Select Inscriptions Bearing on Indian History and Civilization from 600 B.C. to 18th Century A.D.*, 2 Vols., Calcutta. University of Calcutta.

Skanda Purana, 1981-82. Nag Sharan Singh, (ed.), Nag Publishers, Delhi.

Smith, P. E. L. 1972. Land use settlement patterns and subsistence agriculture. A demographical perspective. *Man Settlement and Urbanization*, Thringham, R. and Dimbleby, G. W., (eds.) P. J. Ucko, pp. 409-425. Cambridge, Mass. Schenkman Pub.

Spate, O. and Leamonth A. T. A. 1954. *India and Pakistan: a General and Regional Geography, with a Chapter on Ceylon*, London. Methuen and Co.

Stein, A., 1928. Innermost Asia: Detailed Report of Explorations in Central Asia, Kan-Su and Eastern Iran, 3 Vols. Oxford. Clasendan Press.

Stein, A., 1929, *An Archaelogical Tour in Waziristan and Baluchistan.* Memoirs of the Archaeological Survey of India, No. 37, Calcutta.

Stein, A., 1931. *Archaeological Tour in Gedrosia* (with an Appendix by Sewell, R. B., and Guha, B. B.) Memoirs of Archaeological Survey of India, 43. Calcutta.

Stein, A., 1937. *Archaeological Reconnaissances in North West India and South East Iran,* London: Macmillan.

Stein, A., 1943. An Archaeological Tour along the Ghaggar Hakara River (1940-42); App. I, Ghosh, A., The Rajputana desert; App. II, Mughal, M. R., Recent archaeological researches in Cholistan; App. III, Misra, V. N., Climate: A factor in the rise and fall of the Indus civilization; App. IV, Yash Pal, Sahai, B., Sood, R. K., Sensing of the lost Saraswati; (Indian edition), Gupta, S. P. 1989, Kusumanjali Prakashan, Meerut.

Sthavirvādicharita or *Pariśistaparva* of Hemachandra, (ed.) Jacobi, H., Calcutta, 1932.

Strabo, *Geography,* Jones, H. L., (tr.) 8 vols. (*Loeb*), London 1917-33.

Sutta Nipāta Khuddaka Nikāya, 1959. Kashyap, Bhikku J. (ed.) *Nalanda Devanagari Pali Series,* Bihar Government.

Sutta Nipāta Commentary, Paramatthajotika, 1916. Vol. I, *Uragavagga Cullavagga* (ed.) Smith, Helmer *Pali Text Society,* London.

Suraj Bhan *see* Bhan, Suraj.

Taittirīya Brāhmaṇa of the Black Yajur Veda, 1939. Mitra, R. L., (ed.) 3 Vols. 1859-70. Dikshitar, V. R. R., (tr.) Oxford, Calcutta.

Taittirīya Saṃhitā see *Yajur Veda.*

Taittirīya Saṃhitā, 1871-72. Weber, A., (ed.) *Indischen Studien,* Band 11 and 12. Leipzig.

———, (tr.) Keith, A. B., *Hos.,* Vols. 18 and 19, Harvard, 1914.

Tamaskar, B. G., 1989, *Geographical Knowledge in Upanisads*, New Delhi. Indian Publishing.

Taranatha, 1944. Datta, B. N., (tr.) *Mystic Tales of Lama Taranatha*, Calcutta, 1944.

Tevijja Suttanta, 1965. Rhys Davids, T. W., (tr.) *Buddhist Suttas trans. from Pali, SBE*, Vol. XI, Oxford, 1881, (Reprint), Motilal Banarasidas, Delhi.

Thakur, V. K., 1981. *Urbanization in Ancient India*, New Delhi. Abhinav Publications.

Thera-Therī-Gāthā, Psalms of the Early Buddhists, Vol. II, *Psalms of the Brethren*, 1951. Mrs. C. A. F. Rhys Davids, (tr.), London. (tr.) P. T. S., Vol. I, IV.

Thomas, K. S., 1979. Palaeoecological studies in the Bannu basin: The sources of evidence. *SAA*, pp. 227-32.

Thomas, K. D., 1983. Tarakai-Qila: Site, economy and environment. *Site, Environment and Economy*, Proudfoot, B., (ed.) pp. 127-144, *British Archaeological Report, International Series*, No. 173, Oxford.

Thomas, K. D., 1983. Agriculture and subsistence systems of the 3rd millennium B.C., in N. W. Pakistan: A speculative outline. *Integrating the Subsistence Economy*, Jones, M., (ed.) pp. 279-314, *British Archaeological Report, International Series*, No. 181, Oxford.

Thomas, K. D., 1984. The faunal background of the chalcolithic culture of western India. *Animals and Archaeology: III, Early Herders and their Flocks*, Clutton Brock, J. and Greigson, C., (eds.) pp. 355-362, *British Archaeological Report: International Series*, No. 202, Oxford.

Tosi, M., 1969. Excavations at Shah-ri-Sokhta. Preliminary report on the second campaign, September-December, 1968, *East and West*, Vol. 19, pp. 283-386.

Tripathi, Vibha, 1976, *The Painted Grey Ware: An Iron Age Culture of Northern India*, Concept Pub. Co. Delhi.

Upadhyaya, B. S., 2017. B. S., *Buddhakaleen Bharatiya Bhugol. Prayag*, Hindu Sahitya Sammelan, Prayag, Allahabad.

Upanīṣadas see Max Muller, F. 1879-82 and Hume, R. A., 1921.

Uttarādhyāyana Sūtra see Jacobi, H., 1964.

Uvāsagadasāo, Hoernle, A. F. R., (ed.) Calcutta, 1890.

Vājasaneyī Saṃhitā see Yajur Veda.

Vaśiṣṭha Dharmasūtra, see Buhler, G., 1969.

Vats, M. S., 1940. *Excavations at Harappa*, being an account of excavations carried out between 1920-21, and 1933-34, 2 Vols., Manager of Publications, Delhi. Govt. of India.

Vāyū Purāṇa, Tarakratna, Panchanana (ed.) Vangvasi edition, Calcutta.

Vedic Index see Macdonald and Keith, 1958.

Vinaya (texts), 1974. Rhys Davids, T. W., and Oldenberg, H., 3 Vols. *SBE*, Vols. 13, 17, 20, Oxford, Clarendon Press, 1879-1883, (Reprint) Motilal Banarasidas, Delhi.

Viṣṇū Dharmasastra, 1880. Jolly, J., (tr.) *The Institute of Visnu*, *SBE*, Vol. 7, Oxford.

Vishnu Mittre, 1969-70, Status of barley in India archaeology with remarks on Aryan hypothesis, *Puratattva*, Vols. 3 p. 1.

Viṣṇū Purāṇa, see Wilson, H. H., 1979.

Viṣṇū Smriti, see Jolly, J., 1880.

Vyākaraṇa Mahābhāṣya of Patanjali, Kielhorn, F., (ed.) 3rd edition revised by Abhayankar, K. V., 2 Vols., Poona *VORI*, 1965.

Vyavạhāra Bhāṣya, 1929. Commentary by Malaygiri, Bhavnagar.

Waddell, L. A., 1975. *Report on the Excavation at Pataliputra*, Calcutta, 1903, (Reprint).

Wagle, N. N., 1966. *Society at the Time of Buddha*, Popular Prakashan, Bombay.

Wagner, G. E., 1990. Plant remains from Oriyo Timbo. *Harappan Civilization and Oriyo Timbo,* Rissman, B. C., and Chitalwala, Y. W., (ed.) New Delhi.

Watters, T., 1904-05. *On Yuan Chwangs, Travels in India,* 2 Vols. London. (ed. by J. W. Rhys Davids and S. W. Buhell. 2 Vols. Asian Educational Service, 1988).

Wheeler, J. T., 1973. *India of the Vedic Age,* 2 Vols. Cosmo Publication, Delhi.

Wheeler R. E. M., 1953. *The Indus Civilization, Cambridge History of Indian,* suppl. vol., Cambridge. The University Press.

Wheeler, R. E. M., 1959. *Early India and Pakistan to Ashoka,* London: Thames and Hudson.

Wheeler, R. E. M., 1968. *The Indus Civilization,* 3rd edn., The Cambridge. History of India. Cambridge: The University Press.

Whitney, W. D., 1905. (tr.) *Atharva Veda Samhitas,* 2 Vols. Harvard University Press, Cambridge.

Wilson, H. H., 1979, (tr.) *Visnu Purana,* 3rd ed. Calcutta Punthi Pustak 1979 (Rpt. 1961 ed.).

Wheeler, J.T., 1987. *India of the Brahmanic Age, with reference to the Ramayana,* 2 Vols., Cosmo Publications, New Delhi.

Yajñavalkya Smriti, 1936. Gharpure, G. R., (ed.) Poona, 1903-4, (tr.) *Collection of Hindu Law,* Bombay. 1936.

Yajur Veda, Taittirīya Saṃhitā (Black Yajur Veda), 1914. Keith, A.B., (tr.) 2 Vols., *HOS* Vols. 18, 19, Cambridge, Mass. 1914.

Yajur Veda, Vājasaneyī Saṃhitā (White Yajur Veda), 1899. Griffith, R. T. H., (tr.) Benaras. E.J. Lazarus and Co.

Yuga Purāṇa See Mankad. D. R. 1951.

Zimmer, H., 1951. *Myths and Symbols in Indian Art and Civilization,* Campbell, J., (ed.) 1990. First Published. New York. Reprint, Motilal Banarsidas, Delhi.

Index